C000260439

The Spirit of O'Reillys

The World At Our Feet

By Peter O'Reilly

With my best wishes.

Peter O'Reilly

The Spirit of O'Reillys

ISBN 978-0-646-49601-6

Written and published by Peter O'Reilly
Copyright © 2008 Peter O'Reilly
First published August 2008

All rights reserved.
No part of this publication, either text or images, may be reproduced or transmitted in any form or by any means without the written permission of the author and publisher.

Edited and produced by Endless Summer Publishing Pty Ltd.

Design by Zoik

Printed by Fergies

Front cover photo: The second generation – Vince, Peter and Rhelma O'Reilly.
Photographer: Marian Smith.

Back cover photo: The first generation of O'Reillys – from left: Joe, Molly, Viola, and Bernard. Their mother Jane is seated and Rose is on the ground.
Photographer: Max Upham.

Inside front cover: Pat's Bluff
Photographer: Max Upham

Dedication

To Vince and all the O'Reillys who have made the Guest House their life and their love. They have given me the inspiration to write this book.

Acknowledgements

To my wife Annette for her encouragement and her love as I laboured to write this book. To Paul and Helen Manias who have been my guiding light and counselor when compiling this book. To our guests for their friendship and the stories that embellish this book. To my first wife Karma who was my soul-mate for thirty five years of Guest House life.

Photo credits.

Max Upham
Jack Justins Family
Marian Smith
Womans Weekly (January 1947)
Sydney William Jackson
Frank Young
Neil Walker
Clare Courtney
Bob Johnston
Glen Trelfo
O'Reillys photo library.
Jon McGhee for his sketches.

The Spirit of O'Reillys – Chapters

The Stockyard Creek Track

The Spirit of O'Reillys

The World At Our Feet

INTRODUCTION

When Vince and I arrived back to take on the responsibility of running O'Reillys Guest House my aunt Molly, who had been a real strength behind the business, told us we were lucky. She said, "You have the world at your feet." We thought at the time that the world that was ours was a long way away at the end of a rough old road. The Guest House owed a considerable amount of money at the time and the original buildings had been standing for thirty years and were looking old and tired.

I realize now that Molly was right – the world was at our feet. All we had to do was work hard to meet the challenge that it presented. We had to make the effort to be part of that world. I now look back and can appreciate Molly's perspective. The generation before us rode up the mountain on horses and built their Guest House on top of a mountain with the nearest road nine miles away. That horse track was their only link with civilization for many years. It was a tough time for the O'Reillys. By comparison we had it easy.

Molly was right also in saying that we were lucky. I believe our generation nestled comfortably in an easy-going era after the war when people were not demanding and had the capacity to enjoy the simple things of life. There was a lot more trust in business and in society generally and we didn't have the regulations to impede our progress.

It is a privilege for me to record our history, the story of the O'Reilly family on the mountain. It is our story. It belongs to all the O'Reillys and to our many friends who have visited us and have an affinity with our Guest House and our beautiful mountains. They were part of our lives and now they belong in our memories. I invite you to walk with me and meet some of these characters as we meander through three generations.

I trust you will enjoy the journey.
Peter O'Reilly

AUTHOR'S NOTE

O'Reillys – A Home in the Hills

There is something magical about that old place in the hills that is known far and wide as *O'Reillys*. It is a Guest House in the mountains that has claimed the hearts of many people who have stayed there or worked there over many years. Three generations of O'Reillys have plotted its course and have certainly added their personalities to the place that has made it what it is today, uniquely *O'Reillys*.

I am Peter, a second generation O'Reilly, who was part of the Guest House scene from the 1950s to the 1990s. My intention is to document the path *O'Reillys* took during the reign of the second generation, when Mick and Annie O'Reilly's sons, Vince and I, took over the reins. I will also outline the history of the first generation that settled here, and of the vision and enterprise they displayed that assured their future on the mountain, and the future of later generations as well. Certainly our aunts and uncles had presented us with a great heritage, a challenge for us to show the determination and faith in the future of the Guest House as they had done.

Their story is real pioneer stuff. It is a moving story that I believe belongs to my uncle Bernard O'Reilly. He takes us up into the rainforest-covered ranges with the family so we can relive their difficulties and their triumphs just as they did. It is narrated with great sensitivity and feeling in his book *Green Mountains*. I do not have Bernard's gift or his descriptive prowess so what you read will not be another *Green Mountains*. What I shall do is record the progress of the Guest House for the fifty years following the *Green Mountains* era and, as all writers do, reveal a little of myself along the way.

There is really no choice when selecting someone to record these events because I am the only person around today who has worked at the Guest House for well nigh fifty years and have played a part in the many changes that have taken place. Vince's death in 1999 left a void in the lives of the whole family and of the many friends who visit the mountain. Unfortunately the more personal side of Vince's story will remain untold. His adventures and feelings as a boy and a young man and his reaction to the challenges of life at that time were never talked about in any depth although we lived and worked closely nearly all of our lives.

There are milestones worth recording that have marked our journey as we toiled for a generation on the mountain. We climbed the hills that were there before us and enjoyed the view for a moment; there is another hill in the distance that lured us on – another challenge around the corner. The culture of not accepting the status quo but having the will to create something special has been with the O'Reilly family since they arrived on the mountain. That culture is still alive today.

I am certainly not an historian; I have never kept a diary and am not one of those meticulous people who can record events in great detail. My habit of putting the highs and lows of everyday life at the Guest House behind me, and focusing on the next day is no help. I tend to forget even rather important events that have happened and I do miss Vince to yarn to about these things. Fortunately, people who have been visitors over the years generally have a story to tell or a drama to record concerning an earlier visit and they often exhibit an emotional attachment to the place that calls them back. I make use of these memoirs that may change the direction of my story for a time, so when you pick up this book be prepared to meander along a winding path as we follow a myriad of stories that reveal the changing personality of the Guest House over three generations.

One of the reasons people returned to *O'Reillys* is because of the family involvement and I think also they came back at times because they were prepared to overlook the family's shortcomings. For over 50 years of Guest House life, when things were rather primitive and it was something of an adventure to visit the mountain, the O'Reilly family was very much hands-on and innovative and did much of the work themselves. If the organization fell down in some respect there was usually an O'Reilly involved. The dramas that happened over the years would put *Fawlty Towers* in the shade and I can just about see some of our 'old' guests nodding their heads in agreement. I make this point because if it were not for our wonderful and tolerant guests *O'Reillys* would not be in existence today. They were loyal to us during the tough times and became our very good friends and we offer them our heartfelt thanks.

I am writing this with no real plan in mind, but a personal desire to record the evolution of the Guest House during our time. Who will read this? I don't know and it is not of great concern to me at present as I relive the memories of a lifetime. As my mind drifts back over the dramas, the happenings, the people who coloured my life, it is all very personal to me. So what you read is, in a sense, my autobiography – my view of the world as it revolves around the Guest House and the O'Reilly family.

Writing personally as I do comes naturally to me and it is the only way I can record the memories that crowd my mind in great disorder as I ponder the task ahead. The weakness, as I see it, is that I become some sort of hero of my own story when there are so many people who have given so much over three generations. Vince and I and the Guest House itself were supported and helped in a very positive way by our wives, Lona and Karma, who were so much part of life on the mountain. So, dear reader, keep in mind that I am just one of many people – O'Reillys, staff and friends – who have played a role in the O'Reilly saga; a continuing story that perhaps a future generation O'Reilly will record some day just as I am doing now.

OUR FAMILY TREE

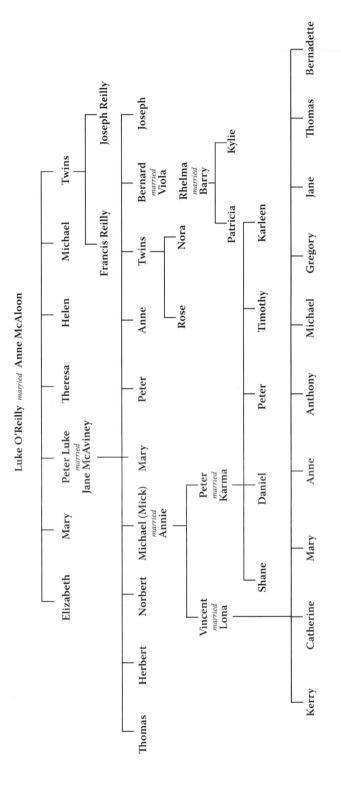

Luke O'Reilly *married* Anne McAloon

The O'Reilly boys (L-R) Cousin Joe, Herb, Norb and Mick (standing).
Photo: Bob Johnston

The O'Reilly Dream

L ife's journey is never straightforward. There are many hills and turns and shady parts along the way and only occasionally do we see a sign that points us in the right direction. I think of the O'Reilly boys who came from sheep properties in the Blue Mountains of NSW. These properties were not large and it seemed to be a tradition for the older boys to come to Queensland and find work so they could help support their younger siblings. Luke came to Beaudesert on one of these journeys and heard of land that could be selected in the high country on the northern slopes of the McPherson Range. He spread the word and by 1911 eight O'Reilly boys, from two sides of the family had arrived to take up the challenge.

The land they selected was advertised by the Queensland Government as dairying blocks. The country was high and rugged, around 3,000 feet above sea level and covered in rainforest. It was also isolated and one could imagine the original selectors walking sixteen miles up the mountain to their future home overloaded with food, tools, blankets and equipment. There would be no grass on the selections to support horses so they were the human packhorses.

The difficulties involved in establishing dairy farms and taming this wild country were obvious and it is not surprising that the only selectors were eight O'Reilly boys from the distant Blue Mountains. They would have been accustomed to rough country and maybe the rugged beauty of these mountains appealed to their Irish heritage. I know that some of the locals had looked at the land and declared the country to be too rough for dairying. Considering the difficult terrain, the land was not cheap. They paid thirty-five shillings an acre for it and it could be paid off over thirty years at five percent interest.

There were five brothers: Tom, Norb, Herb, Mick and Pete who belonged to one family, while their cousins – Pat, Luke and Joe - belonged to another O'Reilly family. Luke and Tom were the only members who had inspected the land previously so for most of them they were heading into the unknown. They would have had no contact with rainforest before and one could imagine the spirit of excitement and adventure that accompanied these young men as they walked from the Kerry Valley towards these rugged mountains. They climbed a steep ridge out of Cainbable Creek that they named 'The Heartbreaker' and then scrambled along a dense rainforest range to claim their selections.

The two families settled in different areas of the mountain and built their huts about three miles apart near spectacular cliff edges. Open eucalypt forest grew around these cliffs and this friendly forest provided open space to build their huts, and also the bark for the walls and roof, as well as good firewood. These were temporary bark humpies that were used till enough land was cleared to allow the construction of a more substantial slab hut on each block. The first job that had to be tackled was clearing the forest. The wall of rainforest confronting them would have looked daunting. The tangle of vines and giant trees with interlocking branches would have made it dangerous work too, so the O'Reilly boys had to learn the trade quickly if they were going to stay alive.

The first bark humpy on the mountain. Photo: Bob Johnston

Clearing the land was heavy work and involved a series of activities carried out in sequence to gain the best results. First they moved through the area to be cleared with brush-hooks and axes and cut the vines as well as the shrubs and small saplings. Then they armed themselves with axes and crosscut saws to fall the trees and that was certainly the biggest job. They soon became skilled at using springboards to get above the buttresses and the gnarled root systems of the large trees and that made the job easier. Standing on a springboard while chopping or using a crosscut saw requires good balance and Herb particularly was skilled at it and was considered to be the best axeman on the mountain.

The cleared timber was trimmed to assist the burning process and then allowed to lie there so it could be burnt later after it had dried out sufficiently. This process could take six months or more depending on the weather. Rain showers in the mountains could put off the burn for months. Rainforest is not combustible under normal conditions and generally will not burn. As a result rainforest flora has no tolerance to fire and a 'good burn' will kill every living plant. Rhodes grass seed was then scattered around as soon as the ashes had cooled so this vigorous tall grass could beat the weeds. It is a slow process from the clearing of the land to eventually having enough grass to support a milking herd.

Also, yards had to be built and cattle bought and driven up the mountain. I imagine the boys would have had a bit to learn about dairying too, considering they all came off sheep properties. They may have milked a house cow before but that would have been the limit of their experience. Milking a whole herd by hand would have been 'hard work' for these novice dairy-farmers. They would have relied on their farming friends at Kerry for advice. A separator was brought up the mountain by packhorse and in those days separators were operated by hand. The precious cream was their money earner and was collected in cans and taken to Beaudesert. The separated milk was fed to the calves that were weaned, as well as to the pigs when they arrived.

The cream heads to the valley. Photo: Keith Hooper

The time it took to establish their dairy was prolonged as various family members went away to get work elsewhere so they could have some money coming in to support the efforts of the ones left at home. Later when Norb, Mick and Pete went away to the war and left Tom and Herb on the mountain the development of their land would have slowed considerably. When the rest of the family arrived Tom and Herb also went away to earn some money and left a young Bernard on the mountain to keep the dairy going for a time. He said during that time he made friends with the wildlife and gained a greater appreciation of the rainforest.

In the early stages times were tough and food was not plentiful, they were limited to what they could carry in supplemented by the occasional scrub turkey or pigeon. Pete or Ped, as he preferred to be called, was only fourteen when he came to the mountain and said that he was hungry most of the time. Turkeys were scarce the first season they were there and Mick said they shot only one and that it was a tough old gobbler. They were more plentiful the following year after some clearing had been done. The boys also shot a brown pigeon one afternoon but found when they plucked the bird that it was nearly all feathers and had a very small body. With five hungry men to feed they decided to boil it up and add other ingredients to make soup so they could have a hearty breakfast. Next morning they were surprised to find that the pigeon was missing from the soup. They may have been eyeing each other suspiciously but the problem was solved the following night when an inquisitive water rat appeared from Morans Creek to see if pigeon was on the menu again. It may have been taking a risk of becoming stock for the soup the following day.

Both families operated dairies but Pat and Luke were the real dairy farmers and their dairy was one of the best scrub dairies in the Beaudesert district. It was operated by them, and later their family, for over fifty years. The dairy belonging to the five brothers was the first to get underway on the mountain but it was also the first to stop operating as a commercial dairy when the family turned their attention to running a Guest House. After they stopped supplying cream to Beaudesert Butter Factory the herd was still milked for another forty years to satisfy the needs of an expanding Guest House.

When the land was opened up for selection the Government's vision was for a series of dairy farms to be established along the Sarabah Range and a road was to be put through to access them. This plan was shelved when a movement to establish a National Park gained momentum resulting in the rest of the land being withdrawn from selection. The idea of a National Park was initiated by a local grazier Robert Collins and after his death carried on by Romeo Lahey whose family had saw-milling interests in Canungra.

At the time there was also a movement headed by Romeo Lahey to remove the O'Reillys from the mountain because their selections were within the proposed national park boundaries. The proposal was for the government to compensate them for the work they had done that would allow them to select land elsewhere. At one stage they were told by Romeo to stop clearing as an approach was to be made to buy their land. They waited for a time but after receiving no official notification from government the boys started clearing again. Negotiations broke down during the First World War but resumed in the 1920s. By this time the O'Reilly boys had been on the mountain for ten years and more and their dairies were operating effectively. Also, more people were visiting the area, and Tom O'Reilly with the support of the rest of the family was making preparations for building a Guest House.

The idea of starting all over again somewhere else did not have much appeal. Fortunately for the family by this time they had some influential people on their side including well-known naturalist and editor of the *Daily Mail* in Brisbane, Alex Chisholm. He could see that accommodation was necessary if people were to access the newly established National Park and used his connection with government to assure them of this. The result was that the O'Reillys weathered the storm and stayed on.

There was nothing personal about Romeo Lahey's efforts to remove the O'Reillys from the bosom of the National Park. It is not considered desirable for private land to exist within a national park and that was Romeo's motivation. The O'Reillys however, did not agree. They had been there for years before the national park was proclaimed and had worked hard to establish a home and a viable living. They considered they had a right to stay. It was a very personal issue for the O'Reillys and a sensitive one for Romeo as well. I believe Romeo would have been happy with the end result because earlier he had proposed that a Health Resort be built on O'Reilly property if the government reclaimed the land.

The National Park was gazetted in July 1915 isolating their properties that were surrounded by the Reserve and this turn of events left them with no possibility of an access road to their land. The O'Reillys anticipated this and had already carved a track around the side of Lukes Bluff and then down a ridge into Stockyard Creek. The track then followed the creek out to the Kerry Valley. The Beaudesert Council supported them in their track building efforts by supplying tools and explosives. Constructing the track around the precipitous side of the bluff was a challenging exercise. Holes had to be drilled in the hard rock to accommodate explosives and the boys clung on to the steep side as they belted away at the drills with a heavy hammer. It was slow and tedious work. They had already packed a forge and a small anvil up the track to the foot of the bluff, which were used to sharpen the drills. Tom was the leading 'powder monkey' and they would set up a series of charges usually late in the day and light the fuses to set the lot off. The noise of the explosions would bounce off the ridges along the Kerry Valley for miles.

The Stockyard Creek route was much shorter than the Cainbable Creek track and it made their home more accessible. The cream was taken nine miles down the mountain on packhorses where it was transported in to Beaudesert. Their first trip down the mountain did not end well when the motion of the packhorses churned the cream that arrived as butter to the butter factory. This resulted in the cream being down-graded and they received less for it. To counter this problem they developed the habit of taking the cream down at night when the afternoon milking was finished so they could poke the packhorses along nice and quietly.

The separated milk was fed to the pigs and that was the easy part. Getting the weaners up to the mountain in the first place would have been an interesting exercise. They were put into bags a few at a time and arrived up on a tolerant packhorse or at times on the pommel of someone's saddle. It sounds as if it would be a difficult undertaking but the little fellows soon settled down with the movement of the horses. When they arrived they were put into a dingo-proof enclosure because these young porkers would have appealed to the tastebuds of these wild dogs. Poultry was carried in the same way but this time a small slit was put in the bag so the fowls could put their heads out.

When the pigs were big and fat they had to be driven to market. I can remember my father Mick telling me how he and Herb took three days to drive pigs over some rough country to the railway at Hillview. It would have been 'all hands on deck' to persuade the pigs to leave home and driving them along a narrow rainforest track for the first three miles would have been a real challenge. The boys succeeded in herding them into a makeshift yard at the top of the cliff where the Stockyard Creek Track commences and they penned them there for the night.

The pigs were not fed that evening but they were hungry enough next morning to follow a trail of corn down the track with the boys watching, no doubt satisfied that their plan was working. They drove them cautiously around the cliff so the pigs would not bunch up or become startled in any way. If this happened they could easily lose them over the edge. Once they were in new country the pigs forgot about home and were much easier to handle. They drove them down the mountain and then through the rainforest along Stockyard Creek. Although they had to do some 'scrub-dashing' to keep them on the track they stayed together fairly well and were not too hard to handle. They had little trouble penning them in Larry Keaveny's pigsty at Kerry that night. On the third day they drove them up a steep ridge over the Jinbroken Range through open forest country to Hillview where they were yarded to await the train to Beaudesert.

The activities of the selectors on the mountain were subject to government regulation and these laws stated that they had to clear their land and establish pasture to support cattle and also that they had to earn their living from dairying. Also, each selector had to build a residence on his land and in theory live there. The boys built their huts according to the rules but the five brothers preferred to live together in their main hut on the banks of Morans Creek that was their home for fifteen years. This hut was built over the boundary of two blocks with half the hut on Herb's land and half on Ped's land. This action satisfied the residency qualifications for both men and saved them building a second hut. I could almost imagine a government official arriving in the middle of the night to check if Herb and Ped were sleeping on their own land in their end of the hut. The result of the government regulation was they had spare huts around that they soon put to good use.

The rugged beauty of the country had wide appeal and from 1914 the O'Reilly boys welcomed visitors who were invited to stay in their spare huts. The visitors were supplied with milk and vegetables and made use of the tracks that the boys had cleared to waterfalls and lookouts. They had reopened the track to Mount Bithongabel on the crest of the McPherson Range that was originally put through by John Buchanan acting under Robert Collins instructions in 1906. By making the area accessible to people on horses Collins hoped to create interest in preserving the area as a national park.

The increasing number of people arriving on the mountain would have given Tom the idea that the future looked brighter for the O'Reilly family if they built a Guest House and catered for these visitors instead of milking cows for a living.

The O'Reilly boys home from the valley

Tom's Vision

The rest of the O'Reilly family arrived at the old slab hut on Morans Creek in 1917. They included Molly, Ann, Rose, Bernard and Joe and their mother Jane. Their father Peter died in Brisbane that year after suffering a stroke and never made it to the mountain. The day before the family was due to leave the Blue Mountains and head for Queensland Peter rode around the district to say goodbye to his good friends. That night he became ill and ended up in hospital for four weeks. He recovered sufficiently to travel to Brisbane where they stayed for a time because of Peter's condition.

This gave young Bernard the opportunity to attend school there. Peter died later that year and two days after the funeral Jane received word that her third son Norbert had been killed in the war. It would have been a traumatic time for Jane and for the whole family. As a result she decided to leave Brisbane and join the rest of the family on the mountain. Tom and Herb were holding the fort with Mick and Ped still away at the war. The dairy was operating by this time but no doubt Tom's idea of accommodation for visitors would have been discussed with the new arrivals. After the war ended he was keen to move forward and soon had the wheels in motion.

Tom and Herb were both noted for their ability to construct roads or tracks in rough mountain country where it was all manual work. Tom camped down in the Stockyard Creek Gorge for months while he extended a road, which was formerly a rough logging track, through the rainforest to about a mile from the start of the climb. To even the grade up the steep ridge out of Stockyard Creek he constructed about a mile of zigzag track that he dug out of the steep side of the mountain. He worked on widening the rest of the track, not only for the convenience of guests, but also wide enough to allow slides to be dragged up the mountain. The slides were a necessary part of Tom's plans for the future. Slides are made up of a low platform nailed to cross members that were attached to two heavy runners that are tapered at the front to allow it to be pulled along by horses. They were often used in rough country.

It took time to raise the money to buy an engine that was a necessary component of a mill that Tom planned to use to cut timber for the new

Clockwise from top: Herb on the Pit Saw, his mate on the other end is in the pit below; Sketch of a slide; Guest with packhorse loaded with stretcher beds Photo: Max Upham; Guests returning down the Stockyard Creek Track. Photo Jack Justins.

enterprise. The engine was eventually purchased and arrived at the foot of the mountain. It had to be pulled to pieces so the smaller parts could be taken up on packhorses. The bed of the engine and the heavy flywheel were placed on separate slides and the horses dragged them through the rainforest from the end of the road to the foot of the climb without great difficulty. From then on it was a different story. They dragged the slides up the steep spur by fastening a pulley block to a tree a short distance up the ridge and passing a wire rope through it to allow the horses to pull down hill as the slide went up. When one slide went up about fifteen yards the next one was attached and up it went. The pulley was then taken up to another tree further up the hill where the process was repeated.

It was slow work and there were plenty of difficulties along the way for it took two days to tow the slides a mile up the first steep ridge out of Stockyard Creek. The horses would have been due for a spell when they arrived at a level ledge known as Rogers Camp. It had always been the traditional place to give the horses a spell on the climb up the track. When they bought cattle up the mountain they rested them there for the night and next morning they found that a calf had been born and was lying in a clump of 'stinking roger', a leggy weed that grew there. The calf had to be named Roger and the place from then on was known as Rogers Camp.

From Rogers Camp onward the grade was not as steep, allowing the horses to tow the individual slides in tandem. They nearly lost horses, slide and engine bed over the edge in the cliff section where the track curved into a gully and the pull of the horses was partly across the gully. It would have been a desperate situation for a few minutes. One of the slide's runners went over the edge but Tom held the horses to keep them under control while the boys levered the slide back on to the track. Fortunately they all survived to eventually arrive at the proposed site for the Guest House after a five day journey.

Bob Miller, an experienced sawmill hand, helped set up the mill which had to be done professionally to produce the standard of timber that was required for the new building. Tom and Herb fell the trees that were needed. They were all rainforest species such as hoop pine, rosewood and red ash while lignum vitae and crows ash were used for the stumps and uprights. They had no access to eucalypt forest at the time.

We replaced these buildings over a period of time forty to fifty years later. Rosewood is a rainforest softwood and because of the natural oil it contains has great lasting qualities. It was used extensively in these buildings and I remember the vibrant red colour and the beautiful rosewood scent of the timber we retrieved from the old building. It was used generally as structural timber such as joists and studs that, because of the exposed position of the building, the O'Reillys made a great job of filling up with big nails. Unfortunately the nails made the timber unusable for anything else.

The timber was well cut considering the difficulties they experienced at the time. The engine powering the mill was a four and a half horsepower Crosley that did not have the power to do the job effectively. Each log was cut in fits and starts with pauses to allow the engine to pick up revs. When cut, the timber was arranged in airy stacks to season and prepare it for the first stage of the Guest House construction.

They must have had some tolerant packhorses roaming around O'Reillys at the time when you consider the difficult loads they had to carry up the mountain track. Equipment for the saw bench such as pulleys, spindles, belts and circular saws would have been awkward to pack. The wheels and axles for the trolleys were heavy and the lengthy rails for the trolleys to run on would have been awkward indeed. Oil and fuel for the engine came up the same way as well as the nine-foot iron for the roof of the building. The sheets of iron were rolled four sheets at a time into a cylinder and then tied to the pack-saddles on either side of the horses. The rolls of iron were longer than the horse carrying them and you could imagine that a horse would have required a quiet disposition to accept these loads. They had restricted vision ahead so piloting them along the mountain track would have been a work of art.

Maureen White, a resident of the Kerry Valley all her life, remembered riding up the Stockyard Creek Track in the 1920s as a girl and her horse being frightened by the O'Reilly packhorses ahead carrying iron up the mountain. The noise of the long sheets of iron bumping against trees along the track would have been a new sound for the horses. Maureen had to dismount and hold her horse till the packhorses moved on up the mountain.

One thing that had to be done before a log could be sawn at the mill was for a flitch or a cut to be taken from the log so it would have a flat side that would run smoothly along rollers on the saw bench. This had to be done by hand using a pit saw. A pit saw is a very large saw and to operate it one man had to stand on top of the log controlling one end of the saw while another stood underneath the log in a pit and took control of the other end. The saw cut had to follow a chalk line on the log. The men could not see each other and although they had to work together, cohesion was difficult. The movement of the saw up and down makes it awkward to operate and the fellow underneath has to look up to follow the chalk line but gets sawdust in his eyes every time he does. It is considered to be one of the worst jobs in the world.

Bernard recalled that when he was a young fellow he was appointed to partner Bob on the pit saw. Probably his elder brothers were smart enough to find something else to do. Bernard was new to the game and asked Bob why he was clearing an area close by. Bob replied that no two men had ever been pit-sawing together for a day without having a fight so he was just clearing a space for it. We've tried different incentive programs at the Guest House over the years but Bob Miller's idea seemed to work very well. The impressionable young Bernard said he never worked so hard in all his life.

A carpenter was employed to direct building operations and he had any number of O'Reilly offsiders to assist him. You could imagine what a great thrill it would have been for the family members to see their dream taking shape before their eyes. Tom, as well as Herb, must have felt a sense of accomplishment when the building was completed. They had achieved what would have seemed like an impossible dream. It was three years since Tom started working on the track and his commitment never faltered. They moved out of the slab hut on Morans Creek that had been home to them for fifteen years and took up residence in the new building.

The packhorses still toiled up the mountain track with a seemingly endless variety of loads that would have tested the skill of their handlers. Everything that was needed was packed up the mountain from carpenters tools and glass windows to guttering and ridge capping for the roof. Then there were the goods that were required to operate the Guest House. A stove had arrived earlier in pieces but pots and dishes for the kitchen were essential as well as beds and bedding for the rooms.

It could not all be carried on horses though. The bath, as well as tank iron needed to construct the tanks, had to be carried up by manpower. Both these items would have been at least awkward or more realistically backbreaking to carry up the steep mountain track but I think it illustrates the determination of the family to build their Guest House and provide at least some comfort for their guests. The accommodation would have seemed grand by comparison with the slab huts that some of the visitors had stayed in previously.

O'Reillys Guest House welcomed its first visitors for Easter 1926 and the doors have been open ever since. The first guests were a group of hardy souls led by Bert Salmon who was a well-known bush walker and rock climber. The O'Reillys had friends in Brisbane who had already visited the mountain and they spread the word so the Guest House had reasonable occupancy from the start and proved to be popular at holiday times. Generally it was the family members who arrived later – Molly, Rose, Anne and Bernard – who injected enthusiasm and energy into the new venture to get it off the ground. They also showed the commitment necessary to keep it operating effectively over the years. Tom's effort and that of his brother Herb in setting it up, and his contribution in the early days of the Guest House would have been invaluable too.

The guests at that time came to Beaudesert in a mixed goods and passenger train from Brisbane and after lunch at the hotel boarded the Kerry Coach for the next stage of their journey. This horse-drawn coach delivered empty cream cans and essential goods to the farms along the way and arrived at the Kerry Hotel around 8pm where the guests stayed the night. Next day they were met by one of the O'Reillys with horses for the fifteen mile ride up the mountain to the Guest House. Luggage, as well as goods needed for the operation of the Guest House, was carried up on packhorses.

The family certainly showed some enterprise in the early 1930s when they formed a company to raise capital that would allow them to expand the Guest House and also buy a car. The car was used to transport people from the railway station at Beaudesert to Stockyard Creek where they mounted horses. It reduced the travelling time of their journey from Brisbane to one very long day. Quite often the journey was prolonged by a wet road over the black-soil flats or a rise in the Albert River that made the crossings difficult or impossible. At times the horses were required to travel further along the valley so the guests had a longer ride.

A holiday at *O'Reillys* in those days was quite an adventure and riding up the track around the cliff at night would have set the scene. The horses liked to walk close to the edge of the track where the going was easiest on their feet. Some of the earlier guests said it was better to go up in the dark when you couldn't see the drop below you than to come down in daylight when it was obvious and very much on your mind. When your horse put its head down to eat some kangaroo grass you certainly had the benefit of a good view over the edge. Bernard, and particularly Rose, were the people who did most of the horse work and it had to be done rain, hail or shine.

Keeping the Guest House supplied with food would have been a big job. Molly's work at the business end of the operation supplying sumptuous meals for the guests was not easy either without benefits of refrigeration or easy access to supplies. They kept sheep in those days and would have killed them in the summer during the hot weather while cattle carcasses kept well during the cool winter days. They milked cows and made butter, grew vegetables and supplied much of their own food. While this was going on, building extensions were being carried out. There was no rest for anyone including the packhorses.

Things improved as time went by and during the mid 1930's a timber road was completed up the Sarabah Range from Canungra to end four miles from the Guest House at a spot known as The Dump. The guests still had to ride in from The Dump but it was a big improvement. The graveling of the last four miles of horse track was finally completed in early 1947 and allowed the service car to arrive at the front door of the Guest House for the first time. The horses could have a spell at last.

The Guest House was twenty-one years old and the O'Reillys had been on the mountain for thirty-six years when the road finally arrived. It brought about what was effectively the end of an era. The aura of remoteness, that certain magic that surrounded the Guest House and the O'Reillys that lived there, faded a little with the arrival of a road. I believe it was a major change in the history of the Guest House and the expectations of visitors who stepped out of the service car at the front door would have changed too. The arrival of the road would require a shift in direction for the Guest House management in the years to come and guide the next generation when they took over.

It is a little sad that the older O'Reilly men, the ones responsible for opening up the country originally, were not there to enjoy the occasion. The original selectors had given a significant slice of their young lives to their goals of a home and a life on the mountain for the O'Reilly family. The formation of a national park thwarted these ambitions and made life more difficult for them. On the other hand it opened up other opportunities that presented challenges of a different order that had to be overcome. The younger family members who arrived later accepted these challenges with great enthusiasm but one could understand the older men drifting away. They had fought their battle with determination and now their bodies and their spirits needed a rest.

Norb was killed in the First World War but Tom and Herb were both involved in establishing the Guest House. Later Herb left to buy a dairy at Kerry where he married and spent the rest of his life. They had no children. Tom stayed with the Guest House much longer but would leave to go prospecting or working in North Queensland for lengthy periods. Ped left much earlier and worked in New Guinea and North Queensland. His experience in the tough early days on the mountain when he was just a lad seemed to leave its mark on Ped. Although he came back at times he never really called the mountain home.

Mick left soon after the First World War and worked around the district but would return to the mountain that he seemed to regard as home till he married. His heart must have still been there because he returned later to play a major role at the Guest House. Only three of the original ten of the Guest House O'Reillys married and there were only three children of the next generation. They included Rhelma – Bernard and Viola's daughter – and Vince and I – Mick and Annie's sons.

But later generations should keep the vision before them of the O'Reilly boys as they first walked up the Heartbreaker into the mountains to follow their dream. The rest of the family were instilled with the same spirit when they arrived. Building a Guest House in the hills became their dream and in spite of the many difficulties along the way they shared their home with many thousands of visitors who were welcomed as one of their family. I believe it is the duty of later generations to keep their dream alive.

The Stinson

There is one event that has had a crucial impact on the efforts of the O'Reilly family to expand their Guest House and have it renowned as a place to visit. That is the Stinson drama that was enacted in the rainforests of the McPherson Range in February 1937. Many people, especially the older generation, associate the name O'Reilly with the sensational events that followed the loss of a Stinson airliner in these mountains and the episode was recorded by Bernard O'Reilly in his book, *Green Mountains*. The drama is now firmly entrenched as a part of Australian history and is certainly a crucial part of O'Reilly history. Without the publicity that surrounded this event *O'Reillys* Guest House would have had difficulty surviving some low points in its existence. The drama gave the O'Reilly name a prominence that it had never enjoyed before.

Airlines of Australia operated four Stinsons on a regular route between Sydney and Brisbane and then connected to other major centres in Queensland. The disappearance of a Stinson airliner with seven people on board while on a flight from Brisbane to Sydney took place in the early days of commercial aviation in Australia and created wide interest all over the country.

There was a cyclonic disturbance off the coast east of Brisbane at the time and strong winds were being experienced in the area. Brisbane had received a buffeting from the cyclone but as it drifted south the winds seemed to be easing a little. This influenced the pilot Rex Boyden to take to the air and fly due south over the McPherson Range directly towards Lismore where there were passengers waiting. Another Stinson had flown up from Sydney that morning but it did not land at Lismore because of low cloud and then flew on to Brisbane around the coast to avoid the ranges. Rex took off from Archerfield Aerodrome at 1:10pm with five passengers and an off-duty pilot on board who was flying back to Sydney.

In those days it was up to the pilot to assess the weather conditions and make a decision on whether to fly and it was also the responsibility of the pilot to choose the course to be followed. There was no radio on the plane so when Rex Boyden took to the air he was on his own and the authorities were unsure which route the plane had taken. The job attracted people of Rex's calibre who enjoyed a challenge. He had a distinguished war record first with the Australian Army where he fought at Gallipoli and was severely wounded, and then with the R.A.F in England. He was an experienced pilot and his comment that day was that he had flown in worse conditions.

The Stinson flew south past Beaudesert and along the Albert River Valley at rather low elevation keeping under the cloud. It crossed into the Christmas Creek Valley as it climbed into cloud that enveloped the McPherson Range. The plane never landed at Lismore but this was accepted because of the low cloud present and the fact that the morning plane had not landed there either. It never arrived in Sydney and as the time passed when fuel would have run out it was suggested that it may have landed elsewhere because of the bad weather, possibly on the beach somewhere.

As days went by its disappearance created great interest around Australia and reports started coming in that it had been heard and sighted from Coffs Harbour south to the outskirts of Sydney. The weight of the evidence pointed to the plane having been lost in the wild Hawkesbury country north of Sydney or perhaps in the sea in the same area. The most intensive aerial search in Australian history had taken place. It was concentrated in the southern half of its flight-path and there were numerous ground searches as well but they failed to find any trace of the plane. Wreckage was supposedly seen off the coast and after a week it was generally accepted that the plane had been lost at sea.

The cyclone had left its mark on the rainforest around *O'Reillys* as well, with trees down over tracks. The telephone line had been brought down by fallen trees and branches and was lying on the ground in a number of places. Bernard and his wife Viola, rode down the Stockyard Creek track a week after the crash to do some work on the telephone line as well as get supplies and visit his brother Herb, at Kerry.

Bernard avidly read Herb's old newspapers and noted that the plane was thought to have flown down the coast and not over the mountains. The disappearance of the Stinson was the chief topic of conversation with the farming community at Kerry for they had seen it fly up the valley towards the ranges. Herb believed that the plane could possibly be up in the McPherson Range somewhere. Bernard and Herb talked extensively about it and Bernard made up his mind to search the ranges for it.

He and Viola rode home that afternoon with Bernard mulling over his plans for the search that he was about to undertake the next day. He rang Bob Stephens who lived at the top of the valley and was one of the people who saw the Stinson as it disappeared into the clouds. Bernard found out the position and direction of flight of the Stinson and then laid out his own map and drew a line from where it was last seen to Lismore where it was heading. The highest point of his pencil line was where it crossed the crest of the McPherson Range near a spot called Point Lookout. This area was the target of his search and as he looked at his map he hoped to get a view over the area from neighbouring Mt. Throakban. Bernard had never been into the headwaters of Christmas Creek before and he knew if the plane was there the odds of finding it in the dense rainforest and wild gorges were extremely long. The convincing reports in the papers of sightings of the aircraft further south he put out of his mind as he prepared for his journey.

Bernard packed provisions. There would not be a varied menu once he was on the way. A billy, tea, sugar, bread and some onions was all he packed. Why onions? Well they seemed to be traditional O'Reilly food and were part of our lunch packs at the Guest House for sixty years. In those earlier times when there was not much to choose from they had the advantage of keeping well and travelling well and they also added some real flavour to any meal. There was a horse track up to Mt Bithongabel and Bernard rode the first four miles to the top of the range and then let the horse go, there would be someone looking out for it back at home.

He followed a track to the Valley of Echoes Lookout. From there on the tortuous McPherson Range was clothed in rainforest and lawyer-vine in dense clumps armed with long wait-a-while tendrils made the going difficult. Bernard said his speed was reduced to less then one mile an hour. When light faded he went down to the head of the Albert River where he boiled the billy and prepared to stay the night. He had been there once before but had not explored any further.

Bernard spent a miserable night on the damp ground, no doubt comforted by a smoky fire and glow-worms on the surrounding banks. He was glad when morning came. The steep climb up Mt Throakban soon had the blood coursing through his veins and the stiffness out of his joints. This mountain is often shrouded in mist and when Bernard arrived that was the way he found it. He waited for a time and the clouds opened to reveal the rainforest-covered McPherson Range as it wound snakelike to the west. On the southern side of the range the rugged escarpment dropped precipitously over three thousand feet into New South Wales. On the northern side the ridges dipped off to the right from the main range dividing the various streams that would join to become Christmas Creek. There was a high range beyond the Christmas Creek catchment that also ran to the right that he took to be Lamington Plateau. If he were right, then the high round mountain where it left the McPherson Range would be Point Lookout.

His heart would have missed a beat when he noticed a brown tree on the side of Lamington Plateau almost hidden by a closer ridge. It looked to be just under a mile from Point Lookout and very close to where his line on the map would have crossed the range. The one brown tree in a sea of green stood out to Bernard even from a distance of some seven miles. It was unusual because the brown leaves covered the tree in a continuous canopy. It looked to him as if it died quickly possibly as a result of some outside influence and not gradually, limb by limb, as trees normally do. Could the brown tree be dying because of fire fuelled by petrol from the crashed Stinson? Lightning can cause this same reaction but there had not been an electrical storm for some time. Bernard put his head down and tore off into the rainforest. He had to find out.

He selected a course that he estimated would take him towards the brown tree. It was impossible to follow a direct line and his bush skills would have been put to the test by the dense rainforest and the topography of the country. He did not have a compass but would rely on the sun when he could see it, the lie of the land and his own sense of direction to get him into the area of the brown tree. He crossed various branches of Christmas Creek and climbed over the ridges in between. He had something to eat beside a stream and toiled up the next range. He was getting very tired and despondent and with the rainforest enclosing him on all sides, he said the utter hopelessness of his task became apparent to him. He climbed a tree in an attempt to obtain a view of Lamington Plateau but the dense rainforest defeated him.

A human call from the direction of Lamington Plateau revived his spirits and it was followed by another. He did not answer immediately because he thought it may have been someone mad like himself searching. Surely if the Stinson was there, no one would be alive after ten days even if they had survived the crash. He called as he dropped into yet another gorge and thought he heard an answer from the range ahead. He cooeed as he toiled up the steep ridge on the other side and there was an immediate answer from down the hill to his right. He followed the direction of the calls. As he approached he could see where a gap had been torn in the rainforest canopy and he realised that he had found the crashed plane. His search was over.

The tangled and charred wreckage of the plane lay before him and as Bernard described it in *Green Mountains* 'a repulsive thing that contained the bodies of men.' He heard voices coming from below the wreck. Two men lay there, both looking as though they were near death. 'Proud, I saw first, his eyes far back in his head like those of a corpse, lying as he had lain for ten days on the wet ground with a leg that was green and swelling and maggoty.' Binstead tried to shake hands with Bernard but his hands as well as his legs were raw flesh from crawling down the mountain to get water. The tragic scene overwhelmed Bernard as he stood there surveying the enormity of it all, but the practical Joe Binstead broke the ice by asking, "How about boiling the billy." As Bernard struggled with the wet wood he heard their story a little at a time.

When the Stinson climbed into the cloud mass approaching the McPherson Range the force of the wind increased, buffeting the plane. The cyclone was now situated off the coast of northern NSW. As it drifted south it generated gale force winds that blew over the valley of the Tweed River to hit the great wall of the McPherson Range. As the wind swept up and over the range it is slowed by the barrier but picks up speed as it funnels down the gorges on the northern side. It is said to reach its maximum speed around a half mile from the crest of the range, and that is where the Stinson came to grief as it was climbing into the teeth of the gale.

The plane was flying blind in heavy cloud and seemed to be at the mercy of the wind. Binstead relates they saw trees through the mist and when the pilot realised that they were not going to make the top of the range he slewed the plane around. This action would have saved the lives of the three men sitting on the port side of the plane. The plane crashed into the side of the mountain hitting a large tree which was chopped off by the impact and came to rest against another one, a giant bollygum that was destined to be Bernard's beacon.

Four people died in the crash or in the resultant fire. They were: the pilots Rex Boyden and Beverley Shepherd, and an American architect, William Fountain, as well as a Sydney businessman, Roland Graham. Three people sitting on the port side of the plane survived the crash. John Proud, who was the first to recover, broke a window and climbed out nursing a badly broken leg. He helped Joe Binstead out and the last to escape was a young Englishman, Jim Westray. The plane was burning fiercely by this time resulting in Jim Westray receiving some rather severe burns.

They would no doubt have been in a state of shock from this tragic experience but as time passed and the fire died down they moved closer to the plane for warmth. They realised that they had been extremely fortunate to survive the crash and as they discussed their situation they believed that search parties would be out looking for them very soon and that they would be rescued in a few days at the most. Jim Westray did not want to wait that long and was impatient to go for help. He left next morning saying he would go down to the stream in the gorge below and follow it to the north where they had seen farms from the plane before it entered the clouds.

The two that were left at the wreck were confident of their early rescue. They drank coffee from a flask that Binstead had found in the wreck that belonged to one of the pilots and then he took the flask with him as he searched for water. He was relieved to find a spring about 300 yards away down the steep side of the mountain. He scrambled through dense lawyer vine and over slippery rocks as he toiled back up the mountain to bring water to Proud. This journey turned into a daily ritual as days passed and the anticipated arrival of a search party did not eventuate. They could hear planes above on their regular daily flights between Brisbane and Sydney and were puzzled by the lack of aircraft searching for them. They were not to know that the search activity was focused on an area much closer to Sydney many miles away.

They maintained a positive outlook throughout the time they were there and to assist search parties they arranged to cooee every hour. They estimated that in such dense forest no one could pass through their range of hearing in

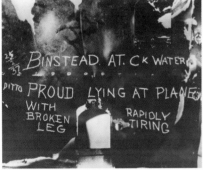

Clockwise from above: Binstead receives a drink during his rescue; John Proud, he had suffered much but his spirit had sustained him; front page news in Sydney; Binstead's message when he went for water.

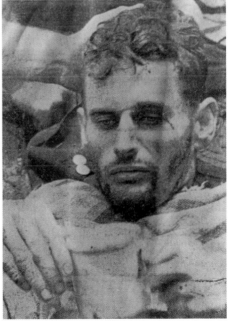

less than an hour. They also realised that if they didn't call someone could be fifty yards away and not know they were there. It was their scheduled call that Bernard heard from across the gorge that eventually drew him to the wreck. Around day four they would have realised that something must have happened to Jim Westray, and as you could imagine, doubts about their survival began to surface.

Their situation was serious and would have forced Joe Binstead to consider his next move. He could stay at the wreck with Proud and trust that help would arrive or he could attempt to reach civilization himself. The surrounding rainforest, the rugged terrain, and the fact that Westray very likely did not make it, would have seemed ominous to someone from Sydney who had never experienced these conditions. Nevertheless I believe that Proud's deteriorating condition is what influenced Binstead to stay. Proud was becoming feverish and the wound where the bone had broken the flesh of his leg had become gangrenous. He certainly needed water and without it he would not last long. Proud unselfishly encouraged Binstead to leave and at least save himself. Joe Binstead was forever the optimist and believed that help would arrive.

Binstead found some fruits from a small palm that grew in the forest locally known as the walking stick palm. The fruits had very little flesh over a large seed and were not all that nourishing but at least they may have lifted their morale. After a week Binstead was too weak to walk and just crawled to the spring to get water. His hands and feet as well as his clothes were torn by lawyer vine. Each trip was now an ordeal for him and as one long day followed another his strength was almost gone. He took the precaution of scratching a message on the metal shell of the plane in case he did not make it back.

25/2/37 Binstead at creek water.
Proud lying at plane with broken leg. Rapidly tiring.

The fact that they were still calling every hour even on the tenth day when Bernard arrived showed their determination to survive. They could not have lasted much longer. Their strength was almost gone but their spirit was still alive. Bernard made tea for them and gave them what food he had, just a small portion of bread. They told him about Jim Westray who had left the crash site nine days earlier. They indicated the direction he took and that he intended to follow a stream out to the north and make contact with the farming community there. Bernard approved of his plan and intended to do the same.

Bernard realised that he would have to return quickly with a doctor and medical supplies as well as food and shelter for the men if they were to be saved. In his heart he thought Proud was too far gone and would not be alive when he returned. He left the men with a supply of water and received their good wishes for a safe journey as he promised to return with a doctor and a hundred men. He followed Westray's tracks in the soft leaf-mould as he descended into a branch of Christmas Creek. He had to negotiate two rather dangerous cliffs, with wet rocks that had bird-nest ferns clinging to them. He could hear the stream below swollen by the recent rains, crashing against the rocks well before he could see it. Westray's tracks turned and followed the stream down and he like Bernard was forced into the stream-bed, by the cliffs on either side.

The going was difficult even for Bernard who had experienced these conditions before and knew how to handle them. The boiling torrent surging around large moss covered boulders offered little grip for wet boots and would certainly have been a challenge for Jim Westray nine days earlier. Bernard came to a waterfall not far down the creek that he found difficult to get past. The drop of the waterfall met the cliffs on either side of the gorge and Bernard had to feel his way carefully over the drop of the fall. He was relieved that Westray seemed to have negotiated this obstacle without harm.

Proud's desperate condition was on his mind as he bounded off down the creek acutely aware that he must try and get out of the rainforest before dark to organize help for the two survivors. He had left the wreck at four-thirty so that meant he had three hours at the most. He passed waterfalls and cascades along the creek and eventually came to a larger fall and looked for the easiest way around it. It was to the right it seemed, and as he walked that way he noticed where the giant helmholtzia or stream lilly had been torn away from the cliff of the waterfall and concluded that this may have been the cause of Westray's downfall. The sword-like leaves and large size of these plants offer good hand and foot holds and give the impression of stability. These plants however are brittle and have very little hold on the rock and would just fall away with the weight of a person.

The route around the waterfall to the right was easy for Bernard as it would have been for Westray but in his haste the Englishman had made a grave mistake. Bernard searched the area under the waterfall but there was no sign of Westray. He was optimistic that he may find him alive with a broken leg or similar injury. After all the two had survived at the plane and at least Westray had a plentiful supply of water. The country was not quite as steep here and Bernard rock-hopped down the creek as fast as his legs would carry him. At every corner he looked ahead expecting to see Westray.

There he was at last, sitting with his back against a rock looking downstream. He was in such a natural position Bernard called out to him but received no answer. He went up to the Englishmen and one glance was enough to tell him that he was dead. He had received head injuries and was bathing his broken ankle in the water when he died. He had John Proud's cigarette case beside him and a burnt out cigarette was still in his fingers so he would have died quite peacefully in the end. He had the roughest part of the journey behind him and was gazing down Christmas Creek where there was help and the comforts of home.

Bernard took a wallet containing a considerable amount of money from Westray, and the cigarette case that lay beside him. He noted that it was getting gloomy in the forest already. Time was slipping away and he still had a long way to go. The finding of Jim Westray's body seemed to cast a shadow over Bernard that followed him as he threw caution to the wind and charged off down the creek. He fell on numerous occasions and waded through the water, at times waist deep, and as darkness closed in he did not let up. After what seemed to him to be an endless battle he saw the country open up and left the stream to walk through tall flooded gums. He followed a snigging track for a time and then heard a shot about fifty yards away. He called and was asked where the hell he had come from. Two Buchanan boys were shooting flying foxes on their fruit trees and they were the first to hear that the Stinson had been found and that there were two survivors.

Bernard drank tea while the boys ran in horses and as he sat there he became conscious of a thousand cuts and bruises and a great tiredness enveloped him. There was no time to rest though, the horses were ready and they rode off down the valley to the Burgess house where Henry promptly drove them to John

Buchanan's house where there was a telephone. They rang Airlines of Australia and it was suggested that Bernard and the local people were in the best position to organise a rescue for the survivors. He discussed with John Buchanan how this could be done and then they continued on to the settlement of Hillview.

Gracie Silcock operated the exchange at Hillview and she spent the night on the telephone. When the sensational news hit the airwaves the press were clamouring for information but first there was a rescue to organise. The party line servicing the upper Christmas Creek and Albert River valleys had around a dozen subscribers and Gracie rang the code for each place in quick succession so people knew that there was some emergency and picked up the phone. The result was they were all on the phone together so they could all talk to each other and have a discussion, a round table conference over the phone. It was one of the advantages of the old party lines.

It was decided that the country was too rough to bring the survivors down the creek the way Bernard had come and that the more even grade along the top of Lamington Plateau would be the best route to carry the stretchers out. To this end John Buchanan who was an experienced timber man and dairy farmer in the district would direct every available man up on to Lamington Plateau. At dawn they would start cutting a track through the rainforest towards the crash site – a distance of around ten miles. They had a big job ahead of them. Gracie Silcock had the task of contacting people from the district to join the cutting party. They were to gather at Hillview during the night with axes and brush-hooks as well as food to take with them.

Bob Stephens from Darlington on the Albert River side, would arrange for a doctor to come to the Stephens home 'Cedar Glen' without delay. A small party accompanied the doctor and took him over a low divide into the Christmas Creek Valley. They had arranged to meet Bernard there at 2:30 in the morning. This plan had the advantage of landing the party with the doctor higher up the valley, thus shortening the difficult creek section. The plans could not be improved on and if the men were to be saved the will and the organization was there to do it.

Bernard restocked his food supply while he was at Hillview and he also rang the Guest House to tell them the good news. It was now time to leave if his small group was going to keep its 2:30 appointment. They travelled first by car then on horseback and Bernard was not looking forward to plunging into the streambed again. The party with the doctor was waiting when Bernard's group arrived and the billy was boiling. Bernard looked as if he needed a doctor himself by this time, so he was given some medical treatment and they were on their way. The going was slow in the dark and it was extremely difficult floundering along a rocky streambed while loaded with gear. Daylight came and Westray's body was moved out of the creek and into a palm grove nearby. His grave is there today in a tranquil and beautiful setting of piccabeen palms and tall rainforest trees.

The creek was rougher and steeper now and they found it difficult avoiding cascades and waterfalls. At last they came to the spot where Bernard knew they must leave the creek and head up the steep side of the mountain. He and Bob Stephens went on ahead carrying some sustenance for the men at the plane and were relieved to see that both were still alive. They boiled the billy and while this was happening whipped up some brandy, eggs and milk in a pannikin that was given sparingly to the men. The doctor arrived and examined both men. He treated Proud's leg and stated that he believed the maggots eating the gangrenous flesh had checked the spread of infection. They had saved Proud's life and the doctor believed his leg could be saved as well. When the doctor had sedated the men they were moved up on to a level area and a tarpaulin was erected to make a dry shelter for them. They would have to spend another night on the mountain.

A question that people ask at times is – who took the photos of the men at the wreck before they were moved away from the plane? It was a coincidence that a freelance photographer, Herb Meissner, who did work for the newspapers, was staying in the Albert River Valley at the time. He made the most of the opportunity and came up with the doctor's party. He was guided out before the stretcher track was completed and believed that his film was ruined because of the rain. It was soon proved otherwise and his photos appeared in every daily newspaper in Australia.

A track was cut from the crash site to the top of Lamington Plateau and contact was made with the track cutting party about sunset. They had done a tremendous job cutting ten miles of track in a day. Both groups spent a long wet night generally standing together around smoky fires drinking tea and telling yarns to while away the time. Daylight was welcome and the task of carrying the stretchers fourteen miles to the waiting ambulances soon began. Men went on ahead trimming the track so there would be no encumbrance to the stretcher-bearers. Water was carried to nourish the group along the way and to boil the billy later in the day. Relieving carriers were needed because the stretchers were kept moving. They had gone many miles when they came to the lead group who had boiled the billy and the stretchers were put down while they had a mug of tea.

They emerged from the rainforest at the end of the plateau and then the stretchers were carefully taken down the steep side of the mountain and along the valley to the waiting ambulances. There was a tremendous crowd there to greet them including many people from the press. I have viewed some film of Joe Binstead being put into the ambulance. He had survived a near-death experience but that did not stop a reporter asking him if he had anything to say. I admired him for his reply. He said, "I would like to thank the men who carried us out, they did a terrific job. I would also like to offer my condolences to the relatives of the people who died."

An interesting event that resulted from the loss of the plane was that a memorial service was being held for Joe Binstead in St Matthew's Anglican Church at Manly in Sydney that was attended by his wife and daughter. As the rector was delivering the eulogy for the deceased a police officer came to the door and interrupted him and gave them the incredible news that Joe was one of two survivors of the crash. All present were ecstatic and the memorial service turned into one of thanksgiving.

That is where the drama ended as the ambulances drove away but the story is still alive today. It is now part of our history. Bernard would have taken quite some time to recover from his ordeal but the episode had propelled his name and even that of the family into the newspapers and on to everyone's lips. He was invited to Sydney and was met at the train by the mayor and given a civic reception at the Town Hall. People everywhere wanted to meet him even many years later.

In 1967, thirty years later, we had a Stinson reunion dinner at the Guest House and I met the survivors Joe Binstead and John Proud for the first time. Quite a number of the stretcher-bearers came back for the celebration. It was a moving occasion and we enjoyed hearing first hand the stories of the people involved in the drama.

The following words were written by Bernard and distributed as a memorial of the occasion. This small booklet had space for signatures that people made use of and concluded with a poem composed by Bernard.

1937 STINSON 1967

Tonight we remember an event
which brought out all that was best
in human endurance and human nature.

We, the actors in that drama of
thirty years ago look back on
those golden hours.

IN RETROSPECT

When the valleys turn to purple
And the sun is riding low
We'll be sitting on our doorsteps
And we'll dream of long ago –
When our backs could bear the burden
And our arms were young and strong
We'll be dreaming of the old days
With the shadows growing long.

Bernard O'Reilly.

Mick

The management of the Guest House for 50 years from the 1950s was in the hands of Mick and Annie O'Reilly and their family, and now is under the control of their grandchildren. Mick's contribution was significant so I shall go back and follow his trail. After the First World War he spent quite a bit of time working away from the mountain and did not have a major involvement with the early Guest House. His trail will eventually lead you to Conondale in the Mary River Valley of Queensland where Vince and I were raised. Although our time there has little relevance to the Guest House, Conondale naturally is the heart of Vince and my childhood memories and somehow I do not want it to be a blank space in our history.

I believe life on a dairy farm as we experienced it, in the latter stage of the depression and during the war, was a good grounding for two lads who would later take on the responsibility of managing *O'Reillys* Guest House. Our parents were no different from many other families on dairies at that time; they could not afford to pay labour so the running of the dairy was the responsibility of Mum, Dad and the kids. We all had our jobs to do and the dairy was the focus of our lives. The Guest House demanded the same all-consuming life. Whether on the dairy or at the Guest House we never worked any particular hours but did the job that had to be done. Both these occupations demanded the same commitment – you put your life into it. To quote my old mate Reg Cullen, "When you are on a dairy the cows are the boss and when you run a Guest House the guests are the boss."

I will go back in history to pick up Mick's trail at their old home on Long Swamp Creek. When he was not much more than a lad he started his first job at Kanimbla Station which was a large grazing property in the Blue Mountains area of NSW. It was situated on the Cox River not far from the O'Reilly home. It was managed by John Berghofer who, for some unknown reason, had a disagreement with the O'Reillys. In an interview years later he said he knew them well and wouldn't say what the disagreement was about. His son, also called John, took over the management of the property in 1903 and it would have been him that Mick worked for.

DISTRICT _Brisbane_

MAXIMUM
AREA ALLOWED } _144 Yacs._

"THE LAND ACT OF 1910."

APPLICATION TO SELECT AN AGRICULTURAL FARM.

RECEIVED this _20th_ day of _Sept_, 19_11_, at _12·50_ o'clock.

A. Mallaber
Land Agent at _Brisbane_

*State Christian
Name and Surname
in full.

†State Occupation.

I, *_Eugene Michael O'Reilly,_ of _Katoomba_ _new_
†_Labourer_, hereby apply to select the Crown Lands described in the Schedule hereto, as an Agricultural Farm, under the provisions of "_The Land Act of_ 1910," and I herewith lodge the sum of _Five_ pounds _seventeen_ shillings and _seven_ pence, on account of the First Year's

‡Insert "Natural
born" or
"Naturalised."

Rent and Survey Fee. I am a ‡ _natural born_ subject of His Majesty, and of the full age of _sixteen_ years. I apply to select the land in order that I may hold and use it for my own exclusive benefit according to law, and not as a trustee, agent, or servant of or for any other person. And the said land, together with all other land now held by me as Agricultural Selections in the same District, does not exceed _100_ acres, and the area of all such lands held by me in the State does not exceed 2,560 acres.

I offer that the Selection shall be subject to the condition of personal residence during the first five years of the term of the lease, and I undertake to perform that condition.

SURVEYED

SCHEDULE.

Date of Notification : _19. 5. 11_   Portion Nos. _43 4_

Page in _Gazette_ : _1750_   Area of each Portion : } _99. 1. 0 4_

County : _Ward_   Total Area applied for : }

Parish : _Roberts_   Purchasing Price per Acre : _35/-_

Particulars of other Selections held } _nil_
or applied for by Applicant }

DATED at _Katoomba_ this _25th_ day of _September_ 19_11_

[Signature of Applicant] _Eugene Michael O'Reilly_

WITNESS : _Edward Dowdell_

Area of Land applied for.			Annual Rent per Acre.	Deposit.			COMMISSIONER'S DECISION :
A.	R.	P.		£	s.	d.	
99.	1.	0	10½	4	6	11	_Accepted_ _Wm A Ath_
							Land Commissioner
⅕ Survey Fee	_£7..13..0..._			1	10	8	_7/10/11_
TOTAL				£5	17	7	

DUP. TO S.O.

44

He had a number of skills that he later passed on to us that he would have picked up from John Berghofer who was an experienced property manager. Mick knew how to break down a carcass of beef correctly so the meat could be used most effectively. He was also skilled at sharpening butchers knives and crosscut saws and could spay heifers and castrate the bull calves and do many other jobs he would have learnt on Kanimbla.

Mick with four brothers and three cousins, selected land on the mountain in 1911 when he was eighteen years of age. The block he selected, Portion 43, includes the area where the Tree Top Walk and Gardens are now located. I cannot remember my father looking robust and strong. He had rheumatic fever as a child and was dressed in red flannel by his mother, that was considered the thing to do at the time. It kept him away from school for the best part of two years but I was always impressed by his general knowledge and his excellent handwriting. If we didn't know how to spell a word we asked Dad.

'Falling scrub' in the cool wet conditions on the mountain took a toll on Micks health. When he became sick he would head to his friends, the Doherty family in the Kerry Valley, and Mrs Doherty would nurse him back to health. She was heard to say that young Mick will never make old bones, he is too frail. They were very good to him and he had great affection for them all. I always enjoyed Mick's yarns about the family, especially about old Hughie who was the local butcher and a bit of a character.

Mick would have fallen most of the rainforest on his block before the First World War with the help of his brothers. He fell hoop pine on Flying Fox Creek for Lahey's sawmill at Canungra to earn some money during that time. He enjoyed his time there and although he was not one to talk much of the past he would give us glimpses of life there at times. There was a huge flying fox or fruit bat camp there and many of them were killed when the tall hoop pine trees came crashing down. The area was also frequented by numbers of big fat carpet pythons that were living on the fruit bats. Mick had great respect for David Lahey who was in charge of the organization and spoke well of him. He said that they were good employers and treated their workers well.

He was a good worker and would have appreciated being part of life as it was in Canungra at the time. The mill employed a large workforce and in those earlier times was the reason for the town's existence. A train-line had been put through up the Coomera River Valley from Canungra to access the good timber there and Mick worked on Flying Fox Creek which was a tributary of the Coomera. The upper Coomera River Valley is known locally as Pine Creek. He would have had his horse with him in Canungra but may have travelled to work on the train at times because of all the gear they required. An axe, a brush-hook, a cross-cut saw, a wallaby jack and maul and wedges were all necessary and had to be carried quite often over rough country to the trees that had to be felled.

Bullock teams cross Canungra Creek to the mill

Some of the trees were in difficult situations and it was the duty of the faller, the fellow who fell the tree to cut a track to it for the bullock team to haul the logs out. The bullock drivers were known for their colourful language and if the track into the log was not up to scratch the bullockies were not very complimentary. The tall hoop pine trees were cut into manageable lengths by the faller and then the bark was stripped off them. The leading end on the log was tapered to make it easier for the bullock teams to haul the logs to the railhead.

Bullock teams were an essential part of the operation. They even brought the train and the rolling stock in to Canungra in the first place because there was no rail link at the time. As well as hauling the logs on their way to the mill they hauled the sawn timber from Canungra to the railway at Jimboomba that was about twenty miles away. During the severe drought of 1900-1 the operation of the mill ground to a halt because there was not enough feed for the bullocks.

Canungra was a full day's ride away from the O'Reilly selections at the time and Mick would have made an early start if he hoped to get home before dark. He talked of riding home up the Canungra Creek Valley and climbing up over the Sarabah Range. He crossed the range near the first two hairpin bends at what is now known as 'The Racecourse' on the Canungra-O'Reillys road. He then forded Cainbable Creek and rode up the Albert River Valley to arrive home via the Stockyard Creek Track. The O'Reillys had many friends in the Kerry Valley and as was the custom in those days he would have called in for a yarn and a feed along the way. I imagine the Kerry Hotel would have had some appeal for Mick as well.

He went to Europe in the First World War, sailing over with his brother Ped. While he was there he received word that his father had died in Brisbane and soon after that his elder brother Norb had been killed in France. It was a distressing time for all the family. Mick was always skinny and felt the cold and said that he was not warm all the time he was in Europe. He spent time in a hospital in England with a leg injury and was eventually sent home because of his health. This saved him from taking any further part in what was a terrible war.

Mick spent time in a military hospital after returning home and took months to recover his health. He then applied for the position of National Park Ranger and was employed as a working overseer on four pound a week by the Forestry Dept. His temporary appointment lasted from 1919 till 1923 and thus Mick became the first Ranger of any national park in Queensland. He supplied his own horse and rode around the park boundaries checking that the extensive logging that was taking place at the time did not encroach on the national park. He was given a compass as part of his equipment to check the lines and it is still in the hands of the O'Reilly family.

He continued his association with the timber industry when he took on a pine falling contract for the next two years. The work was carried out on Boldries, a block of land about five miles north of the O'Reilly huts. He had men working for him both fallers and bullockies and one of these was Wally Grout, father of the famous cricketer. Wally was a good worker and Mick thought a lot of him but if they were working late and it was getting dark Wally would say, "Mick have you ever been bitten by a Possum?" and Mick would know it was time to knock off. I think he would have made good money there because the trees were tall and straight and he was paid by the super foot for the timber that was sent to the mill. Falling pine in rainforest could be dangerous for the inexperienced but Mick had been at it for a while and knew the game quite well. He camped at the top of what is now known as Mick O'Reillys Creek.

Mick told us that if a hoop pine grew on the boundary line between two blocks, the direction the tree was leaning indicated who the tree belonged to. He said that a faller could encourage the tree to fall away from the lean provided the lean was not too pronounced. This was done by putting a belly or an open cut on the side that you wanted the tree to fall and then by putting in a cut with the cross-cut saw on the opposite side above the belly. As the cut deepened the faller would follow the saw with wedges belting them into the saw cut to bring the head of the tree over and change its centre of gravity till eventually the tree fell on your side of the boundary. Mick was generally very honest but there must have been a bit of the rogue in him. Maybe it depended on who owned the block next door.

Tom and Herb O'Reilly both worked on Boldries putting tracks around the sides of the steep country for the bullock teams. They were both considered to be good workers and were noted for their road-making skills. Tom utilized his experience as a 'powder monkey' if explosives were needed and they certainly were needed when he worked on the log chute on the Cainbable Creek side. Pat O'Reilly had a bullock team working there as well and hauled logs to the chute where they were shot down the mountain-side into the Cainbable Creek Gorge. A good taper was cut on the leading edge of the logs that were to go down the chute and they were normally slippery if they had just been barked so once they started moving they gained speed quickly. It was an impressive operation and was certainly worth watching. The log chute itself is quite spectacular and is still in evidence today.

Mick later bought a block of land lower down on Cainbable Creek that he cleared to grow bananas. These blocks were originally surveyed as banana blocks and Mick built a hut and lived down there for a time. He found from experience that the soil was too heavy and the bananas were slow to develop. One night when he was there he heard a rustling noise outside and took his gun and went out in his socks hoping to shoot a rat that had been raiding his tucker each night. He was wading through some weeds and felt something tugging at his sock. He gave a wild kick and in the lantern light saw a tiger snake flying through the air. It had latched on to the end of his sock that was sticking out past his toes. He was by himself in an isolated place and if he had been bitten that would have been the end of the story.

Mick, like other members of the family, rode to the Kerry dances and he would arrange for the lady in the Kerry Hotel to wash and iron his good clothes so they would be ready for the next dance. He always liked to be neatly dressed. There were two sides to his personality – he was serious and focused when it came to getting a job done but there was a lighter side to him. Before the First World War, when groups of young people rode up to the mountain from the nearby valleys, Mick and Luke appear in most of the photographs taken so they both enjoyed these occasions. He had a good sense of humour and liked nothing better than spinning a few yarns over a rum or a beer. He had a loyal band of friends who thought the world of him but he was not an outgoing personality.

Bernard when writing in *Green Mountains* records some of the tricks Mick got up to as a child like putting a match under the thermometer just when the men were coming outside to see how cold it was. For the people who knew him this seemed to be out of character and even I have trouble seeing him as a mischievous youngster. I know some of the antics of his second son did not amuse him all that much.

He talked of trapping rabbits that were in plague proportions when he was a lad and had driven many families off the land. He, with one of his brothers, decided to blow up a warren that was somewhere near their home. Mick had trapped a rabbit and tied a half a plug of gelignite to its chest, inserted a detonator and fuse, which he lit and let the rabbit go. The rabbit was probably a bit dazed from being in the trap and ran to the entrance of the burrow and stopped. There was a hell of an explosion but the amazing thing was when the dust settled the rabbit was still standing there. Mick reasoned that because the explosion occurred at the entrance to the burrow its force was directed into the air behind the rabbit. I don't know if their parents had any knowledge of what they were doing but looking at their adventure from today's perspective it does seem pretty wild. How standards have changed over a hundred years.

Mick's hut on Portion 43 was only small but I imagine he made use of it himself when the other family members arrived and the hut on Morans Creek became crowded. Visitors made use of his hut at times as well and the naturalist, Sydney William Jackson, stayed in there in 1921 when researching the rufous scrub-bird. It rained almost every day during his five weeks stay and he ended up christening it 'The Ark'. He was confined to the hut for long periods and the monotonous call of a wonga pigeon day after day became too much for him. He ended up shooting it and having it for dinner. Jackson spent a lot of time in the bush and was used to living off the land. He is seen in the accompanying photograph cooking scrub turkey eggs outside Mick's hut.

Sydney William Jackson cooking turkey eggs

If Mick were around today I would ask him a few questions. I am not sure what association he had with the mountain during this time but he is not recorded in *Green Mountains* as having any significant involvement with the Guest House once it opened. Mick was of a practical frame of mind and I imagine he couldn't see that a living could be made for all the family members present, first from dairying and later from the Guest House. Another thing that may have influenced him was his intention to marry Annie O'Neill. I imagine Mick, who always liked to do the right thing, wanted 'a few quid in his pocket' when they tied the knot. He would have made good money while pine falling although the banana growing venture was a failure.

When Mick and Annie married they bought a dairy at Mooloola so there must have been some money somewhere. I imagine it wasn't Annie's money as she, like Mick, was one of a family of ten children and was born and bred on a dairy farm. Her face appears in some old photos taken on the mountain before the First World War when large groups of local people rode up there. How long he was courting her I don't know but Mick never rushed into things. He wrote to her in 1917 from a hospital in England when he was in the army. He was recovering from an injury to his leg, which must have been rather serious, because he said he would be able to walk on it again before too long. It was just a chatty card so there was nothing serious in the air at the time.

Mick and Annie were married on November 20th 1929.

The following item appeared in the *Beaudesert Times,* Friday December 6th 1929.

Wedding

A picturesque wedding took place in St Mary's Roman Catholic Church, South Brisbane on November 20th, when Rev. Father Hennessy (Beaudesert) solemnised the marriage of Mr. Michael O'Reilly (son of Mrs R. O'Reilly and the late Mr. P. O'Reilly, National Park Beaudesert) and Miss Anne O'Neill (second daughter of Mrs K O'Neill, and the late Mr T. O'Neill "Glandore", Beaudesert). Miss Julie O'Neill, was bridesmaid, and Mr Bernard O'Reilly was best man.

Conondale Our Childhood

Mick and Annie bought a dairy in the Mooloola River Valley north of Brisbane in early 1930, during the Depression. Vince was born in 1931 in Brisbane because of some difficulty with the birth and I was told that Vince was a sick little boy for a time. They sold the dairy at Mooloola and with newborn baby Vince travelled to Conondale where they bought a dairy on the Mary River. I was born in Maleny the nearest town in 1933 and with Vince I spent the first eleven years of my life there.

My parent's decision to leave Mooloola and buy a larger dairy at Conondale would have been influenced by Mick receiving money for his original selection on the mountain. A company had just been formed to raise money for the expansion of the Guest House and a decision was made to buy the original selectors out. According to the company minutes Mick was to be paid £800 in 1931 and the remaining £400 ten years later in 1941 for his land.

Mick had never worked on a dairy but Annie had been born and bred on one and could really milk cows. This was just as well because for the first six years or so they milked by hand. It would have been a tough time for my parents. The Depression lingered on in country areas and the Second World War was just around the corner. Mick had never been a farmer either but he had to learn quickly if they were going to make the place pay. I have a book that he bought while at Conondale that would have been his bible while on the farm. *The Farmers Handbook* was compiled by the NSW Dept of Agriculture and is an amazing book that covers every aspect of farm life. Everything from how to use a broad-axe to harnessing horses to planting crops and sharpening tools are all there described in great detail.

My father said he was pleased to see me when I was born, which is understandable when he gazed on the face of his second son. He added, with a glint in his eye, that the child endowment seemed like a fortune to him at the time and that he was desperately short of cash. The depression hung over the land and Mick said his cream cheque for the month was £10 and he couldn't meet the repayments on the farm. Fortunately for him he had bought the dairy from a well-known local family, and they did not foreclose and told Mick they knew he would pay them when he could and of course Mick did.

My mother stayed at a boarding house in Maleny that was run by the Madden Sisters when my birth was imminent. It would have been the sensible thing to do because my parents did not have any means of transport or a phone at the time. Two-year old Vince would have stayed with Dad and I imagine one of his sisters would have come down from the mountain to help out. I think of my Mother and the workload she must have had at the time caring for a baby and a toddler as well as milking cows, cooking meals and doing a thousand other jobs around the house and the dairy. There was no refrigeration and the copper had to be lit to heat water to wash nappies. It was no more and no less than what other dairy farmer's wives were doing at the time but they never stopped. There were dairies everywhere along the coast in the first half of the twentieth century run by families and an essential part of that family was the lady of the house who literally did everything.

Peter and Vince O'Reilly at Conondale

I find it a pleasant experience to let my mind drift back to the Conondale of my childhood. Dad and Mum are working hard to pay the bills but that was not a worry for us kids. Life was free and easy and revolved around the farm. I was very young and one of my earliest memories takes me back and I am with my father. There is a truck backed into the ramp at the pigsty and Dad with the local carrier are forcing pigs up the ramp and into the truck to the accompaniment of much squealing and shouting. There is a calf tied up to the fence and Dad unties it and gives it to the carrier who pays him two shillings (20 cents) for it. It is my birthday and Dad walks over and gives me the two shillings. It is a lot of money and I have never seen a coin so bright and shiny before. I keep turning it over in my hand admiring it but then Dad takes it off me in case I lose it.

When I was older and went to Maleny for the day to go to the dentist, Mum would give me two shillings to spend. That would buy a penny ice cream when I arrived and a pie and vegetables for lunch sitting down at a café that we thought was the ultimate in luxury. I also had enough left for a malted milk and a bun before getting on the cream truck for the trip home. I've always loved those old-fashioned buns with lots of sultanas and not spicy as they seem to be today.

I remember my mother relating an instance that I must have been too young to remember. There was a wire netting fence around the house and a bush stone-curlew had landed inside it during the night. In trying to get out it had put its head through the wire netting and taken all the skin off its neck. Dad had to do away with it and times were tough so Mum cleaned it and cooked it for dinner. We kids really enjoyed the treat and are soon back with our plates saying, "More curlew Mum, more curlew."

The Conondale and Maleny districts were all dairy farms so we shared our way of life with the children at school. Our only means of transport other than horses was the cream truck that went to Maleny three times a week and brought back supplies for us. We didn't have a car so it was a real adventure for us to go to Maleny in the cream truck. It was a thirteen-mile trip, which included what was then the tortuous climb up the Conondale Range. A real test for the heavily laden 'Maple Leaf' was negotiating the Devils Elbow, a steep sharp bend near the top of the range. There were many stops along the way picking up cans of cream. On the trip home bread, meat, mail and a hundred other items were delivered to the various cream boxes along the way and if there was a drum of fuel aboard it meant a trip into someone's dairy.

We did not have a telephone but Mrs Sleba in the exchange left any messages for us in our cream box. We bought an ice chest later that never seemed to be a success because the ice was nearly all melted by the time the cream truck brought it from Maleny. Flies were a number one enemy and there was a real battle in the house to keep them at bay. Flypapers hung untidily from the ceiling in long strips with dead flies stuck all over them. They had a job to do but the interior decorators of today would have trouble matching them with the décor of any kitchen. Glass flytraps were also used with sugar placed under them to attract the flies and were a continual source of amusement for us kids. We didn't mind watching the flies come to grief.

Another scourge, as far as I was concerned, were those little black ants that seemed to get into everything. I hated the flavour of them and they had a habit of sneaking into the bread or meat unnoticed. The legs of our food cupboard stood in used jam tins that were filled with water to keep the ants out of our food. There were no chemicals around in those days that could be used and we were probably all the healthier for it.

We had kerosene lamps in the house and a lantern was always handy if we had to go outside to bring in wood for the stove or to visit the 'dunny' that stood in lonely isolation further down the hill. When we were older our parents bought a rather cumbersome 'cabinet wireless set' and listening to serials became an important part of our day, *Dad and Dave* and *Mrs Obs* couldn't be missed. We had to be quiet while Dad listened to the news to get the latest reports on how the war was going. We hated the storm season when static interrupted proceedings or when the battery went flat on the wireless and had to be taken to Maleny in the cream truck to be charged. It would be away for a couple of days.

We kids were always expected to give a hand at the dairy. Dad and Mum would get up early and milk and then call us to go down to the yard at half past six. Some of the kids at school had to get up much earlier. Vince helped finish the milking and I swept the bails. We fed the calves and then I took the cows out to the paddock that had been selected for them that day. It was then up to the house for breakfast and off to school. On Monday morning it was my job to go out to the day paddock and bring in the draft horses. Dad didn't work in the cultivation on Sunday so the horses had the day off. If the fog was thick and I had trouble finding the horses I was sometimes late for school.

After school Vince and I took it in turns to take a crust of bread that enticed Shirley our little black pony to be caught and then go for the cows. The one at home went down to the dairy to help Mum set up for the milking. The separator was assembled and a fire lit so there would be hot water for the washing up later. Vince helped with the milking while I shelled corn for the chooks with the help of the two Sleba girls from the exchange who come over to get milk. I fed the chooks, collected the eggs and helped feed the calves with Vince and then drove the cows out to their selected paddock. We relied on tanks for water and when the tanks were low mum sent us down to the river for a swim in lieu of a bath.

When Mick first bought a pony for us he probably couldn't afford a saddle so we rode bareback. We had a few 'spills' but we accepted that as a normal occurrence. If we hit the ground Shirley would wait for us and then stand patiently beside a log or a stump while we made hard work of climbing aboard. We would canter up and down the river banks after the cows and I believe that riding bareback helped us acquire good balance and that we were better riders as a result.

Dad eventually bought a small saddle and when he put it on Shirley for us to try he thought we would be really pleased. We soon found out that the leathers pinched our bare legs and really we didn't like anything about it at all. Our reaction must have been a disappointment for Dad who ended up giving it or selling it to one of his neighbours. When we went to the mountain years later we still rode bareback until we grew up. We found that riding home from the Dump on a cold night was a lot warmer sitting bareback on a horse then on a cold saddle.

The local dairy farmers all separated their milk and the cream was sent to the Maleny butter-factory and the separated milk fed to the pigs. We had some good cultivation paddocks on either side of the Mary River and Dad grew crops mainly for pig and cow feed. He also grew potatoes and other vegetables at times. He had two beautiful draft horses, Prince and Star, and did his cultivation work with them. We never had a wagon or a dray but Dad made a slide that was used to bring in crops such as corn and pumpkins. Mick had a frame built on to the slide and fording the open crossing of the Mary River with a load of pumpkins was always a thrill for us. He also took the cream out to the road on the slide to be picked up by the cream truck. I remember him cutting lucerne with a scythe and digging sweet potatoes by hand.

One of our neighbours gave me a half sugar-bag of peanuts which was a highlight for us and I suppose Mick was encouraging me to be a farmer and suggested I plant some to have to eat next year. He came home one afternoon and said he had left a row down in the cultivation for my peanuts but by that time I had eaten most of them which didn't impress him very much. I had a few left which Mum made room for me to plant in her vegetable garden and it gave me a thrill to harvest a mini crop of peanuts.

I have pleasant memories of the Conondale State School but I seemed to be at the wrong end of the class most of the time and I can never remember putting much effort into my schoolwork. We had a slate to write on which I managed quite well and a smelly wet rag to clean it after each lesson. My worst memory was of those copybooks where we had to copy the very neat writing at the top of the page. This was done by dipping a pen into an inkwell and wiping off the excess ink on the side of the ink well, then proceeding. Well, as my friends know, I am not the neatest person in the world and it was always a disaster with blots of ink and wobbly writing.

Some things must have sunk in because I can rattle off the tables we learnt at school as if it were yesterday. I still have a scrapbook that I put together at school featuring the Royal Family and battleships and tanks that were fighting in the war. We must have been real patriots at the time because the Australian flag was raised on the flagpole each morning and we lined up and saluted it before marching into school. We sang *God Save the King* on all special occasions and we even learnt *Advance Australia Fair*, which I thought was a dirge and still do. I am a *Waltzing Matilda* man myself.

To me it was a carefree time as your childhood should be and the only shadow that hung over our heads was the war and what would happen if the Japs arrived. The families who worked on dairies worked as a unit and the whole family shared the same problems, the droughts and the good times, the highs and lows of dairy-farming. When we went to school we had much in common with our friends there who were nearly all from dairies. Some children rode horses to school while some came in the cream truck and others walked quite long distances. We played games during lunch hour that we really enjoyed. On Friday we had a religion class and us Catholics would go over to my Mother's place and she would teach us our prayers.

We had a calf club at school and each child selected a calf or at least our parents did. We groomed it and taught it to lead and on calf club day took it to school to join a parade. There were four milking breeds represented – Jerseys, Guernseys, AIS and Friesians and each breed was judged separately and ribbons awarded. Vince received a ribbon in the Jersey breed with his calf 'Minty'.

We never wore shoes to go to school or even to go to Maleny so it was real torture when we had to put them on to go to Mass, which only happened occasionally. Our friends the Aherns and the Daltons both had cars and would sometimes take us to either Maleny or Kenilworth to Mass. Our shoes always seemed to be too tight as we had probably grown a bit since we had last put them on and Mum would have to put up with a couple of whinging kids.

Guns were a part of life on the farm and Dad taught us how to handle a firearm safely. One Sunday afternoon when Mum and Dad usually had a rest Dad sent me down to the cultivation with the .22 to give the lorikeets a scare. There were clouds of them on the sorghum. I had a shot at them and hit two with the one shot, there were so many birds. I fired again and hit another one and then decided to go home with three birds from two shots. Dad would have got a shock because all he wanted me to do was frighten them away. I remember being really disappointed because it was Sunday afternoon and Mum was having a rest and didn't feel inclined to get up and clean them and cook them for dinner. It would seem an odd thing to do for a little bloke who had at least a casual interest in birds to shoot lorikeets but protecting the crop was important to us all in those days.

The incident illustrates the freedom our generation had that was with us right through to adulthood. I was lucky to be part of a generally unsupervised and not over regulated generation who took some responsibility for them selves and were prepared to contribute to the wellbeing of the family. We survived without warning labels on containers, without helmets and without a thousand rules and regulations we have today that seems to negate your own judgment and common sense. For kids to grow into responsible adults they should be given responsibilities in their formative years and be encouraged to contribute to family life.

The War

The War was coming closer. Trenches were dug in the school ground by volunteers from the district and we enjoyed doing air-raid drill. Mrs Sleba, the lady in the exchange, had to identify and report all aircraft that flew over to headquarters in Brisbane where the searchlights were visible of a night. Planes flying at night were rare when I was a little bloke and I can remember my parents pointing out a plane flying past to the east of our house one night and wondered why I couldn't see it. No – all I could see was a bloody star moving along.

The second time I broke my arm it was a nasty break from a buster off a horse and I was taken to Maleny Hospital by Mr Garret the schoolteacher at Conondale. Doctor Para who set my arm was not happy with it and advised that it should be X-rayed. This could not be done in Maleny so it meant a trip to Brisbane and the quickest way to get there was in the *Courier-Mail* truck. It normally took two days to travel to Brisbane from Conondale because the cream truck did not arrive in Maleny in time to catch the bus to Landsborough that connected with the train. The *Courier-Mail* truck was not supposed to carry passengers but during the war the authorities seemed to be more lenient. The driver was an obliging man and after Mum arrived from Conondale and lumbered me out of hospital we were soon sitting up in the back of the *Courier-Mail* truck with bundles of newspapers and bags of charcoal for the gas producer that powered the truck.

By the time we arrived at Brisbane in the enclosed back of the truck I was not feeling too well, my arm was swelling under the plaster and aching like blazes. After a long wait the X-ray indicated my arm had to be set again. This meant another dose of the dreaded ether and a stay in hospital. The worst memory other than the ether during my stay in the Mater Children's was being so thirsty yet not being allowed to have water for twenty-four hours after the anaesthetic. I was not allowed to drink after my Maleny anaesthetic and had drunk very little since before I broke my arm. My mouth was so dry and parched. I nearly drove the nurses mad bringing me glasses of water after my time of abstinence had ended.

We went to my mother's old home 'Glandore' at Laravale south of Beaudesert after I left hospital and then over to her sister May Smith at the Kerry Hotel which was a country pub. I listened to the men talking in the bar about what would happen when the Japs arrived, at that stage it seemed to be accepted by many people that they couldn't be stopped. I went to bed and worried about it and it was on my mind till the end of the war.

Dad was part of the VDC, the Voluntary Defence Corp., at Conondale and when I think about it *Dad's Army* had nothing on them. Men from around the district turned up with rifles of all shapes and sizes and even a shotgun and were trained and drilled by a retired army officer. I remember them marching around the school ground and a few of us kids put sticks over our shoulders and marched along behind them until the officer told us to get the hell out of it. They all had target practice on a stump down in the paddock afterwards. It is amusing to look back on now but it was deadly serious at the time as the Japs were not far away in New Guinea.

The war effort was all around us. Coupons were required to buy all the essential food items such as tea, sugar, butter and meat as well as clothing. We were lucky to live on a dairy and be partly self-sufficient. We grew some vegetables, churned our own butter and even killed a vealer on occasions. Some of these activities were not legal because of restrictions that were placed on what could be done with farm produce during the war. Clothing was not a big item on the dairy because we rarely went out and Annie did a busy trade in hand-me-downs with her sisters who all had the same problems.

Coupons were also required for petrol and severe restrictions were placed on the amount of petrol used. Private vehicles were only allowed to travel eighty miles (130km) a month and the speed limit was reduced to thirty miles per hour (50kph). Many vehicles including the cream trucks used gas-producers for power that ran on charcoal. They had to be fired up to produce gas and sat outside on the running boards of the vehicles using them. They were not very pleasant things and drivers were never happy with them but they were a common sight during the war. Bags of charcoal had to be carried to feed the fire and were inclined to cover the interior of any vehicle in black grit.

There was an air of uncertainty in the community and it became more personal when a lad we knew well was killed in New Guinea. We, like many of the other families in the district, were offered Italian prisoners of war to work on the dairies. They were conscripts and not interested in the war and were really good people. Mick had just bought the dairy next door and ran both as one large dairy so he was glad of the help. The POWs were dressed in red clothes and lived in a building on the farm. Vince and I liked them and we got on well together. John especially became a real friend and said he was going to migrate to Australia after the war and would come and visit us but by that time we would have left Conondale.

Our aunts and uncles Molly, Rose, Ann, Bernard, Tom, Pete and Joe as well as our cousin Rhelma visited us during the war and for Vince and me they were all highlights. These visits would have reinforced a connection with the Guest House. Rose, who was my Godmother, gave me a torch for my seventh birthday. It was the first one that I had seen and I was thrilled. Vince and I made up a game and he hid in the house somewhere and I would come looking for him with the torch. When I found him he jumped out and frightened me and I dropped the torch and it went out. What a disaster! I started bawling but Rose soon had the torch back together again and all was well.

Tom would help on the farm for a while and then go prospecting for gold in Little Yabba Creek that was down the road a bit. Ann was content to sit beside the Mary River and fish for hours and usually came home with a catfish or an eel. We ate eels in those days. Bernard painted our bodies with blue inkweed berries with all sorts of crazy designs. He and Ped both called while on leave from the war. We had a cat Topsy who was good at keeping the mice population at an acceptable level and she had kittens at regular intervals that would mysteriously disappear after a short time. This happened while Ped was with us on leave and we blamed the goanna that used to pinch the eggs and even the chickens on occasions. Next time it happened we wrote to Ped who was overseas by this time to tell him the bloody goanna had taken the kittens again. We must have been a couple of gullible kids.

Jane O'Reilly my grandmother, came to live with us for a while. Conondale had a warmer climate than the mountain and she had not been well and felt the cold. She was taken to Maleny Hospital when her health deteriorated and I went up in the cream truck one day to see her. Mum gave me a parcel to take up for her. While I was talking to her she had a turn and started bleeding from the mouth. I called the nurses and they shot me outside. I hung around for a while at a loss what to do. She didn't recover and I believe I was the last one to speak to her. She was buried beside her husband Peter in the Bald Hills cemetery north of Brisbane.

I can remember visiting the Guest House from Conondale when we were quite small and at a time when our parents were not there. There was a fancy dress ball in the dining room and Molly or Rose dressed us up and of course we both won a prize. Mine was cut-out wooden animals which I really cherished and took back to Conondale with me. We were not there much in the early years but somehow the mountain seemed like a magic place to us. I remember asking my mother when could we go back there and she replied, "Some day please God!" and I said, "I want to please God right away."

My mother and father had only a casual interest in birds and there didn't seem

Our generation – Peter, Rhelma and Vince in the cool mountains

to be much time to foster such an interest on a busy dairy. I can still remember when I saw my first straw-necked ibis and I walked down the paddock to get a closer look at them but of course they flew away. I recall climbing up a tree to look in a butcher-bird's nest and later finding a nesting brown pigeon. The call of the bush stone-curlews could be heard on most nights and their haunting call still reminds me of my childhood.

A highlight for me was finding a beautiful golden bird in a scrubby gully as I came back from putting the cows out. At the time I thought it was the most beautiful bird I had ever seen and I often went back there to look at it. The bird was always in the same gully. When Rose visited us I described the bird and she told me it was a golden whistler. Birds and nature study generally were to become an important part of my adult life but I believe the interest was always there.

An incident that my parents would not let me forget happened when I was a little bloke. The magpie larks or peewees as we called them would fly at their reflections in the windows and at times break the thin glass. Dad had replacement glass in a box under the house where we kids used to play with our trucks. Dad told us not to go near it but I had to have a look and knocked the box over and broke some of the glass. Dad was very annoyed and demanded to know who was responsible. I volunteered that I thought that the peewees might had done it.

Vince, Peter and Rhelma at the Guest House

Life on the Mountain

It came as rather a shock for Vince and me to find out that we were leaving Conondale. It was the only life that we had ever known and we didn't like leaving all our schoolmates behind. We had been going up in the world too for now we had the phone connected, bought a kerosene refrigerator, and set up a thirty-two volt generator on the Lister Diesel Engine that drove the milking machines. It meant we had one electric light in the dairy and two in the house. My parents had also bought the dairy next door and combined the two. Earlier, Dad had bought a purebred Jersey bull and was upgrading the herd.

There were two things that influenced Mick's decision to head back to the mountain and one was that the general grind of farm life had played havoc with his health. The second reason was that he had some communication from the family that there would be a role for him at the Guest House if he returned. Molly had visited us at Conondale and had a serious discussion with Mick that I believe influenced him and helped him make up his mind. My aunts particularly, had been through a tough time running the Guest House during the war when the men were away and at that stage had contributed twenty years of their life to it. The financial situation at the Guest House was a concern too and meticulous Mick seemed to be the man for the job.

All of a sudden it was over, our carefree life at Conondale came to an abrupt end. I know it is part of growing up but to some extent the magic of our childhood stayed behind us at Conondale. Our rather sheltered world was about to change. I don't remember shedding tears when we left because the thought of going to the mountain of our dreams was enough to get us on the road. We would be welcomed by our aunts and uncles and the memories of an exciting holiday there were still with us. We stayed at Herb O'Reilly's farm in the Kerry Valley on the way and then Rose brought horses down and we rode with our parents up the Stockyard Creek Track to the Guest House.

Mum and Dad left to go back to Conondale to finalise details concerning the sale of the farm and to have a break before starting life at the Guest House but we stayed on to continue our schooling. We walked a couple of miles over to Luke O'Reilly's farm each day and received instruction by correspondence in the company of Rhelma and Luke and Marie's children. The war was still on and there were soldiers everywhere doing jungle training as it was called then.

The local farming community had a send-off for Mum and Dad at the Conondale hall while they were there. On that night Vince and I were in the office at the Guest House and Rose had dance music playing on the wireless. We had memories of lying in bed at Conondale and listening to the music coming from the hall and we were both homesick. I remember shedding a few tears in bed that night. It was winter and we were not dressed for the mountain climate and felt the cold. I would not have been comforted by the fact that I was destined to spend the next fifty years of my life there.

Our Aunts were very good to us and when our parents returned we soon settled down. We made friends with visitors to the Guest House and became good mates with the Johnston boys from Kerry. There were two large army camps in the area - the Americans were stationed at 'Camp Cable' north of Canungra and the Australian Army was based at Canungra itself. Both groups made use of the rainforest in the national park for training. It was exciting to see Jeeps and Blitz-buggies ploughing through the mud to get to the Guest House. The guests themselves still had to ride horses the last four miles along a muddy track.

We were still attending school at Luke's Farm when the war ended. A group of soldiers walked up the Commando Track from the Albert River Valley and we called out and told them that the war was over. One bloke held out his rifle and said, "Do you want this?" We really enjoyed the spontaneous celebration that night around a bonfire down the Pacific Slope. It is the area across the road from the Guest House where the picnic tables are now situated. There were no fireworks available but unbeknown to us Lou Wellish, who worked for the Forestry Dept., put half a plug of gelignite into a stump further down the slope. When it exploded the blast was more effective than Lou anticipated and bits of stump were landing everywhere.

It all added to the excitement of the occasion and next morning we found the remains of an unlucky red-bellied black snake at the bottom of that shattered stump. I will always remember the exuberance of the occasion when the dark cloud of war that hung over us was swept away. We were all united in

At the Dump – out of the service car and onto the horses

Luggage was put into bags then loaded onto the packhorses

Riding up from the Kerry Hotel to O'Reillys 1931 Photo: Jack Justins family

a spontaneous celebration that has had no equal in my lifetime.

Luke and Marie O'Reilly were still dairying over at the farm until Luke's deteriorating health resulted in the family moving to Beaudesert. School was relocated to Bernard and Viola's house 'Goblin Wood' where Vince, Rhelma and I spent time expanding our knowledge under the guidance of a Miss Pierce. I don't think Vince and I adapted very well to correspondence and I repeated the following year at Beaudesert Convent. While we were in school in 1946 word came through that Luke O'Reilly had died.

Life was certainly more exciting and varied at the Guest House than it was at Conondale. We didn't appreciate this at first although we did adjust to some extent. Our schooling was one of the least successful aspects. I think that after attending a larger school it is hard to adapt to correspondence lessons. We missed our mates and the games we used to play and we were not inspired by the governess who taught us, which I suppose was not her fault.

One of the things I really loved about the Guest House was the hot showers that we had never experienced before. We always had baths with very little water and a hot shower was an absolute luxury. As time went by we found it easy to flow along with the routine of life on the mountain and had various jobs like bringing in the cows for milking or Molly sending us out with a billy to collect mushrooms. When the lilly-pillys were fruiting Rose would have us bring in branches laden with the mauve coloured fruits for the vases in the dining room.

The Guest House had a casual routine about it that was dictated by the arrival of the service car that came up four times a week and these were important occasions. Orders for supplies had to be made and the horses rounded up for a trip to the Dump. Other activities fell into place during the week that kept the system in running order. Every Friday tables were stacked and the dining room scrubbed out with buckets of water being thrown around. There was a large fireplace in the dining room and as there was no lounge at the time the dining room was the soul of the Guest House, the place where it all happened. It was where the family members and the guests got to know each other and it was where the guests were entertained. The visitors appreciated these simple pleasures that were on offer and to Vince and I they were new and exciting experiences.

One day after Luke's family left for Beaudesert Pat O'Reilly asked Vince and I to help him drive some pigs he wanted to sell out to the Dump where they would be picked up by truck and taken to the sale. The Dump was about four miles away from the farm. Pat was Luke's brother and lived in a hut on his own property, which adjoined Luke's place. They both had a share in the dairy. We liked Uncle Pat as we called him, he would fill us up with orange cordial whenever we visited him but the older generation thought he was a bit hard to get along with at times.

Driving pigs away from home is not easy at any time but one has to be nimble to pilot them through rainforest. We drove them along a track that was used by the packhorses to take the cream from the dairy out to the Dump. It crossed Stockyard Creek and then entered the rainforest to merge with the main road just short of Snake Ridge. Pat was giving the orders and we were scooting through the scrub like pademelons rounding up the pigs. We lost one in the first half mile but drove the rest to the Dump without further loss. Pat had a small yard built there and we succeeded in yarding all but one pig and try as we might it would not go into the yard. Pat was not the most patient bloke in the world and when the pig eventually cleared out back home he was really annoyed and was grinding his teeth and we expected to see smoke coming out of his ears. Vince and I were impressed when he said he was going to shoot the b... when he got back and decided that we would do our best not to upset Uncle Pat in the future.

Another time Pat asked Vince and me to help him drive some young bulls up the Stockyard Creek Track to his property on the mountain. Bulls were fetching a good price at the sales and his idea was to let them grow up and put on some weight and then he would sell them. What he didn't anticipate was that when these cranky Jersey bulls grew up they would start to fight and when they did they wouldn't let a fence interfere with a good fight and would go straight through it. Pat was forever repairing fences. When guests were going to West Cliff they walked down through Pat's paddock. His bulls were famous by this time and getting past them was part of the West Cliff adventure and would mean a detour through the prickly raspberry and wild tobacco bush. People were creative in the 1940s and 50s and composed humorous parodies on popular songs that were sung with much gusto. The following is a verse from one that was sung to the tune of *Lilly Marlane* where the bull gets a mention.

'You end up bruised and bloody from a crawl up Bull-ant Spur
You face the bull at West Cliff and wind up in the burr
And then when you've pulled the prickles out
You cop a clout across the snout with a dirty big bit of Gympie
And boy then you pass out.
They carry you home in pieces, a sore and bloody wreck...
(and so it continues)

NB. The Gympie is a stinging tree that inflects a severe sting

Vince and I also went down with Mick to Canungra to help him dismantle four army huts he bought for the Guest House when the camp was being dismantled there in 1946. I imagine Mick and Annie wanted some accommodation for themselves as well as for Vince and me. When the huts were erected they moved into one and we moved into another. Our hut later became the schoolroom for the next generation and some of the huts are still doing the rounds of the staff village. At a later stage when I came home on holidays from Gatton College with Neil Walker, our hut was known as the 'The Rough House'. I bought a pair of boxing gloves so we were always sparring or clowning around or at least you would expect to get one thrown at you when you entered the place.

My most exciting early memories on the mountain involved Rhelma and the horses. On Saturday it was our job to take Lion the packhorse over to Luke's farm for a can of cream. Luke would load the can on the packhorse for us with a bag of rocks on the other side to balance the load. We enjoyed the outing and placid old Lion would wait on the road while we raced down various sidetracks jumping our horses over logs. While the cream was fresh it was used with sweets and the rest of it was churned into butter. There was a big old churn in use at the Guest House at the time and we kids would take it in turns, wielding the handle to produce the home made butter as it was called. As we did this we had to listen for the splashing sound that told us that the fat had separated from the buttermilk and we had to cease operations immediately. If we didn't the ingredients would stir up together into a real mess.

One day when we were going over to Luke's to get the cream Molly told us a lady who wanted an outing was going to ride over with us. We were not all that impressed but we said we would look after her. All went well but when we came to the Pine Tree on the way home we raced our horses over the flat as we always did. When we looked back we could see the lady developing a decided list to port as her horse trotted along after us till she rather gently hit the ground. Let's say we saw the humorous side of the situation as we rode back but became concerned when she lay on her back on the ground and didn't move. We sat on our horses looking down at her wondering what to do but next thing she sprang up like a jack-in-the-box. I think her idea was to teach these smart kids a lesson but she had been lying on a nest of green ants.

Rhelma and I used to take it in turns to ride our two ponies Scorgie and Rowley around at weekends. We would spend hours over at Moonlight Crag which is a spectacular lookout. The place really appealed to us. We also rode out to the Dump to meet the guests if it was dump day. I remember Rose organising races for us over the flat when some new horses were broken in. We kids also had a small racetrack down near the creek in an area that is now grown over by trees.

Horses seemed to be so much part of our lives and I suppose we had a casual attitude and didn't consider the risks involved. The following incident could have had serious results. Jim and Paddy Smith came up from Kerry to work some of our horses and took others away to be broken in. There was one mare Foalene running around, I don't know what her history was but I had never seen her being ridden. They yarded her and when Jim hopped aboard she bucked around the yard a bit. She soon settled down and some time later I was going to get the cows and Rose suggested I take Foalene. Rose also suggested I put a saddle on her or she might 'get rid of me'. I hopped on barefoot which was not a very smart thing to do because of the risk of a foot getting caught in the stirrup in the event of a fall and being dragged along by the horse.

Foalene always had an entourage of followers and I set off with three of four of her disciples trailing behind. I went down the steep side of the hill and possibly the cropper pulled on her tail and without warning she started to buck. There wasn't anything too violent about it and I think I would have stayed there only my foot went through the stirrup and I ended up on the ground. The horse cleared out but the amazing thing was that the stirrup iron was around my calf muscle with the stirrup leather still attached to it. It is not easy to remove a stirrup leather from a saddle without unbuckling it but there was the whole thing around my leg and the stirrup leather still buckled.

I would have been in real trouble if the leather had not come adrift from the saddle because Foalene was flighty and would have dragged me around the paddock. It was not a common occurrence but it did happen and a lad near Beaudesert died by being dragged around a dip yard by a panicked horse. Anyhow I got to my feet and eventually caught the mare and had some difficulty attaching the stirrup because she was touchy on the off side. I hopped back on and chased the cows in and didn't think much about the incident till very much later when I realised how lucky I was – the Lord was watching over me that day.

In the early 1950s we used to ride down to Kerry to go to the dances at the Kerry Hall. It was usually Vince, Rhelma and I who made the trip and I remember we rode down the Stockyard Creek Track the first time just as the generation before us had done. We usually rode down the Duck Creek Track, which was a shorter distance to Tom Ward's house at Kerry. We put our horses in Tom's cow yard and got a lift to the dance in the back of Ward's truck. They were a friendly crowd at Kerry and we enjoyed the dances. It would be at least 2am by the time we climbed on our horses and headed for home. If it was a moonlit night we could trot along and make good time and it would help us to keep warm. If the night was cold and dark we had to walk our horses in case we copped a cockspur or some lantana across the face and I can remember getting really cold. It would be well and truly daylight by the time we arrived home.

The Magic of the Mountain

When Vince and I arrived on the mountain as children, adapting to the major change in our lives was an emotional experience. It took us a while to absorb the 'Spirit of O'Reillys', to really feel part of it. I think that it would be fair to say that our life at Conondale was generally focused on the dairy and our horizons were more confined. Our lives now were certainly influenced by our aunts and uncles who were colourful characters and also by the passing parade of people who visited the Guest House. The expansive life on top of a mountain where we could see for a hundred miles helped elevate our spirits too and gave us a greater appreciation of life and all it has to offer.

I didn't go on many walks in 1945 but one day my Aunt Rose probably decided that a good walk would keep me out of mischief for a while and lumped me with a group that was doing the Lighting and Echo circuit. I had never been to the border as we called it, that is the interstate border that follows the crest of the McPherson Range and I didn't have high expectations of it. It was a day that I still remember so well and that walk instilled in me an appreciation of these mountains that I have never lost.

Although I saw the Antarctic Beech Forest for the first time and many waterfalls as well the highlight of my day was when I walked out on to the Valley of Echoes lookout – I had never seen anything so rugged and beautiful. Echo is a small crag that juts out from the mountainside. The growth was much shorter on the lookout at that time and one could stand on top and look all around. The valley, three thousand feet below, was all dairy farms, but it was the windswept mountains on my right that really impressed me.

The rainforest there covers the precipitous mountainsides and is buffeted and shaped by the strong winds that whip up from the valley. I had never seen anything like it before and to my eyes there was something mysterious, something almost foreboding about that wall of mountains, a place where you could never go. I didn't know what was behind it. The country there was a mystery to me but that feeling of remoteness fuelled my imagination and even today the 'Valley of Echoes' is a special place for me. We had lunch at Echo that day and as we were about to leave a currawong flew from the lookout across the gorge and away into the mountains. It gave me the strangest feeling as its call faded away and to me it seemed like a lost soul being swallowed up by those wild mountains. I am no poet but a few years later I composed a simple poem to the memory of that currawong. It also remembers a magnificent rainforest that once grew in the valley and those wise old beech trees that looked down from the heights.

'The Call of the Currawong'

An old Beech Tree to a Currawong
"Does man realise that he may be wrong
Does he search for some great Master Plan
From his Guiding Light to understand"
The bird would like to respond to the tree
But turns and flies for his wings are free
Over the hills in the dying rays
His lonely call is fading away
His spirit is lost, it's the end of the day.

There is something about currawongs that to me represent the indomitable spirit of the mountains. It can be winter and there is a cold south-westerly change coming through. Most of the birds are quiet but not the currawongs. They would nearly deafen you as their calls ring through the hills as if to welcome the change.

I really looked up to my aunts and uncles and the way they contributed to life at the Guest House. They were creative and could be relied upon to be imaginative when naming places or describing dramas that took place in the bush. Conan Doyle's book *The Lost World* had been doing the rounds since the early days of the Guest House and his description of an inaccessible place in the jungles of South America that was enclosed by cliffs really appealed to them. According to Conan Doyle many species of dinosaurs and other crazy monsters still survived there. The O'Reillys could see Mt Razorback to the south-west and this rather formidable looking mountain that was generally surrounded by cliffs became their 'Lost World'. It was capped by a plateau with a small stream that ran through rainforest. To add some colour to the O'Reilly legend people who braved the climb to get there would sketch the monster that they had seen as a record for all to see. Two of these sketches still hang on the Guest House dining room wall and I know as kids we were suitably impressed by them.

ONTISPRONKUS SMITHYCUS

Inhabitant of the Lost World as depicted by a guest

There was a large hoop-pine tree on the crest of the hill where the camping area is now and somehow it occupied an important place on our landscape and in our history as well. It was a magnificent tall tree that could be seen from Beechmont, Tamborine Mountain and Mt Barney as well as from the Richmond Range in NSW. If a view could be obtained of our mountains from anywhere we would always look for the Pine Tree that stood out like a sentinel.

Locally too it was a well-known feature. People liked to camp there and the milking cows too seemed to prefer the flat area around the tree to spend the night. Guests would walk there after dinner in the summer and it was traditional to canter our horses over the flat from the Pine Tree. In more recent times this beautiful old tree was struck by lightening and we watched it deteriorate over the next two years before it died. We were all saddened because it was like a death in the family. Many of our guests would remember the Pine Tree and miss its stately presence.

The Family Who Showed Us The Way

Vince and I arrived on the mountain while the war was on but we really settled in to the place the following year in 1946. I believe it was good for us to be a part of life when the Guest House was still isolated to some extent and the first generation ran it as a family. We could experience the mountain of old with my aunts and uncles and a way of life that had existed for a generation. I think visitors then adapted themselves to be part of the O'Reilly family but as time went by the Guest House adapted to suit the visitors.

The family tradition of saying the rosary after dinner of a night is an example. Guests who chose to be part of it would go into the staff dining room where Molly would preside over the family rosary. The room was often crowded and sometimes people who had never said a rosary in their lives would come in to feel part of it. Visitors were also welcome at *Goblin Wood* in Bernard and Viola's lounge room where mass was celebrated when a priest visited the mountain.

I remember my Uncle Tom quietly saying the rosary by the staff dining room fire seemingly oblivious to a noisy game of cards that we kids were involved in close by. I believe now that I was privileged to share life on the mountain with the first generation of O'Reillys who operated the Guest House, and to feel the strength of spirit that was a natural part of their lives.

The mystique that accompanied my aunts and uncles when they visited us when we were children at Conondale never faded. They were real personalities and like any family they had different strengths and weaknesses but between them they established a Guest House and ran it for a generation in the most isolated of conditions. They were always good to us and I have pleasant memories of them all.

I would like to introduce you to them and let you see them through my young eyes from the distant 1940s. Their names were always preceded by the title 'Uncle' or 'Aunty' for us kids though the guests often referred to them as Miss Molly or Miss Rose, which seemed to be the accepted practice at the time. It is an enjoyable experience for me to recall my early memories of them all, and a way of life that was new to Vince and me, so different from a dairy farm at Conondale.

Aunty Molly was a central figure at the Guest House. I can remember her in the kitchen adorned with a liberal coating of flour as she made dampers or apple pies or lifted heavy dishes of roast meats or vegetables. She had a strong build, which she needed for the job, a good head of curls crowning a pleasant smiling face and the kitchen was always a welcoming place when she was there. Molly was good to us children and we would go in to make some toast on top of the stove or maybe cook a mushroom that I found while getting the cows. Standing beside the large wood stove was a good place to warm up on a cold day.

Molly would throw slabs of steak on the hot stove with plenty of fat that fuelled flames that leaped up to singe the front of her hair. Guests would drop into the kitchen to see her and have a yarn while she poured them a cuppa. She had a good singing voice and would take part in sing-a-longs in the dining room at times and be persuaded to sing *The Mountains of Mourn*. In spite of her workload she was a motherly person and a natural hostess. She loved a smoke and like most other members of the family was seldom without a cigarette. Her pleasant manner concealed a strong will and determination that she displayed throughout her

Molly O'Reilly

life. She was a tireless worker and no doubt she put her heart and soul into the Guest House but she also liked to be in charge. She would not let anybody or anything stand in the way of what she considered right for the Guest House and would do anything to protect it

If there was a special occasion coming up and poultry was needed on the menu Molly would round up us kids and herd us down to the chook-house. She pointed out hens that she suspected of not laying any more and we would fly around after them and present them to Molly for inspection. It was exciting stuff for us but the fate of the hens depended on her decision that would be influenced by the fact that she needed eight birds for dinner.

Usually a few members of the family were involved in the plucking and the dressing of the poultry. There was a certain skill involved if the hens were to be plucked easily: the hot water had to be the right temperature and the hens dipped in it for a limited time. Molly considered herself to be an expert and said that she could pluck a fowl in ten seconds. I said this to Reg Cullen who worked at the Guest House before and after the war and his sardonic reply was, "But it would take me half an hour to clean up the feathers."

Molly seemed to have an answer to any problem that surfaced and one day a new guest had arrived who spoke very well with an English accent. Molly showed her to a small single room, which at that time lacked furniture. She looked around and enquired of Molly, "Where am I going to hang my clothes?" Molly said she would fix that and went out. She arrived back in a minute with a hammer and nails and proceeded to belt them into the walls. She said, "There you are dear!" and then shot back to the kitchen to put the roasts on for dinner probably leaving the lady in stunned silence. The lady in question soon became a regular visitor and a good friend of the O'Reilly family and especially of Molly.

Aunty Ann, the aunt with the red curls, was a trained nursing sister. Ann was an attractive lady and although she did not have Rose's outgoing personality there was a quiet dignity about her that commanded respect. She valued her privacy and generally avoided being photographed. Ann was a good cook and would take over from Molly at times to give her a day off. Molly liked to rule the roost and as far as her siblings were concerned I imagine she was not always easy to get along with. Ann was cooking one day and Molly came in and lifted the lids on a few pots on the stove to see what Ann had on for dinner and maybe give a little advice. At this point Ann walked out and Molly was left in charge – the things that happen in families.

Ann would get up before daylight and light the fire in the old wood stove so it would be full steam ahead when Molly, who often arrived late, hit the deck to do the cooking. Ann would also light the fire in the boiler so there would be hot water for the washing up. She also grew vegetables for the kitchen, especially lettuce for the salads. She grew them around the Guest House but the satin bowerbirds had a liking for lettuce so we made a vegetable garden for her that we completely enclosed with wire netting. In earlier times she had a vegetable patch down on a flat area beside Morans Creek about one hundred metres below the Wishing Tree where she had access to water.

Aunty Rose was a real outdoor person and the horses were the love of her life. Like Ann she was a trained nursing sister. Rose was a natural horsewoman and looked good on a horse. To me as a kid she had a lot going for her, she had a lean, angular frame, attractive strong features and a head of dark curls that complimented her bright personality. The cold, wet conditions of the mountain didn't faze her and she was often out at night piloting visitors through the dark of the rainforest to the Guest House.

Rose also did the washing and would fire up the copper to give the dirty linen the treatment and then hang the sheets out on the 'miles' of clotheslines. It was a big job because it all had to be done by hand even wringing out the sheets. Washing the linen was straightforward enough but getting it dry was in the lap of the Gods if the south-easters were bringing showers to the mountains. If guests were due to arrive there was often a crisis situation as sheets were needed for beds. The kerosene iron would be working overtime with flames curling from its sides as sheets and pillowcases were ironed dry. If it showered while the washing was on the line everyone within cooee would come running to give a hand to bring it in. Even the guests were not exempt.

It was Rose's job to cook on Sunday night when she would make a curry using any meat that was left over from the weekend meals. It paid to taste it before helping yourself because sometimes she was really generous with the curry powder. Rose was one to spin a yarn and she did this with a certain flair. When we were going out to the Dump with her she would often sing and encouraged us to sing as well. We all had favourite songs and most of Rose's songs were about horses.

What we really enjoyed as kids were her ghost stories that she used to tell in the dark after the lights went out at night. One of Rose's jobs was closing down the engine about 9.30pm or 10.00pm or sometimes later of a night. That was the time for ghost stories. We would sit around and listen to them in the dark and for us kids it was a spooky experience. Molly used to tell them at times as well and I believe it helps your imagination to have some Irish blood in your veins, whether you are telling ghost stories or listening to them. Like so many of the old traditions this one has faded too with our changing times.

Uncle Tom was the dreamer or the visionary of the family who conceived the idea to build the Guest House in the first place and he did much of the work setting it up. He had red curly hair and seemed very much at home in the scrub chopping wood for the fires or making tracks. The forest seemed to be his real home and to me there seemed to be something of a leprechaun about him. He was quiet and reserved and liked to keep to himself but the people who knew him really liked him. One thing I remember about Tom is that he liked to bring in an enormous backlog for the open fire in the dining room that would burn for days. He had worked hard during his life and was very strong.

Tom had a restless nature and often went away for months at a time prospecting for gold in places that only the prospectors knew about. It was something he loved to do and being out there alone never daunted him. Tom had a simple faith in God and a love of wild things and wild places and it seems fitting that his restless spirit would finally find rest in the country that he loved. His grave lies beside the Mitchell River in Queensland's Gulf Country where he died in 1958 while looking for that seam of gold.

Most of the guests who came to the Guest House in those days knew of Bernard and wanted to meet him. He was famous because of his great effort in finding the Stinson and also many people had read his book *Green Mountains*. But to Vince and I as children these attributes did not mean very much. We liked Uncle Bernard because we found him easy to talk to and he always had time for us. He invariably had a story to tell and his way-out sense of humour was always there to add some flavour. I remember Bernard returning from the war with souvenirs for all of us and some great yarns about seeing orang-outangs in Borneo and about lots of other exciting things. His wife Viola played her part with my aunts in keeping the Guest House going during the war. She got on well with the O'Reilly sisters, particularly Rose, and seemed to be a natural part of family life on the mountain.

Bernard entertained the guests with stories and conducted quizzes beside the fire in the dining room. He would choose a rather straightforward question for me that I still seemed to struggle with. This was all done with much good humour. I remember well when there was the build-up to a federal election and the currawongs were calling with their usual exuberance. Bernard put words to their calls and invented political slogans so that one was a Menzies supporter and the next one a Chifley supporter.

He would go for a stroll with the guests and there was no formality about it. He wandered about the place and pointed out distant mountains or a flowering tree or a nesting bird and added a bit of O'Reilly history along the way. He invariably started out with a cup of tea, black and strong that was drunk in a leisurely manner along the way and the cup placed on the nearest stump or rock with the thought that he would be back to pick it up later. If it was a busy time and cups were in short supply Molly would have us kids scouting around the hills to round up any stray cups that we could find. The whole O'Reilly family exhibited a love of nature, but it was the way Bernard brought the wildlife and rainforest into everyone's life that was special.

I must include Joe in these memories because he was part of the Guest House for so long. Uncle Joe was the youngest of a family of eleven. He was an epileptic and would be called a slow learner in today's terminology. He never went to school and so couldn't read or write. He had a lean raw-boned frame and when he was older I remember having trouble finding slippers that would fit his size thirteen feet. We were a bit scared of him when we were kids but he never did us any harm and was really a kind person. He was a simple soul and he liked nothing better than squatting down in the front garden of the Guest House and having a yarn to the guests while smoking his pipe.

He visited us at Conondale and would ride out to bring in the cows to be milked. He had not been with us very long and we were milking over seventy cows at the time. He would drive them into the laneway and although he couldn't count he sat on his horse and looked at them for a while and then he could name any that were missing which was a good effort. They all had names of course. His sisters cared for him while up on the mountain and Rose particularly was like a mother to him.

Pat and Romeo

Two forthright personalities who contributed to life on the mountain were Pat O'Reilly and Romeo Lahey. They were poles apart in a way, Pat was a son of the land and knew no other way of life while Romeo was an engineer who settled on the mountain and was originally part of a big organization, Laheys Ltd of Canungra. They were both pioneers in their own way and naturally viewed life from different perspectives. I think it was inevitable that there would be some disagreement between them.

Of the three cousins who came to the mountain Uncle Pat was the only one that I really knew. I never met Cousin Joe who died earlier and Luke died in 1946 soon after we arrived back. Both Vince and I liked Uncle Pat and he was always good to us. There was no doubt that he had a temper and could be hard to get along with at times. My father Mick and Pat had a good relationship and Mick had great respect for Pat who he said was a good worker and a skilled builder. You have only to look at his log cabin to appreciate that. Pat would have worked for Mick snigging logs with his bullock team on Bolderys when Mick had the pine-falling contract there. To me Pat was a real character but he could be a bit of a villain at times.

Pat O'Reilly's log cabin. Photo: Max Upham

He had a dust up with Romeo Lahey in earlier times that was fuelled by their forceful personalities and their different ambitions in life. The relationship between the O'Reillys and the Laheys was good. Mick assured me of that. But I imagine it would have been a bit frosty at times between the O'Reillys and Romeo considering his aspiration for the O'Reillys to leave the mountain because their properties were within the National Park.

An incident involving Pat O'Reilly and Romeo would not have helped the relationship. The story goes that Romeo was walking around the park as he often did and met Pat and had afternoon tea with him. He must have walked on down to Pats Bluff and noticed that Pat had fallen timber over the survey line that was in the National Park. Pat's theory was that grass did not grow close to the rainforest so he fell the scrub a chain or twenty metres over the line so that he could make use of all of his country. He did this along roughly a half-mile stretch of land fronting the park. He was in the wrong of course and Romeo had every right to report him to the authorities, which he did.

The matter came before the court in Beaudesert and Pat was convicted and fined an amount of over thirty pounds. He was also ordered to cut and stack the timber he had fallen over the line. Now Pat's fiery nature came to the fore. When the verdict was read out he jumped to his feet and said, "My grandfather had been sent out from Ireland for shooting an informer and I am satisfied that the breed must be slipping." His meaning was obvious and the magistrate hearing the case told him to sit down and be quiet otherwise he would be charged with contempt of court.

Pat did not have much money and paying the fine was bad enough but hiring labour to trim the timber would have been very difficult for him. Pat went down into the valley to hire labour and while he was away Luke must have been a bit careless with matches because by the time Pat returned it had all been burnt and there was nothing much left to cut and stack. I have heard both Mick and Bernard tell the story of Pat and Romeo's incident that was related by both men as a yarn for the humour they saw in it with no hint of rancour. These yarns never lost anything in the telling and both men certainly appreciated Pat's fiery disposition.

Pat's grandfather, Robert was deported to Australia with his brother Michael and the crime they were accused of was murder. I do not know the finer details nor if the victim was 'an informer'. One would think that if they did murder someone in Ireland they would have been executed there. Robert did quite well for himself in Australia and ended up owning land, marrying and raising a family.

Our branch of the family, that is the Guest House O'Reillys, had its origin in Australia from a different direction. My great-grandfather, Luke O'Reilly was the first of our family to arrive from Ireland and his son Peter was the father of the family who started the Guest House. Peter's sister Elizabeth married a second generation Robert O'Reilly and they were Pat's parents. It's a bit complicated because an O'Reilly married an O'Reilly who was no relation. It meant the O'Reilly names of the two families who settled on the mountain came from two separate lines.

The Guest House O'Reillys did not escape without a bit of drama either. When they originally cleared the land they fell the rainforest on the road alignment in front of what was later to be the Guest House. It's the area where the picnic tables are now but in earlier times it was called the Pacific Slope. Possibly they wanted to get a view to the north and east to impress their early visitors. I remember when I was young people would retreat to the warm aspect of the Pacific Slope to shelter from the cold westerly winds. There is no doubt they went further than that and fell country to the east of the road alignment in the National Park. This was brought to the attention of the authorities and the O'Reillys looked as if they could be in some trouble. The boys decided that their brother Norb would not mind shouldering the blame for the good of all the family. Norb had died earlier in the war but he could still help his brothers out and the matter was dropped by the authorities.

Romeo believed people should enjoy their National Park and that tracks should be kept in good order and was practical in his approach. In those earlier times he would always have a brush-hook with him when he went for a walk in case a track needed clearing or a lookout needed trimming. He was very proud of the National Park and never tired of showing it to people.

The relationship between the O'Reillys at the Guest House and Romeo was quite friendly during my time there. He would often take visitors for a walk in the National Park and call in for a cup of tea or a meal. He lived further out on the mountain where he ran two dairies that were operated by families on shares. They were situated on land that was originally logged by Laheys after the road was put through and then cleared for dairying. He showed some enterprise when he cut up land and sold them as housing blocks back in the 1950s. A good view of the National Park could be obtained from this land and it would have been part of Romeo's ambition to share the National Park with the people. He also donated some hilltop land to the National Park that is now Kamarun Lookout.

Romeo never tired of walking around the mountains and gorges and as a story of Mick's indicates he was a tough walker and good at scrambling through rainforest where there were no tracks. In very early times Romeo arrived at their slab hut on Morans Creek with a young friend after an extended expedition exploring the mountains for a number of days. They had very little food left and Romeo's companion was exhausted and just about starving. According to Mick, Romeo did not seem 'any the worse for wear' and looked as if he had been on a normal hike and as Mick recalled, "He could live on the smell of an oily rag."

Later on during my time at the Guest House there was an incident where one of our guests was at Coomera Falls Lookout after having spent a night at *Binna Burra*. He was part of a group that was walking back to *O'Reillys*. He put his haversack down and as he looked away it rolled over the cliff. It contained some items including a camera that he was keen to recover if possible. Romeo heard about this and offered to take me over to *Binna Burra* and guide me down the Mystery Track into Coomera Gorge to look for the haversack under the cliff. As we drove over in Romeo's car he related the history of the road and various other historical facts that I wished I had taken more notice of. He pointed out where he considered Captain Logan, who was Commandant of the Moreton Bay Penal Settlement in 1826-27, had crossed the Sarabah Range as he endeavoured to find his way through to the coast on one of his explorations.

I was reminded of Mick as he talked about Romeo's driving on the mountain in earlier times. He was an engineer and surveyed and constructed the road up the mountain that took years to build. He would have been responsible for its maintenance as well and complained about the drivers of the logging trucks who followed the same wheel-tracks down the mountain each time. This action would cause a rut that the storm water would flow down and scour out the road. To counter this when he drove on the mountain he would have one wheel in the middle of the road and the other one on the edge kicking stones down the side of the mountain. This action would encourage the water to flow off the road. His passengers would be sitting on the edge of their seats because he was short of stature and one had the impression that he could hardly see over the bonnet of those big old cars.

The manager of *Binna Burra* came with us as well and we had a pleasant day but alas we saw the haversack hanging from some growth protruding from the cliff well above us. I said goodbye to Romeo and decided to run the ten miles back to the Guest House that afternoon. I did return a week later with the intention of retrieving the haversack but it was not there.

Robert Collins was the one who initiated the movement for a National Park to be reserved on the northern slopes of the McPherson Range and his persistence was responsible for the act in parliament that made this possible. He was a man of great vision and determination and he should be remembered for his tremendous contribution. His unexpected death before his dream was realized would have been tragic at the time. Romeo Lahey took up his cause with tremendous vigour.

Romeo certainly was a visionary and it was his opinion that if we were going to protect the national park we needed to get people involved and let them see that this magnificent area was worth fighting for. To this end he could see a great future in what we know today as eco-tourism. In the 1930s when he put the timber road through to the mountain he had in mind that it would be a tourist road in the future and surveyed it to take advantage of the excellent views. It is also a spectacular engineering feat and some of the rock walls supporting the road are worth stopping to look at, especially the one under the hairpin bend known as 'Quick-and-Lively'. The road was an expensive exercise and was probably the reason David Lahey said to Mick one day in a light-hearted way, "Young Romeo would break the Bank of England."

The O'Reilly family can certainly feel thankful that the vision of both Collins and Lahey to conserve this beautiful area as a national park was successfully concluded. The construction of a road to the mountain was a tremendous help as well and we can thank the Lahey Family and Romeo particularly for that. It was a private road in those earlier times but there is no record of the

Lahey family ever charging the O'Reillys a toll for it's use. These actions have helped make our Guest House in the hills a viable undertaking. If it were not for these two men and the vision of Tom O'Reilly who conceived the idea of a Guest House the O'Reilly family would not be living on the mountain today, a hundred years after the boys first walked up the 'Heartbreaker'. There is also a continuous stream of people who have stayed at *O'Reillys* and developed an affinity with the beautiful Lamington National Park who would appreciate their efforts as well.

Pat O'Reilly with guests

Vince and Peter

Vince sat for the scholarship exam at the end of primary school in 1945 but did not continue his schooling. He had a flair for machinery and was skilled with his hands so I imagine Mum and Dad decided that an apprenticeship in the engineering trade was the way to go. He may have been too young to take up an apprenticeship and did not go to Brisbane till after his fifteenth birthday in May 1946. He spent some time working at the Guest House as odd-job man and assistant to the yardman Dan. He would have served his time with Mick on the end of a crosscut saw as well.

The forestry camp was set up two miles south of the Guest House after the war and men who worked on the National Park tracks were billeted there in Norb O'Reilly's old clearing. There were quite a number of people working there at the time and some had their wives living there as well. During 1946 Vince had the contract to pack supplies out there for them twice a week. The old riding track was still open and Vince would load a couple of pack horses with goods and his arrival would have been welcomed at the isolated camp.

Horses were still an important part of life and 1946 was the last year that guests, luggage and goods still had to be transported from The Dump on horses. Vince would have enjoyed that part of his work. It didn't seem to worry Vince that he had to work while Rhelma and I were either going to school or riding around the countryside but that was his nature. He spent some time in hospital during the year to have a sliver of steel removed from his leg. He was splitting firewood with a maul and wedges in the rainforest and when he hit the wedge with the heavy maul to drive it into the timber, a piece of steel flew from the wedge and lodged in Vince's thigh muscle. I remember him riding the first four miles on his way to hospital. I can also recall later that year Mum and Vince riding off to Kerry to stay with our friends the Johnstons to go to a three day Mission at the Kerry Church.

Vince started a five year apprenticeship during the year in fitting and turning with F.L. Hudson at West End in Brisbane. It would have been a big step for him at the time because at fifteen he was unfamiliar with the city having only

Peter and Vince O'Reilly
with Mrs Walker

visited it on a few occasions. He certainly had the temperament to meet the biggest challenge that life had thrown at him so far. He had Mick's dedication and commitment and would have focused on the job at hand. He boarded at Kangaroo Point, and I remember getting off the tram at the Morrison Hotel and walking up the hill to visit him. To go to work he would take a tram to South Brisbane and another one to West End. He later moved to West End to board closer to his work. He returned to the mountain most weekends in the bus and being Vince always gave a hand around the Guest House.

I boarded with a lady in Beaudesert in 1947 and went to the convent for a year to be 'knocked into shape' by the nuns. The following year the brothers at Marist College Ashgrove continued the 'knocking into shape' routine to the extent that when I landed at Gatton Agricultural College for the following two years I thought I had arrived in heaven. I was interested in cattle and life on the land so Gatton was the place to go.

I enjoyed sport while away at school and when I was in Beaudesert I joined Father Brosnan's boys' club that was made up of boys from the State School and the Convent. I played my first rugby league and cricket there and of course sport was big time at the other boarding schools that I went to as well. I spent quite a bit of time with the Luke O'Reilly family while I was in Beaudesert and Marie O'Reilly was like a second mother to me. It was a wet year and Jane Street where I boarded often looked like a cow-yard from mobs of cattle being driven along it to the sale yards. Quite often through the year we couldn't cross Spring Creek to get to school.

The next year at Ashgrove I did not set the place alight with any outstanding academic or sporting achievements and like many country kids I found it difficult to adapt to the regimented life at boarding school. We had no real time to call our own and every hour of the day was taken up with some activity. That was probably why my mate Les and I decided to make the best of a free day we were given to relax before sitting for the scholarship exam the following day. We had not ridden a horse for quite a while so we decided to catch the local hack that hung around the college and go for a ride. It was known as the butcher's horse and was used to pull a cart around occasionally by the groundsman. We pinched the bridle that they normally used and attached some rope for reins and caught the horse. We had never seen anyone ride it but that didn't worry us. We went to the main oval out of sight of the college and I hopped on bareback and raced him down the oval in fine style.

I had ridden bareback much of my life so that side of it did not worry me. All went well till I tried to stop him, he had no mouth at all and I couldn't even steer him let alone stop him. I doubt if he had ever been ridden and seemed terrified of the lump of human on his back. We went flying through the trees at the northern end of the oval and I think he was doubtful about heading too far into the bush and we came around in a wide circle and next thing we were heading up towards the college buildings. I was terrified at the thought of me on this mad horse careering through the well-ordered college grounds with Brothers and students jumping for their lives. Luckily this was avoided as I managed to lug him around and aim him at the tennis court fence. As he propped I slid off and held him.

I led him down to my mate Les and said, "Don't get on the bugger he's mad." Les was undeterred and decided to ride him the opposite way up the oval where he had a hill to slow him down. Les flew up the oval but when it came to the hill Les couldn't hold him and he went flying through the trees till Les came off and skinned his face on a stump and looked a real mess. The stinking horse took off into the suburbs with the college bridle and we would really be in trouble if the Brothers found out.

We spent all day looking for him in the drizzling rain and didn't even have time to stop for lunch. We followed his tracks but I am sure we confused them with carthorses that were used to deliver milk and bread to the suburbs at the time and we ended up wandering around aimlessly and couldn't find the damn horse. Luckily late that evening it came sneaking back to the college so we grabbed the bridle and put it away before anyone saw it. So much for a relaxing day before Scholarship!

Gatton College was much more my style and at least we learnt things that I had an interest in, but on looking back, study did not have a high priority. We slept two to a room not thirty-five or whatever to a dormitory as we had at Ashgrove. Neil Walker who is still a friend was my best mate there and we had some great adventures together. We walked along Lockyer Creek looking for bird nests or snakes or anything else we could find. We would also walk down towards the train-line where the owls roosted in the palms. I suppose what you do in your spare time reveals what your interests are and tells you something of your personality. Our greatest adventure was walking from the college back to O'Reillys.

This is how the idea was conceived. I always loved to climb mountains and there was a double-headed mountain that I could see from the college that took my eye. It was on the Little Liverpool Range beside Laidley Creek. Mount Beau Brummell, I believe it is called, and I intended to climb it when I had a chance. On Sundays we Catholics would go to Gatton to Mass in the back of a truck while the rest attended a general service at the college. After that we all had to attend cadets. I soon realised that by the time we returned from Gatton the roll had already been called so no-one really knew whether I was at cadets or not. This was my opportunity to climb Mt Beau Brummell.

I told Neil where I was going and took off on my bike. As I pedalled up Laidley Creek I couldn't see the mountain I wanted to climb and passed by without knowing it. I ended up climbing Kangaroo Mountain near the top of the valley rather late in the afternoon. To my surprise I could see both Mt. Barney and Mt. Lindesay and other familiar sights that were visible from the Guest House. I completed the long trip back to college pedalling along in the dark without a light and then I collapsed on the bed exhausted. Fortunately, Neil had sneaked some food from the dining room for me and then it was off to study for an hour but I wasn't really with it.

The mountains I had seen from Kangaroo Mountain seemed to virtually be in our back yard when I was at home. Well they were thirty miles away and more, but seeing them convinced me that it would not be too hard to walk home next holidays. Neil said he would join me and I had a road map that also showed the mountains so we looked at it and made our plans. My mother must have had confidence in us being able to handle it because, when I wrote and told her what we were going to do, she sent us two tins of beef and a haversack to carry our goods. We raided the vegetable storeroom under the kitchen the night before we left and collected a bag full of spuds and onions that we intended to cook in the coals along the way – some traditional O'Reilly food.

We left next morning and walked to Laidley where we bought one loaf of bread which of course wasn't going to last very long. That's how smart we were, I must have thought that there would be shops along the way to buy more. We walked up Laidley Creek and camped the night in the forest at the top of the valley. It was not a comfortable night as the weather was hot and muggy and the mosquitoes ate us. Next morning we climbed up the steep side of Little Liverpool Range just south of Mount Castle and followed the eastern side of the Great Dividing Range. We travelled too close to the range and had to climb in and out of steep gullies all day. My mother's tinned beef and our bread supply was soon exhausted and we cooked our potatoes and onions and boiled the billy for each meal. We were really tired by the time we reached the Cunningham's Gap Highway in late afternoon but as neither of us had seen Cunningham's Gap we decided that we would go up there and have a look at it.

As we trudged along the road a transport truck passed us on a rather level stretch of road but slowed as it came to a steeper pinch. We were dying for a lift so I took off after it with Neil in hot pursuit. We caught up to it and climbed up and hung on to the vertical back of the heavily laden truck. Trucks climbed very slowly in those days so we were in no real danger and we would have no trouble hopping off at the top of the range. We travelled along happily for a while and a car that passed must have signalled to the driver that there was something odd about his load and he pulled up. We knew we were caught and didn't know what to do but we climbed down and endeavoured to walk casually to the edge of the road and looked at the view. The driver walked back and looked at his load and scowled at us for he would have remembered passing us quite a distance back down the road. He hopped back into the truck and drove off but we were not game to hitch another ride.

We arrived at Cunningham's Gap to see a 'no camping' sign so we climbed to the top of Mt. Cordeaux and camped beside an old mine shaft. There was a wild southeaster blowing and we did not have the equipment for cold weather so we froze but we were so tired we lay down on the rocks and went to sleep. We were just about out of food by this time and had to head for civilization next morning to get more. We got a lift in the back of a truck down the road and then walked towards Boonah. We stopped along the way and were in the process of counting our precious money on a stump beside the road when a woman who was taking her cream into Boonah stopped and asked if we would like a lift. In the confusion of getting our gear into the car we left some of our money on the stump. Things were not going at all well.

We bought some food in Boonah and headed out along the nearest road that we thought must lead to Beaudesert. We were getting tired and finding our way home by the shortest route was our plan now. We walked a long way and admired some beautiful views of the Great Dividing Range before two footsore young fellows were picked up by a truck. It was then that we discovered that this truck was heading to Maroon and that we were on the Rathdowney road, a slight error in direction. We eventually arrived in Beaudesert via Rathdowney. We had certainly travelled the long way round.

We then walked 20kms to my uncle Herb's place at Kerry and we camped along the way. Food and money were in short supply so we hoped to pick up a feed at my uncles place. We didn't start well because Herb and his wife Agatha were doing the morning milking and as we walked up to the dairy the cows took fright and backed out of the bails with the milking machines going everywhere. Herb sent us up to the house to wait while they finished milking and eventually Agatha came good with a hearty breakfast.

We had about nineteen kilometres to walk up the mountain to the Guest House but we were in luck. As we passed the only property on the way Tom Dunne was getting his horse in to ride up there to see Josie the lady who would eventually be his wife. Josie worked at the Guest House. Tom offered to catch another horse and Neil and I ended our journey riding double-bank on a horse called 'Big Sister' up the mountain. We arrived home about lunchtime and after a feed we lay down and went to sleep. We'd had it.

I know I was surprised at the interest that was shown in our trip by the older folk at home especially by my aunts. The venture seemed to appeal to them. The way we communicated then was by letter rather than by telephone so our parents would not have heard from us since well before the trip started and would have been interested or concerned about how we were going. Neil's mother would ring my mother but she had nothing to report. They seemed to have confidence in us and I admire our parents for letting us have our little adventure and not constraining us.

I enjoyed my two years at Gatton and the experience certainly enlivened my interest in cattle and I left there with a strong desire to own a cattle property some day. Running the Guest House was certainly not on the horizon as far as I was concerned.

Good mates – Neil Walker and Peter O'Reilly

Guests at Elabana Falls in 1940s
Photo: Max Upham

The Guest House in the Forties and Fifties

Many of the adventures associated with *O'Reillys* Guest House over the first thirty-five years of its life have to do with just getting there. I suppose that is to be expected considering the isolation of the place at the time but still that isolation was part of its charm. A holiday on the mountain could be a real adventure and that often appealed to the people who were *O'Reillys* regulars in the 1940s and 1950s.

In the early days of the Guest House visitors used to ride nine miles up the famous Stockyard Creek Track to get to *O'Reillys* after a long journey from Brisbane. When Laheys Ltd constructed a logging road up the Sarabah Range from Canungra in the mid 1930s it became the main access to the Guest House. This road ended at the edge of the National Park four miles from *O'Reillys* at a spot known as 'The Dump'.

Until 1947 the service car would bring guests to this spot where they were virtually 'dumped' with their luggage and supplies to continue their journey on horses. There is some magnificent rainforest around The Dump. That made it a pleasant place to wait and it was just as well because there was plenty of waiting to be done. *O'Reillys* and their guests seemed to be forever waiting for the service car and its arrival was subject to the effects of weather and road conditions or breakdowns. There was no way to communicate with The Dump so if the service car did not arrive in an hour or two they all had to hop on their horses and ride back to the Guest House.

I remember Rhelma and I being given the awesome responsibility of taking the horses out to The Dump to meet the service car when we were still quite young. There were some guests arriving and we had to load the packhorses with luggage and goods. It would have been 1946 and I remember we were quite proud of our effort. We had seen it done plenty of times before when Rose was in charge. The first job was to put the luggage and goods into bags and arrange them into even lots so they would balance each other on the packsaddle. The bags were then placed on the horses and attached with hooks on the packsaddle passing through the bags. When this was done Rose would

All dressed up for the bus trip home

Reg Cullen with a packhorse ready for a trip to The Dump

The O'Reilly family gathered for the opening of the church in 1955

get us kids to take the horse for a short walk to see how the load settled down and if the saddle was creeping to one side it meant that the load was uneven. A rock would be chosen from a stack nearby and one of a suitable size was placed in a bag and hung on the light side of the packsaddle to even the load. These rocks were used quite often and had done many a journey between The Dump and the Guest House.

As kids we would often ride out to The Dump. In those days the weekends were shorter – they began mid Saturday. The service car was due to arrive at The Dump at 6pm. The poor old guests would then alight from a nice warm car and were put onto horses. The horses knew the track well and were quite happy to head for home along a muddy track for over an hour in the dark of night with an anxious guest for company. Molly or Viola would keep a lookout for the arrival of the horses, and the guests were then escorted into the Guest House dining room and given a plate of hot soup. They would comment that the lights of the Guest House when they appeared were a very welcome sight. Rose or Bernard or whoever was in charge at The Dump would have to arrange the luggage and goods and load the packhorses that would take quite some time and the packhorses could arrive an hour after the guests.

You could imagine what an experience it must have been for the guests but quite often, regular visitors were present who knew the ropes and escorted the group on their ride to the Guest House. There was always the possibility of things not going to plan and one Saturday night a lady was riding in when she felt a branch leaning over the track. Instinctively she grabbed hold of it but of course the horse kept going. When Rose arrived later with the packhorses she heard a cooee from where this lady was sitting on a branch beside the track. She arrived home behind the packsaddle of a tolerant packhorse.

The packhorses would often walk along at their own pace and it was not always easy to keep track of them in the dark. One of *O'Reillys* famous packhorses was Lion and he would trundle along at a pace that suited him and if it was a cold windy night he would renege on crossing the exposed flat near the Pine Tree and poke off into the bushes for the night. The weight of the load did not seem to worry solid old Lion and maybe the warm packsaddle on his back was a comfort to him. He was almost impossible to find on a dark night and the guests were cheerfully told that their luggage would arrive some time

The Dump – our station in the bush

Guests relax in a sunny spot

Before the campground people
camped anywhere

Director Charles Chauvel filming *Sons of Matthew*
based on Bernard O'Reilly's *Green Mountains*

in the morning. When the sun came up to warm the air next morning Lion would saunter in without a care in the world.

The operator of the service cars at the time was thought to be cranky by us kids but when you consider the conditions he had to put up with I suppose you couldn't blame him. He was always grumbling about the gates he had to open on the way up and we were amused to see him arrive at The Dump one day with a wire gate draped across the front of his car. He must have decided that he had opened enough gates that day.

It was a great step forward for the O'Reillys in early 1947 when the gravelling of the old horse track was completed and a generally all-weather road had finally arrived. It meant that a regular coach service could now be established to the front door of the Guest House for the first time. Filmmaker Charles Chauvel's decision to produce a film *Sons of Matthew* based on Bernard's book *Green Mountains* influenced the Beaudesert Shire Council to do something about the road to make the Guest House more accessible. This move brought to an end the reign of the horses as an essential means of transport for the Guest House after thirty-five years of service. It also ushered in a new era, one where our home that nestled peacefully and serenely on the crest of a mountain range for a generation in glorious isolation was being dragged into the real world.

The floods and landslides of early 1947 heralded a series of wet years and our adventurous guests often had to overcome flooded creek crossings and slippery roads to breathe the cool mountain air of *O'Reillys*. It had been dry in 1946 but in January 1947 the big rains came and, as often happens after a dry spell, there were landslides everywhere. The mountain road to Canungra was a mess and was closed for three weeks while council employees with heavy machinery worked to reopen it. The service car was diverted through Beaudesert and guests rode up the Stockyard Creek Track as they did of old. I can remember the horses ploughing through knee-deep mud along the Stockyard Creek Valley as I went off to school in Beaudesert.

After the war Mr Burling, who operated the service cars, bought an ex-army 4WD Blitz-buggy to transport passengers. The back of the Blitz was completely enclosed except for a manhole in the roof where people could stand and take it in turns to put their head out and get some fresh air. It could certainly handle the road conditions better than the service cars but it was not what you would

The Bus about to push the service car through Canungra Creek

Just getting there was an adventure in earlier times

The 'Butter Box' the Guest House's first bus

'The Duck' loaded up for the trip home

call luxuriously appointed and was the No.1 'get sick' vehicle on the winding mountain road.

Ron Ramsey, who later became our accountant and a good friend, remembers coming up from Canungra in Burling's Blitz, which he said was an armoured car with holes in the sides for the firing of guns. It was about dark when Ron arrived at The Dump and it must have been a busy time because there were not enough horses and the young people walked to the Guest House holding hands in the dark. Ron's comment was, "We knew the girls pretty well by the time we got there."

Ron also remembers travelling up to the Guest House with his brother Allan on a motorbike in 1946 before the road was gravelled. They had a rough time coming up but were surprised to find that the place was booked out. They were not interested in going back so my mother Annie said that there were a couple of bunks in the saddle shed they could use. They were pretty rough and had potato bags on them and Annie gave them some blankets to throw over them. They asked how much the tariff would be and Annie said one pound for their stay and Ron who has a dry sense of humour asked, "Have you got anything cheaper?" Annie probably hit him in reply. That night they found there were lumps in the bed and on investigating found there were some potatoes left in the bags.

The bus run was sold to Rex Law in 1947 and he invested in an ex-army duck to make crossing the flooded Canungra Creek possible. It worked fairly well but the duck had to be attached to the far bank by a rope to stop the whole outfit, guests and all, ending up in Moreton Bay down the fast flowing Canungra Creek. People sat all over the Duck and often the driver could hardly see the road for luggage.

Rex also bought the first bus into the Guest House, an ex-army international, square in shape and was known as 'The Butterbox'. O'Reilly's butter arrived in wooden boxes of a similar shape at the time. It was a great machine and was used on the *O'Reillys* run for many years. Vince O'Reilly would often drive it up when he came home for weekends while working in Brisbane.

The photograph of the Butterbox attempting to push a service car through the floodwaters of Canungra Creek is well known around the Guest House and to an extent exemplifies the carefree spirit of the era. The time was Easter 1947 and the flooded creek prevented travel to *O'Reillys* on the Thursday night or Good Friday so an attempt was made to get through on the Saturday of Easter. A log of wood was held between the two vehicles to prevent damage to the service car. The bus conked out because the fan sprayed water over the motor and the fan belt was removed. People were sitting up in the service car as if they were going to town but they almost were sitting in water. It all turned out well and eventually they all arrived at the Guest House.

When the bus left Brisbane one could never be sure if it would make it to the mountain. I travelled in the bus with Rose in 1948 when I was coming home from boarding school at Ashgrove in Brisbane. We arrived at Canungra to find that there had been good rain in the mountains that made the crossings of Canungra Creek impassable. There were three open crossings through Canungra Creek at the time.

Rose said that I could join her and get a lift to Beaudesert and then go out to Herb O'Reilly's place at Kerry with Bob Johnston in the cream truck and ride home the following day. I decided that it would take too long and choose to walk home from Canungra. I gave Rose my gear to take including my shoes. We preferred to walk barefoot in those days.

Rose gave me advice and asked Ken Curtis, a local farmer, to give me a lift to his place where he had a bridge over Canungra Creek. She'd told me to call on Fred Adkins at the bottom of the mountain for advice on the best route to take. Fred told me to follow the creek up till I came to Caswell's dip and then follow a spur up from there that would lead me up to the top of the range near Mt. Cainbable. It would be much shorter than following the winding mountain road. He also told me I would have difficulty getting around a steep side above the creek that was covered in lantana but whatever I did I was not to attempt to cross the creek. The lantana was dense on that side of the creek and I battled my way through it on my hands and knees and escaped with plenty of scratches. The rest of the climb went well and I arrived at Mt Cainbable with plenty of daylight to spare.

I thought I was as good as home but I had overlooked the fact that I had nine miles to walk to reach the Guest House. When it grew dark I still had miles to go and although it was showering there must have been some sort of a moon because I could make out the road through the rainforest quite well. I arrived home about 9.30pm and thought Mum would be expecting me but she had no idea that I was walking home and imagined I was still with Rose. She took me down to the kitchen and cooked me a very welcome meal.

Another event worth recording happened on Friday of the June long weekend in 1949 and this time I was coming home from boarding school at Gatton College. Two buses left Brisbane at the normal time of 6pm and, because of the wet conditions, Mick brought the ex-army Blitz-buggy from the Guest House down to the bottom of the mountain. The road was very greasy and it was decided to leave one bus at the bottom and tow the Butterbox up the mountain with the Blitz.

The girls boarded the bus and the boys piled on to the back of the Blitz. Why this was done I am not sure but people did dress well back then, even to go to O'Reillys, and asking the girls in their dresses to climb aboard the muddy old Blitz did not seem the right thing to do. Chains were put on the wheels of the Butterbox to help with traction and with a bus driver behind the wheel of both vehicles we set off. The Butterbox slid around a bit but all went well till, as we looked back from the Blitz, we saw the headlights of the bus begin to tilt at an angle and we realised that it was sliding over the edge of the road. It went so far then stopped. The boys jumped off the back of the Blitz to hang on to the bus, adding their weight to stop it rolling over. If it started to roll down the steep mountainside it would just keep going.

It looked a terrifying sight as the right front wheel of the bus was three feet off the road. The tow-rope helped to hold it while the differential ploughed into the dirt on the edge of the road to stop it going any further. The only door on the bus was facing downhill into space and the ladies made a valiant effort to squeeze their figures through the small square windows of the Butterbox to safety. They were assisted and encouraged by the boys on the road. This took quite a time with much squealing and wriggling to evacuate them all from the bus and it was to the relief of everyone present when the last person made it out on to the road.

Wire from a nearby fence was used to tie the bus to a tree and that must have satisfied Rex Law the proprietor because he crawled back into the bus to have a sleep. The Blitz took off for the Guest House loaded with bodies and perishable goods while all the younger fry started to walk the 24kms to the

Guest House. They arrived somewhat jaded and tired but still in good spirits in time for breakfast.

Mick and I waited with the luggage and goods for the Blitz to arrive back. Mick said it was a shame that we had nothing to eat and was amused when I pulled some saveloys and half a loaf of bread from my cadet overcoat pocket that I had grabbed before it all went off in the Blitz. I was 16 at the time so food was an important item. A bulldozer arrived about dawn to tow the bus back on to the road so it all ended well but it was a close call.

Many of the young people present that night knew each other well. They were regular visitors and belonged to an unofficial group known over the years as 'The Gang'. They were a wonderful group of young people with a real spirit of adventure. They enjoyed the dramas that were part of life on the mountain at the time and took it all in their stride. The main topic of conversation over the weekend was how all the girls made it through the rather small square windows of the Butterbox. The Gang was present at Easter 1947 when that famous photo of the bus pushing the service car through the flooded Canungra Creek was taken.

I believe that to some extent The Gang reflected the attitude of the whole community after the war. Many people had been through a tough time and now they appreciated what they had, they were not demanding and most importantly they enjoyed life. People took responsibility for their actions and thank God we didn't have an army of experts to advise us about the dangers in life, and of all the things we should worry about – that breed of 'we know best' people hadn't even been born.

I know the *O'Reillys* really appreciated the presence of The Gang during holiday time because life was never dull while they were around. They organized much of their own entertainment and if they decided to walk to the border they would order lunches for thirty or more people. The dances they arranged were always lively events that went to midnight and later. There were always a couple of pianists to provide music, and as teenagers we were taught some really great dances. There was no hard drink at these events but they were so much fun. The Gang presented a dinner gong to the O'Reilly family with the names of members inscribed on it. It was used for years to announce to everyone for miles around that meals were being served. It is now retired and is retained as a valuable reminder of a great group of people and a wonderful era of our history.

The realigning of the road to avoid two of the Canungra Creek crossings and the construction of a bridge across the remaining one was a big step forward. This work was carried out in the mid 1950s and made travel to the Guest House more reliable. Even so the mountain road could still be unpredictable and in wet times often prevented the buses from getting through.

When Karma England, the girl I would eventually marry, first visited the Guest House she arrived with three friends for Easter 1958. In spite of the wet conditions the bus carrying them made it through to the Guest House but the second one carrying their luggage was stuck at the bottom of the mountain. The girls had come straight from work in Brisbane and were still dressed in their good clothes and that was not the average gear worn at *O'Reillys*. The boys in the next room lent them some garb to sleep in that night and luckily the bus made it through the next day to save what would have been a desperate situation for the girls, especially for the one I married.

It was the era of the buses. Most people used them because the average driver at that time regarded the road as a challenge that they and their car could do without. During busy holiday times two or three fully laden buses would arrive at the Guest House and it was a general rule that if you didn't book early you didn't get a seat. As the road improved people used their cars more but the regular bus to *O'Reillys* from Brisbane continued with day visitors making the run viable when guest numbers dropped off. The arrival time of the bus never altered for many years and the bus days were Sunday, Tuesday, Thursday and Friday night. Now we have a daily service from both Brisbane and the Gold Coast.

Mick and Annie on the Mountain

When my parents Mick and Annie arrived from Conondale in 1945 it seemed to be accepted that Mick would play a role in the management of the Guest House. I am not aware of the discussions Mick had with the rest of the family but I believe that my aunts and uncles certainly needed a break from the continuous grind of running the Guest House. The family had formed a company to raise money and guide the business and it was recorded at a meeting in 1946 that Mick be appointed manager of the Guest House on a salary of £4 a week. This would increase at the end of twelve months corresponding with any improvement in the financial position of the Guest House. It is interesting to see that Mick was given an incentive to improve the finances of the business similar to the incentives that are used in business today. In addition to the salary the company would provide keep for his wife and family.

For a number of reasons the business at that time was not in good shape, it owed a considerable amount of money but it had done well to survive the difficult periods of the Depression and the Second World War. It is very likely too that the business had never completely recovered its establishment costs and the rather stormy birth of the company had put a severe financial strain on the family. Knowing Mick as I did the financial situation would have worried him and I imagine he would have made a few changes and kept the money situation strictly under control. Mick was not brilliant but he was methodical and dedicated to any cause that he believed in. The figures had to add up and the books had to balance otherwise he would pore over them half the night. I know he thought that the financial situation was serious and he had a rule that the bills had to be paid first and the family members were the last on the list.

I don't think it is too hard to imagine that there would have been some teething problems with Mick's arrival. My aunts and uncles had run the place for over twenty years their way and Mick, who liked to do things his way, was bringing in changes that he considered necessary. Molly encouraged Mick to return but knowing her nature, she had a mother hen approach to the Guest House and liked to have a say in everything that went on. I imagine there would have been a battle of wills but just what happened I don't know for after three years, in 1949, Mick and Annie left the Guest House and were share dairying over at Luke's farm.

They ran Luke's dairy on shares for over twelve months from mid 1949 till well into 1950. I didn't like leaving the dairy at Conondale but the experience at Luke's farm certainly cured me of any ambition to be a dairy farmer. According to the general opinion around the mountain there was only one day between Christmas and Easter without at least a shower of rain. The yards at the dairy were a quagmire with mud to a depth of some three feet and when the cows entered the bails we had to spend about five minutes washing the mud off before we could put the machines on them. They would wade through mud again on the way out that would harden up nicely by the next milking.

I remember extending my Easter holidays for a week when I was home from boarding school at Gatton to give my parents a hand on the dairy and later Vince took a week off work to do the same. Mum would get up in the morning and light the primus and that was the signal to get up and tackle the wet and the mud again. When I arrived back at boarding school I awoke to hear the roar of a train on the distant line and for a second I thought I was home and could hear the primus. I thanked the Lord I was at boarding school and rolled over and went back to sleep.

Mick bought an ex-army left hand drive Jeep and it became our car for the next thirteen years and a work vehicle for a considerable time after that. Mick had never driven before and would have gone for his licence in his mid fifties. I also learnt to drive in the Jeep. Packhorses had been used to take the cream out since the dairy started operating over thirty years earlier but now Mick was using the Jeep to do the job. The era when horses were an essential means of transport on the mountain had at last come to an end.

We spent an enjoyable Christmas on the farm with just Mum and Dad, Vince and me, and our cousin Paul Coote from Beaudesert, whom we felt was one of the family. In those days Mum would put coins in the pudding, threepences and sixpences, and I remember teasing Paul who was an intense little bloke by pretending I found two shillings in my pudding. Paul liked counting his money and couldn't hide his disappointment of not finding it in his pudding. It was a happy time for us all but it was the last quiet Christmas we would experience for a long while with just our own family. The next year would be the first of many back at the Guest House.

Later in 1950 Mick and Annie left the farm to live in Pat O'Reilly's hut. Pat moved to another hut near the dairy. They started working at the Guest House again doing the trip over and back in Mick's Jeep. I remember staying in Pat's hut with them when I was home on holidays from boarding school. I have fond memories of the place and enjoyed eating heaps of potatoes that Annie cooked in a pressure cooker on the wood stove. The old hut was a bit primitive I suppose for we were back in the era of kerosene lamps and wind whistling through cracks in the walls but I still liked the place.

Our faithful Jeep towing a load of rocks on a slide along with some guests

I never asked questions of Mick at the time about his future or what was behind the job swapping. I did find out later that the bank manager from Canungra contacted Mick and told him he was concerned that the business was going deeper into the red and if this continued they may lose the place. There must have been some discussion between Mick and other members of the family before he left the dairy because even while we were still staying in Pat's Hut he and Annie made plans to build a house near the Guest House.

The business had survived the Depression and the War and was now struggling through a post war period when people, to a great extent, deserted the mountains and went to the coast for holidays. Guesthouses in the Blue Mountains and in areas of SE Queensland struggled or went out of business during that period. The family members who established the Guest House had stuck with it during its long period of isolation in difficult times and had endured the most physically demanding period of its history. The thing in their favour I believe was that the people who rode in on horses would have some appreciation of the rigours of life experienced on the mountain and to some extent have an empathy with the O'Reilly family by the time they arrived. This was now changing.

The arrival of the bus to the front door solved a transport problem but in the end would create many others. It demanded a different response from the family. More would be expected of the Guest House from now on. Enjoying the hospitality of the pioneering O'Reilly family would never be quite the same again. It was the end of an era. Mick and Annie's arrival back at the Guest House was all part of a change that was inevitable. Although Mick was one of the originals on the mountain he was not part of the original Guest House and in a sense he and Annie ushered in a new phase in its history that would be carried on by Vince and me.

Mick would have taken control of the money when he arrived back. He was always concerned about the financial situation of the Guest House and that concern stayed with him till the day he died. Other members of the family were still involved and there was no dramatic change but over a number of years Mick and Annie gradually took over the running of the place. Bernard at that time was going through a low period in his life and was not the dominant personality at the Guest House that he had been. He worked away from the Guest House for a time and then he and Viola opened a small accommodation establishment of their own at Darlington on the Albert River.

Fortunately, in a large family there are different personalities that have the capacity to complement each other and to stand up when needed. Mick was not a flamboyant character but his dedication and strength as well as his business acumen was needed at the time and he had great support from his wife Annie. He steadied the O'Reilly ship and set a standard for Vince and me to follow that would guide us for a generation.

The family members all contributed in their own way but I believe Bernard's effort of finding the Stinson and his ability with a pen of creating the masterpiece that is *Green Mountains* was crucial to the survival of the place. The publicity was invaluable then as it still is today. It was largely through Bernard's creative ability that what could be called O'Reilly folklore blossomed, and a certain aura surrounded the family. The deeds of the boys who climbed the mountain to establish the dairies, the Stockyard Creek Track and the packhorses, the finding of the Stinson and the building of a Guest House all in the isolation of their mountain home was presented to the world in *Green Mountains*. The book was given terrific impetus because Bernard was a national hero at the time and the Stinson epic is part of Australian history.

Another benefit we inherited was the reputation the family gained from their interest in and their knowledge of the rainforest that surrounded their home. Almost since the O'Reillys first arrived on the mountain they attracted naturalists from far and wide. It was to the mutual benefit of the O'Reillys and their visitors. The O'Reillys would have gained enlightenment and a deeper insight into the local botany and wildlife from the visitors and they would have benefited from the observations and local knowledge of the O'Reillys.

My aunts and uncles certainly had a great appreciation of the natural world. Visitors, who were considered part of the family, were invited to share this experience. In a sense that tradition set a standard for the next and future generations to follow. We may not have inherited a strong financial situation but I believe we inherited something more valuable, a love and an appreciation of nature and a direction to follow. Also I would like to think that their calmness, the strength of spirit that surrounded them would become part of our lives as well. Their simple faith in God as the creator of their beautiful world was indeed a strength to them as it is to me today.

People Who Helped Us Follow
The Nature Trail

My mind goes back to the O'Reilly boys when they first arrived on the mountain.

They would not have had much money but they were confronted with thirty-five shillings an acre payment for the land or the five percent interest that was due if they extended the payment time. A considerable amount of money was needed to develop the land as well so it was an uphill battle. They would have been working hard to narrow the time gap of a number of years that normally existed before there was any return from their dairies. They still had to fulfil the conditions laid down by the government for the development of their blocks otherwise the land could be forfeited.

You'd think that they would have been working under a deal of pressure and the rainforest they were battling would loom as the enemy. This did not seem to happen. Even though they were clearing the land they developed an interest in the rainforest and some affinity with it. They would have been helped in this regard by a well known naturalist Alex Chisholm. Alex became a good friend of the O'Reilly family and was always ready to help them.

A booklet produced by The Intelligence and Tourist Bureau, Brisbane, Queensland and titled 'NATIONAL PARK *Queensland*' tells us a little of life on the mountain as it was then. It described the National Park in glowing terms and the following text refers to the area around *O'Reillys*:

'When established as a resort, with all the necessary artificial advantages, it will assuredly be the show park of the Commonwealth'.

The text continues referring to the O'Reilly boys as the Reillys:

'Three miles beyond is the Reillys main dwelling, and on three other selections are comfortable huts suitable for any visitors who care to stay there and take their own provisions and camp requisites. There is plenty of excellent water and unlimited

firewood at all those huts, and plenty of milk and butter is obtainable from the homestead of the Reillys – young men who have done a lot of clearing, and whose uniform courtesy to visitors is gratefully remembered by them all'.

Another more polished booklet was produced later this time by The Queensland Government Tourist Bureau, they seem to have lost their 'intelligence' along the way. Both books contained the same wording and were well written by an unnamed author. The script was quite comprehensive and detailed and contained accounts of the history, topography, vegetation, wildlife and means of access to the National Park. It referred to the Christmas Creek, Lamington Plateau area as well as the country around *O'Reillys*. The text was accompanied by many photographs of good quality. Both publications are undated but described conditions as they were when the original selectors were there before the rest of the O'Reilly family arrived in 1917. Also, it was before Mick went away to the war so I guess it refers to a time soon after the National Park was gazetted in 1915.

The texts end with the following words:

'To the Reilly brothers, sole inhabitants of the Park, we are indebted for the clearings which enable the visitor to see the scenery after leaving the edge of the Summit, for paddocks for visitors' horses, for a residence and provisions for tourists, for much quite unselfish work, useless to them but valuable to visitors, and for uniform courtesy and assistance as guides and entertainers.'

The 'unselfish work' in the preceding quotation probably refers to the tracks the boys put through to scenic spots especially the lookouts on the crest of the McPherson Range that really impressed the author. The original selectors laid a platform for an O'Reilly culture where the rainforest that surrounded their home was very much part of their lives, which they were proud to share with their guests. This way of life has not changed and ninety years later goes under the rather trendy name of eco-tourism. It was still early days but after reading what was written and enjoying the company of the visitors one could easily imagine Tom having thoughts about a future Guest House. It would seem attractive when compared to milking cows for a living and carrying cream to Kerry.

Alex Chisholm was editor of the *Daily Mail* as well as a member of the Royal Society of Queensland in Brisbane when he bought a group of naturalists and scientists up to the mountain in 1919. Their aim was to visit the Antarctic Beech Forest on the crest of the range. This isolated plant community was new to the party that included the Government botanist Cyril White. They travelled up the mountain on horses from the Kerry Hotel and stayed in the O'Reilly slab huts. With Herb O'Reilly as guide they walked the seven kilometres to Mt Bithongabel where they camped for five days. The beech orchid *Dendrobium falcorostrum* was named as a result of this expedition as was a *Pittosporum,* a shrub that is restricted to the beech forest of the McPherson Range area and was given the species name *oreillyanum* in honour of my Uncle Tom.

Not one to waste time Alex found the rare and elusive bird of the high country, the rufous scrub-bird, for the first time in Queensland. This enthusiastic naturalist would have inspired the O'Reilly family to learn more about these complex rainforests that surrounded their home. Some years later he used his influence with government to counter a campaign to remove the O'Reillys from the mountain because their properties were within the National Park. He loved these mountains and realised that accommodation was necessary if people were going to have the opportunity to enjoy the rainforest experience just as he had done. Alex visited the Guest House on many later occasions with a good friend Hilda Curtis from Tamborine Mountain and their meetings with my aunts were like joyous reunions. A walk to Mt Bithongabel to look for the rufous scrub-bird in the Antarctic Beech Forest was always part of these visits.

Alex recorded the highlights of their 1919 trip in a newspaper article, which was entitled *The Green Mountains of Queensland.* He was the first to use the name 'Green Mountains' as he contrasted the area with the Blue Mountains of NSW. His name 'Green Mountains' would have referred to the general mountainous area just as the Blue Mountains name did. It was an appealing name and as a consequence Bernard entitled his book *Green Mountains* and that seemed to set it in concrete as an O'Reilly name. When Vince and I took over the Guest House we liked the name and included it in our address for thirty years. It all came to a head in 1992 when the Dept of Main Roads after

Above: Orange blossom orchid
Left: Our birdo friend Roy Wheeler
Below: *Green Mountains* by
Bernard O'Reilly.

discussion with the National Park Service decided to remove the O'Reilly sign that had been in Canungra since the road went through and replace it with 'Green Mountains'. The result was that the Canungra people were besieged with visitors asking directions to *O'Reillys*. After all those years everyone, whether they were local or from interstate or overseas knew the place as 'O'Reillys' and the name 'Green Mountains' just did not work. To avoid any further confusion the official name of our area is now 'O'Reillys Plateau' but to most people it is just '*O'Reillys*'. When you consider Alex Chisholm's original article, the name 'Green Mountains' would have fitted quite well with the general mountainous area of our region and in my opinion be streets ahead of 'The Hinterland'.

In 1966 Alex Chisholm unveiled a plaque at the site where the original party camped on Mt Bithongabel. Forty-seven years had elapsed since they camped there and the 'originals', including Alex and Herb O'Reilly, were 'getting on a bit' as were some of their friends who made the effort to be there. I pushed a wheelbarrow up there laden with scones and the trimmings for morning tea and had the billy boiling and a cup of tea waiting for them when they arrived. I was feeling the strain myself during the seven kilometre walk and appreciated brother-in-law Geoff who towed the barrow up the incline with a rope. It was a special occasion and those present were enthralled as we sat and listened to Alex as he recalled his memories of 1919. The scent of the flowering native gardenia was in the air and their attractive white blooms were sprinkled on the ground around us as the clouds settled on the Antarctic beech trees overhead.

Roy Wheeler was another person who played a leading role in cementing *O'Reillys* reputation as a place to visit to see birds. He was well known in the bird world and was a member of the Bird Observers Club in Victoria. His love of birds was infectious and he would have large groups of people on his 'bird walk' each morning at the Guest House. He was a people's person and it wouldn't matter to him if you were an expert or that you hadn't looked at a bird before. He would still welcome you. I believe that Roy literally introduced thousands of people to the joys of 'bird watching' both at *O'Reillys* and around Australia during his lifetime.

He took a great interest in the O'Reilly children's correspondence school at the Guest House and gave mini-lectures and showed them slides of birds from around Australia. Every time he came back he brought each child a souvenir ruler that he had picked up in his travels and the kids looked forward to their gift. He also handed out two shillings for each satin bowerbird's bower he was shown. My son Pete would do some homework when he knew that Roy was coming and have a half dozen or so lined up for him. As far as Roy was concerned it was all in the interest of awakening the children's awareness of birds and nature generally.

I was invited by Roy and his wife Vera to stay with them and be a spectator at the 1956 Olympic Games, and son Ken even had tickets for each day that I could use. I had never been to Melbourne before and although I was twenty-three at the time it was a real adventure for me. I enjoyed every day at the games, the atmosphere was laid back and friendly and I just loved the whole experience. I heard an Australian national anthem for the first time. We had to relinquish 'God Save the Queen' and leave it to the British. 'Waltzing Matilda' was played when we had a win with the words of 'God Bless Australia'. It sounded good to me. Vera and I were good friends and after the men had gone to work we would have a cup of tea and a yarn. I went out with the Bird Observers Club while I was there and for the first time in my life saw a southern emu-wren being enticed out of the reeds by making a squeaky noise with the tongue.

Roy would come up for a couple of months each year and take out bird walks and show slides of a night. He bought the first bird group up in the 1950s and played a role in establishing *O'Reillys* reputation as a 'must visit' destination for bird observers. Ever since that time we've had regular visits from American and European birds groups and the bird fraternity both in Australia and overseas have been valued customers. Roy was a great support when I was setting up our first Bird Week in 1978 and was active for the first six events until a stroke ended his career in1984. He certainly helped *O'Reillys* along the way and we have fond memories of him.

Settling in at the Guest House

I came home from school at the end of 1950 and helped Mick and the builder as they worked on erecting what was to be our new home. It certainly showed Mick and Annie's commitment to the future of the Guest House as I imagine their savings and more would have gone into it. It was decided that I would not go back to boarding school and stay on and work at the Guest House when I had finished off-siding for the builder.

Mick was aware that he was building in an exposed situation on the crest of a range and being Mick he always made sure of things. He took time to 'Cobb and Co' that is to wire the studs, top plates, rafters and battens together and the studs to the bearers below. When the house was cut in half and moved to the staff village some thirty-five years later the builder Vince Tomkins was amazed at the strength of the building. Ted Tomkins, Vince's father, did some finishing work on Mick and Annie's house that began a long association between the builders, the Tomkins family of Beaudesert and the O'Reillys.

We moved into our new home in 1951 and Annie set up what she called 'Green Mountains Store' in the front of the building. It had a modest beginning but grew and grew with the demands of the time. Initially she catered for the needs of the guests but eventually the day visitors became an important part of her trade. A ring would come through from the bus driver in Canungra telling her how many day visitors were on the bus and she would have scones and pikelets and a cup of tea waiting for them when they arrived. The present kiosk was given the name 'Grans' by her grandchildren in memory of her and her contribution to the mountain.

1951 was the last year of Vince's apprenticeship in Brisbane but he came home most weekends and often drove the bus from Brisbane. I started a four-year stint working at the Guest House. I had a break away when I was called up for National Service training in 1952 and was required to be part of what we now call the Reserves for a further two years on a part time basis. Once I became used to wearing heavy boots on a hot parade ground I really enjoyed the experience. As an eighteen-year-old I found the shooting and training

Above: Mick and Annie's house with Annie's original shop at the front.

Above: Annie and Josie in the shop.

Right: The Blitz in a spot of bother.

generally to be exciting stuff.

My mate Neil lived in Brisbane. We knew a few girls around town who visited the Guest House so it was all a bit of a holiday for me. Some of the boys were not happy with the money they were receiving compared to their earnings in 'real life'. Mick was my boss at the time and he was watching every penny. I didn't comment but what I was getting looked 'pretty bloody good' to me.

Our ex-army Blitz-buggy had been bought for us by Rex Law and became part of our family for the next twenty years. It was more like an unco-operative teenage son at times especially when the weather was wet and damp. I suppose it had good reason to object to being left out in the rain. We developed affection for the old Blitz as time went by and it would have carried in hundreds of tons of firewood over the years. It had many other jobs as well and had the honour of towing some rather sophisticated looking buses and fully laden trucks up the difficult 'Big Hill' near the Guest House. I remember towing a flash looking Pioneer Tour Bus up the hill one day with the battered old Blitz and would love to have a photo of the episode today.

I had been driving the Blitz around for a while and it was decided that I should get a truck licence to make it legal. I drove the Blitz down to Canungra with Mick on board and asked the police sergeant if I could get a truck licence. He leaned back from his desk and looked out the window of his office and on seeing the Blitz asked if I had driven 'that thing' down the mountain. I said that I had and he replied, "Okay, here's your licence."

The Blitz had a Ford V8 motor and so had plenty of power but it could be cranky at times and we always took the precaution of parking it on a hill to make starting easier. We would prime it by pouring fuel down the carburettor to encourage it to start and if I was too generous flames would leap out of the carbie right beside us. The motor sat between the driver and passenger and we did not cover the motor so we could keep an eye on it. We had trouble with the fuel pump at times till eventually we installed a four gallon fuel drum high up in the cab so the motor could be gravity fed and this system worked really well. The old Blitz nearly killed us a few times when we had to run it into trees after it 'got away' on us in the steep country. One good thing was that the Blitz had no doors so it was easy to bale out if we had to. We had many a battle with her and Mick made the comment one day that, "The Blitz was like your wife, you had to live with her to know her."

The old Blitz seemed to have a charmed life and could have come to a sticky end on a number of occasions. It climbed better in reverse than first gear. One day Vince was roaring up the very steep hill above Balancing Rock backwards with a heavy load of firewood. He looked as if he was going to make it when it slipped out of reverse gear and in a second was gaining speed down the hill. Vince had to make a split second decision. The Albert River Gorge was on the left two thousand feet below and the Morans Creek Gorge on the right was only fifteen hundred feet down. He did the sensible thing and baled out and let the Blitz make the choice. It showed good sense and headed for the only large tree close by which it hit with a resounding clunk. It all ended well. After we did some panel beating work on the Blitz with a heavy hammer and offloaded some of the wood we coaxed her back on to the track. It could easily have missed the tree and ended up in Morans Creek Gorge.

Another time I was bringing up a load of gravel from Canungra Creek in the Blitz and on approaching the sharp Pyramid Rock Corner I found that I had no brakes. My mate Frank baled out. I knew I could never make it around the corner at the speed I was going so I ran it up the bank and after bowling a few saplings over we bounced back down on to the road at a greatly reduced speed. If the Blitz went over at the Pyramid Rock Corner it would have ended up in the Canungra Creek Gorge in really wild country and it is doubtful if we would ever have seen it again. I would not have been with it, baling out was an acquired skill in those days. I ran the Blitz into a lilly-pilly tree one day when I had my young brothers-in-law Geoff and Brian aboard. The lilly-pilly bent over and brought us very gently to a halt and young Brian in the back thought it was exciting stuff.

The Jeep was like a well behaved little sister in contrast to the Blitz and was our car when we left the mountain and a 'do anything workhorse' for the rest of the time. I really liked that old Jeep and it was the first vehicle I ever drove. It received the same treatment as the Blitz and never saw the inside of a shed but it seemed to handle the conditions and would start every time. The Jeep had the flexibility to handle anything and would go anywhere. When the country was more open I would drive down the hill at the back of the Guest House and up the hill opposite to Moonlight Crag without any difficulty. It was a good friend to me too because it was popular with the young girls at the Guest House who would rarely knock back an invitation to go for a spin around the hills in the Jeep.

At the time there was not a lot of traffic on the mountain road and people generally were considerate. There was a cranky bus-driver who was notorious for keeping traffic behind him eating his dust. To counteract this I found a shortcut down a ridge that the Jeep could handle as the road zigzagged down the mountain. It cut about a kilometre off the distance so the bus-driver was not aware that I had passed him. He was not a popular character and I made sure that I was having a drink in Canungra when he arrived. The Jeep was left hand drive and the driver had to rely on his passenger to give the hand signals and I remember upsetting a policeman on point duty in Brisbane one day when Neil pointed one way and I went another. We just kept going.

Killing cattle for beef was part of life at the Guest House at the time and was a regular event. In earlier times there was a set of gallows down the slope within sight of the Guest House that was used, not for hanging people, but for lifting the carcass of a beast off the ground during the dressing procedure. This was necessary if the job was to be done cleanly and hygienically. The gallows was a heavy cumbersome contraption that could be made on the spot by using local round timber and did the job that was asked of it.

I remember earlier when my mate Neil and I were home from boarding school and Mick, who had just taken over the running of the place, decided to kill a beast. He found that the entrails had been left there from the previous killing and that they were too far gone for removal. He asked Neil and me to bury the remains and added that he wanted two feet of soil over it. Well we started with good intentions but found that the deeper we dug the closer our noses came to the offal so we cut short the operation and as a result the buried remains were covered with a thin layer of soil. Mick came down to see how we were getting on and as he walked over the newly filled in grave the earth was springing up and down under his feet. We were watching rather nervously and had visions of him breaking through and ending up being part of it all. This is a rather smelly yarn to include in my memoirs but I think it illustrates that we took on any job that we were allotted and did not have any rebellious thoughts about it. We were a couple of easygoing teenagers who enjoyed life but I must have driven my father mad at times because the welfare of the Guest House meant so much to him.

There were no major building projects carried out in the first four years that I worked at the Guest House, just patching up jobs that didn't require a lot of cash. The emphasis was on improving the infrastructure, especially in areas where money could be saved. There was a need for more staff quarters, as there always seems to be, that would free up accommodation for guests. A cottage on the south bank of Morans Creek that was used in earlier times was dismantled and rebuilt near the Guest House. It was divided into six rooms and in the smallest of these rooms I could put my hands out and touch the walls on either side. "Just big enough for a coffin," as someone commented so the place was named 'The Morgue'. It was known as 'The Morgue' till the day it died about thirty years later.

The old fowl house on the hill below the Guest House had been there for years and was subject to attack by tiger cats, as we called them, and dingoes. One night there were squawks coming from the fowl house and Dan the yardman set off with the lantern followed by Molly with the loaded shotgun ready to do battle. In the haste of it all Molly tripped over a rock and came crashing down with Dan in front with his hands covering his backside expecting a charge of buckshot. Dan came out of it uninjured and I imagine the attacker made his escape.

We built a quoll-proof fowl house near the edge of the rainforest with round timber from the Balancing Rock area. When we constructed a shed in those days we would commence by putting four round tallow-wood poles in the ground at the corners that would make the building very stable. We made use of galvanized iron from the cottage that was dismantled down at the creek. We Cobb & Coed the round timber together and nailed the iron on to it to form the walls. We buried the end of the iron into the ground and put netting around the end of the rafters to keep the determined little buggers out. The building did a good job for ten years but when Vince and Lona married they built their house near the spot and that was the end of the chooks at the Guest House.

It was obvious that a new septic system was a necessity and replacing the old one was Mick's next project. We received a design for a new septic tank that was large and rectangular, shaped like a small room really and it was given council approval. We dug an enormous hole to accommodate the tank with picks and shovels, and boxing was set in place by Ted Tomkins. It was a big job. The concrete was mixed on a sheet of iron and poured into the boxing. Baffles were installed in the tank and even the heavy lid had to be poured while in place and the boxing eventually came out through a manhole. We then dug a hundred yard trench down into the wild tobacco and laid earthenware pipes to take the effluent from the septic tank to pits further down the hill. These pits were of a considerable size and were filled with stones. I can't help but think how much easier the whole job would be today but of course it would have cost a lot more.

Frank Young was a cousin from down south and worked at the Guest House for about thirty years. We tackled many of these projects together that required a great deal of physical labour and I don't remember having the desire to visit the gym at the end of the day. He was a good worker and had a generous nature and we became good friends. He had some funny ways and was called Cranky Franky at times even by his friends.

The gallows where we dressed our beef
Sketch: Jon McGhee

The Big Decision

The name of Reg Cullen keeps popping up in this book as Reg had a close association with the O'Reilly family. The Cullens and the O'Reillys were neighbours in the Blue Mountains and friends of long standing. Reg had worked at the Guest House before the war and then went out west to eventually operate a mobile sawmill that cut cyprus pine. He came back to the Guest House when he sold the mill and worked there until he retired. Reg loved the west and while he was working there invited six of us out to his camp where he had his sawmill.

In 1953 Reg was working in the Tambo area when we made the journey out there. It was a special experience for Vince, Neil and me because we had never been out west before. We went by train to Charleville and then took the bus north where Reg picked us up on the side of the road near Tambo. Neil and I particularly enjoyed the experience of being in country new to us where everything seemed different and the wildlife was exciting. We rose at daylight the first morning and walked along the Nive River hoping to see wildlife coming in to drink. Nothing drinks at that time of the morning but we succeeded in scooping a couple of yellow-belly out of the river with our hands and had fish for dinner.

The purpose of the trip was to visit the Carnarvon Ranges that was one of Reg's haunts and in those days we could stay in a CWA hut there. It had rained earlier and Reg was doubtful, considering the condition of the roads, if we could make it in his ute so he decided to take the tractor and trailer. There were six of us on the open flat-topped four-wheeled trailer with no springs that he normally used for bringing in cypress logs to the mill. What a great way to see the country and we enjoyed every minute of it. We saw emus, bustards, kangaroos and many other birds from the trailer and we drove through beautiful groves of flowering wattles. I was impressed by the size of the cattle that seemed larger and better developed than the coastal population. We travelled through Springsure and Rolleston to the Carnarvons and we ran along the road beside the tractor for exercise.

Above: Our transport to the Carnarvon Ranges.
Left: Peter O'Reilly up a tree after a local monitor.
Below: None of the comforts of home.

The CWA hut was first class accommodation as far as we were concerned and a bit warmer than camping beside the road in the month of August as we did along the way. The Carnarvon Creek Gorge is spectacular and all of us were impressed with the scenery – it remains one of my favourite places today. It was all cattle country then and we followed cattle tracks up the gorge. There were cattle grazing up on Battleship Spur as well. We climbed up there and enjoyed the winter view. When we left, the faithful tractor and trailer took us through Injune to Roma where we caught the train back to Brisbane.

As a result of that trip Vince decided that he could do with a change of lifestyle and left his engineering job in Brisbane and went out to work for Reg. I was still working at the Guest House at the time and although I liked the work I had my heart set on working on a cattle property out west somewhere. Earlier I went horse breaking with a mate Vince Hickey for a time. Vince was an excellent horsemen and I learnt a lot from him. He had worked on Koorongoloo Station on the Cooper and he related his experiences of horse tailing on a mustering camp when they would be out for weeks on a muster going from yard to yard. Each stockman was allotted a certain number of rather lively horses and they would camp in the open in their swags at night. It all sounded exciting to me.

During the early part of 1955 Reg asked if I would like to go out and work for him as well and it didn't take me long to make up my mind to go. He was working south of Mitchell on the Maranoa River at the time. That was new country for me and I looked forward to the experience. I had in mind that this job would be a stepping-stone for me to find work further out on a cattle property. It was a great life with Reg. We would set up the mill in the bush where the cyprus grew and cut timber for a shearing shed or a house. When the job was finished after a few weeks we loaded the mill equipment on to a trailer, hooked the caravan on and towed the lot with the tractor at a leisurely pace to the next job on a property that could be three hundred kilometres away. I was interested in the wildlife as I always was and Vince and I certainly enjoyed our time there. Mick visited us during the winter and enjoyed the warm sunny days after coming from the cool mountains.

It was too good to last. Our mother Annie came out to Reg's camp later in the year to tell us that Mick was struggling at home and that our aunts and uncles felt that they had done their bit and wanted to step back from running the Guest House. When I thought about it I realized that I had been doing much of the outside work at the Guest House and keeping up the supply of meat, milk, wood and water was a big undertaking along with a thousand other jobs that had to be done around the place. It brought home to all the family that they needed some younger blood to instil their energy into the business. Our stay out with Reg would have brought forward the decision to involve Vince and me in the management of the Guest House and the eventual ownership of it as well. It drew us back to the mountain when our lives could easily have headed in another direction. We made a commitment to go back even before Mum left. In the meantime she did about three weeks accumulated washing and the cooking for us as well. Before she left Reg complained that his pyjamas wouldn't stand up in the corner by themselves any more.

I had been out with Reg for a short nine months and on thinking back I could have said give me a year to do my own thing and experience something of life away from the mountain and then I'll come home. Maybe after a year I wouldn't have wanted to come back and really, with the wisdom of hindsight, my destiny was at the Guest House but it took me some time to settle down and realize it. Even after I was married I still took part in land ballots when large cattle properties were being split up but could never win one. I have always said that the younger O'Reillys should find work away from the mountain and experience something of life before coming back and making a commitment to the Guest House and they will settle down much better.

In a sense I had already made a commitment to the mountain before I came out west because I had bought around one hundred acres of Guest House land where I intended to run cattle. The land was on the southern side of Morans Creek and two-thirds of it was covered in regrowth rainforest. I paid £10 an acre for the land and I extended my overdraft from the bank in Canungra to eight hundred pounds so I could pay cash for it. I had already obtained an overdraft to buy a Land Rover that cost £998. The conditions of the overdraft were that I would pay it off over four years at £200 a year plus interest. This meant I was broke at the time so didn't have any cash to put into the Guest House but the Land Rover became part of my commitment.

Mick encouraged me to buy the land because I liked cattle and maybe he thought that if I had some cattle of my own it might keep me at home. The cash would have been handy for the Guest House at the time to help pay off their overdraft and bring forward the upgrading of the buildings. I never regretted buying the land and I ran cattle there for over thirty years. It increased in value over that time and the money I received from the Guest House when I sold it back to them helped me to build my retirement home forty years later.

Vince and I realized that the future of the Guest House was in our hands and took the responsibility seriously. We vowed to continue to upgrade the facilities that Mick had already started and to build some better accommodation when money became available. These plans we discussed with Mick who was the real boss anyway and conservative Mick wanted our debt level reduced before embarking on a building project. He need not have worried we already had a fair sized overdraft and the bank didn't show any enthusiasm for increasing it at the time. In those days we only dealt with one bank and that was the Commercial Bank of Australia in Canungra and they couldn't see a great future for an isolated Guest House way up in the hills that was in need of an upgrade. Tourism was not in favour during the 1950s.

Possibly, if you had met me earlier, at the time of my life when I left school after grade ten with a report card that was not too flash and was told that the future of the Guest House rested on the shoulders of this individual and his brother, you would have been worried. You could probably see that Vince was equal to the task. He was a rather serious young fellow at that stage of his life and committed himself to any task he took on. But Peter, what was he good for other than kicking the football around the hill, or looking at birds and climbing mountains? Vince and I certainly had different interests and personalities but in the long run at the Guest House that would prove to be our strength.

We took responsibility for different areas of Guest House management and had the autonomy to make decisions in our areas and we didn't compete with each other. The bottom line was that I followed the O'Reilly trend and was a naturalist at heart and didn't show a great interest in money or where my next feed was coming from. Vince was the more practical type. Some people who knew me would possibly add 'well someone had to be'. He was a better administrator than I was and took a keen interest in the financial side of things. In the early stages we relied very much on Mick's judgement.

An advantage we had was our close association with our guests, we knew what pleased them and what didn't. There was no need for consultants to tell us what we should do next. I firmly believe that if you own a business you are the one who knows best what changes should be made. You have to look around and see what is happening in your industry and think it through. You are more likely to do this if you haven't an expert breathing down your neck telling you what you should do next. When I was taking a group of people on a walk or a bus trip I would ask them what they thought about certain changes that we were planning and seek their reaction to it. Many of these people were regular guests and took a keen interest in the place.

I was never a confident lad in my teens, especially with groups of people, and it wasn't until later that I really gained in confidence. There was much outside work to be done in my early days at the Guest House and I was not involved to a great extent in guest activities. I lost the end of a finger in the mincing machine at the meat house and that incident really changed the direction of my life. It not only made the guests wary the next time there was mince on the menu but it also meant I couldn't milk cows for a time so it was decided that I would take over guest activities.

This exposure to the passing parade of people, although difficult at first, broadened my outlook and added another dimension to my life. I really enjoyed the friendship of people from every corner of the globe and this became the main focus of my work for the next thirty years. We did not have much time off in those days but I always said that the people you meet made it all worthwhile. We did not have to travel to meet the people of the world – they came to us.

National Park Ltd.

The O'Reilly family had been operating a Guest House for five years when they formed a public company on the first of July 1931 in order to raise money to expand the business. The title of the company then was National Park Ltd and this could be seen as an enterprising move considering that the country was in the depths of a depression and the Guest House was still very isolated.

The company had been operating for twenty-five years when Vince and I arrived back and Mick was its chairman by this time. I knew of the existence of the company but up till that stage had taken very little interest in it and did not know who held the shares. If Vince and I were going to gain an interest in the business in the future, it would be by acquiring shares in the company. At this early stage running the business was more of a concern to us and we gave very little thought to the eventual ownership of it.

Someone who had a major influence on the setting up of the company was a businessman, Humphrey Dare Lea. He would have made a major contribution to the board not only in money but also in experience. He was the original chairman and secretary of the company and together with Bernard and Molly O'Reilly and F.C. Nicholson, a solicitor from Beaudesert; they made up the first board of National Park Ltd. Other members of the family joined the board at a later date. At its first meeting the board resolved that the company buy the land around the Guest House from the owners, the original selectors, Herb, Mick and Ped O'Reilly.

The payments for the land seemed to be rather generous to me. Ped owned portion 42, it comprised ninety-seven acres, where the Guest House stands and he was paid £2,800 for it with £2,400 to be paid in cash and the balance of £400 to be paid at the end of ten years. This figure was said to be incorrect at a later meeting and was increased to £3,600.

Herb's block, portion 41 of one hundred and thirty-nine acres, included the area where the camping ground and the Bowers Development are now. He also owned 17V, a block of four hundred and twenty acres beside the Duck

NATIONAL PARK AND LAMINGTON PLATEAU

O'REILLY'S GUEST HOUSE, NATIONAL PARK, BEAUDESERT

THE National Park Guest House was established under great difficulties ; all essentials for building, furnishing, etc., had to be transported (up the mountain) by pack horse. Owing to the difficulties of transport and the distance from any other habitation, it has always been the aim of the proprietors to create an atmosphere of homeliness and simple comfort, and to supply the Guest House as much as possible from the land, and as the mountain air has a stimulating effect on the appetite, guests will appreciate the abundance of home-grown lamb, poultry, milk, cream, fruit and vegetables, provided. Afternoon Tea and Hot Milk Suppers are served.

TARIFF :

9/- per day—£2/15/- per week.

Holiday Tariff : (Two weeks at Christmas, and one week at Easter) 10/6 per day—£3/3/- per week.

RECREATIONS

RECREATIONS include tennis, riding and swimming.

TRIPS

Guests who wish to find their own way around to the various sights are given full information and are guided by notices.

For those who prefer to ride, horses are available (on certain trips), at the rate of 5/- per day.

Persons who are doubtful about finding their own way may have the services of a guide at the rate of 1/6 per person. Services are optional.

TO BOOK FOR NATONAL PARK, WRITE TO

National Park Ltd., O'Reilly's Guest House, via Beaudesert, Q'land. Ring Kerry 14 S, or through Thos. Cook and Son, or Queensland Government Tourist Bureau.

1931 when people enjoyed themselves and made their own fun
Photo: Jack Justins family

Creek Road. He was paid a total of £2,000 cash for both blocks. Mick's block of ninety-nine acres included the area where the tree-top-walk and gardens are now. He was paid £1,200 for it with a cash payment of £800 and the balance of £400 to be paid at the end of ten years. The remaining money that was owed to Ped and Mick attracted an interest rate of 6% to be paid by the company. Each block extended from the top of the range where the road is, down across Morans Creek to the top of the range opposite.

A mortgage was registered in favour of Dare Lea and the money he lent the company would have to be considerable because £6,000 cash was paid for the land for a start. The confidence of all concerned for this isolated tourist venture seemed unbounded and at that stage there would have been no prospect of a road within nine miles of the place. The accepted interest rate at the time was 6% so the family had put a substantial weight around their neck for a considerable time. One could understand the ambitions and dreams the O'Reilly family had for the Guest House. It was their home, and they could see it as crucial if they were to have a future on the mountain. If Dare Lea was a hard-nosed investor one could perhaps question the wisdom of his decision to pour so much money into it. I would suspect that his decision was made more from the heart than the head but of course I don't know. From a practical perspective the place would have to be run very efficiently with a high occupancy and have a lot in its favour to repay that sort of money. One would anticipate that there could be trouble ahead.

Board meetings were held in Beaudesert and it would have been quite an effort for Bernard and Molly to attend these meetings. They rode down the Stockyard Creek Track and at that time it would have been a long trip to Beaudesert. Both Dare Lea and Nicholson were allotted one share each so they could be on the board but Dare Lea bought three thousand shares later. The other shares were divided between Bernard, Molly, Tom, Rose and Ann O'Reilly.

All went well for about one and a half years and then Molly seemed to upset the external directors. Molly was a determined lady and could be strong-willed as she proved by her dedication to the Guest House over the years. I imagine she would not accept directions from the board all that well and would have been motivated more by the needs of the guests when purchasing items rather than the balance sheet. An attempt was made to move her aside but she responded by arriving at an extraordinary general meeting with proxies from Rose, Tom and Herb in her favour. Mr Nicholson resigned from the board at that meeting and Dare Lea resigned a few weeks later. Molly took over the role as chair of the board. Herb must have acquired shares later because he was not mentioned at the original allocation of shares. He probably invested money in the company. He did attend meetings regularly till the end of 1936.

This dispute, culminating in Dare Lea's resignation, would have put the Guest House in a vulnerable position as far as the O'Reillys were concerned. As well as owning three thousand shares Dare Lea held a mortgage over the Guest House that would have amounted to many thousands of pounds. Bernard wasted little time selling shares and gaining financial support for the company so the O'Reillys could strengthen their financial position.

The following item is taken from the minutes of the extraordinary general meeting 3rd December 1932.

'Proposed by A. W. O'Reilly (Ann) and seconded by A. B. O'Reilly (Bernard) that the Directors of the Company be authorised and directed to execute a Bill of Mortgage in such form as M. T. O'Reilly (Molly) and A. B. O'Reilly think fit and intended to secure the performance of the said Guarantees and the repayment with interest of certain monies amounting to £1,900 advanced to the Company by John Markwell, Edwin Ivan Warner, Doris Symes, and Alfred and Jean Elizabeth Alford'

I believe the present O'Reilly family can look back to 1932 and remember the people mentioned above with gratitude and thank their spirits that they played a role in keeping the Guest House in O'Reilly hands. Bernard made a big effort to sell more shares and received good support from local people around Beaudesert and Canungra districts as well as from O'Reilly guests. These shares were transferred from Dare Lea's ownership although he was still left with 2,165 shares. During 1933 National Park Ltd. gained many more shareholders.

When the dust settled there was much ill feeling and Molly believed that her attempted removal was part of a plot to gain control of the Guest House. One would think that if Dare Lea moved in the early stages to recoup the considerable amount of money that was owed to him he could have made life very difficult for the O'Reillys.

Another person who became involved was Arthur Groom, who was one of the founders of *Binna Burra*. He worked at *O'Reillys* at the time and for one board meeting he was recorded as secretary of the company. He left around that time and it was not on the friendliest of terms. An amount of money owing to him for photographs was also in dispute. There seemed to be friction between *O'Reillys* and *Binna Burra* management in the early days that would have emanated from then. Fortunately it never existed during our generation for we have always been friends with the Groom boys.

That saga is behind us now but one person I have some sympathy for is Humphrey Dare Lea. I have never met him and have no direct knowledge of what went on behind the scenes back in the early 1930s. He had a lot of money tied up in the Guest House that he would have been trying to safeguard and he certainly had a disagreement with Molly. Whether this was a takeover bid I don't know. What I do know is that he had input into setting up the structure of the company that we are still bowling along with eighty years later. I believe Bernard and Molly would have gained valuable knowledge and experience from him.

He held on to his remaining 2165 shares in National Park Ltd. till 1951 when they were acquired by the family. I remember Mick talking of him after he negotiated the buying back of these shares. Mick never went into detail but he did say that Dare Lea was a decent bloke and that he would like to visit the Guest House. Bernard had no objection but Molly would not hear of it. Molly was a determined lady who would not forget things easily. Mick, like me, was not there when the skin and hair was flying and could not make a judgment but I imagine he did hear Dare Lea's side of the story. When I read about him in the board reports it sparks my curiosity and I would have liked to have met him. There is no real evidence in these reports but somehow I believe his heart was in the right place.

Something Mick did when he returned in 1945 was to approach shareholders and offer to buy their National Park Ltd. shares. Some people said they would like to keep them for sentimental reasons even though they had never paid a dividend. Mick explained that the family preferred to buy them back and they were offered the money that they had paid for them, which generally they accepted. A few small parcels of shares arrived back later. Agnes Curtis of Canungra was the last to reluctantly part with her shares in 1965 and in 1967 the company converted to a Proprietary Company so it became National Park Pty. Ltd. The Company paid its first dividend of £315 in 1952 and except for a few hitches along the way has been operating profitably ever since.

The decision to restrict the ownership of shares to family members is certainly appreciated today. It was a wise move considering the growth the Guest House experienced over the next fifty years but it would not have been without some pain at the time. They found £480 in 1948 to buy shares and £2,165 in 1951 to buy Dare Leas shares. Money would have been scarce at the time but the family would have scraped up some and Mick may have had money left from the sale of the farm at Conondale to buy Dare Lea's holding.

A difficulty family businesses encounter at times is at the succession from one generation to another when the original owners are not prepared to step back and relinquish control. Most of the shares held by the older members were transferred to Vince and Peter's ownership in 1957. Certainly, we had made a commitment to the place but the action of the older generation illustrates the good sense and generosity of my aunts and uncles and their strong desire for O'Reillys Guest House to continue.

Mick is recorded as attending his first board meeting in 1947 and joined the board in 1949. He became chairman of the board in 1952, a position he held till he died in 1979. Vince and Peter O'Reilly were elected to the board in 1957 when Molly and Rose retired. Annie, Mick's wife, also joined the board in 1957 and in 1958 Bernard and his wife Viola retired.

There are lots of things easier in life than running a family business. Pressures and jealousies can emerge between family members that have to be handled tactfully and firmly while the business must still be run efficiently if it is to survive. Vince and I worked well together and handled different areas of Guest House management. Our wives, Lona and Karma, both made a valuable contribution too as the children grew older and were appointed directors of the company in 1979 after the death of our parents Mick and Annie. Later some of our children started working at the Guest House and with the passing of time they now control the business. It is good to see the younger ones taking an interest in the Guest House and as I write there is one grandchild working there as well.

In a family business, what may seem simple decisions such as the salaries for family members can be touchy and cause conflict. What is needed is someone outside the business who has something of the wisdom of Solomon about him as well as experience in the business world and the respect of the family. Ron Ramsey our accountant filled this role very well and was in a sense an unofficial external director. Ron was a frequent visitor to the Guest House in the 1950s and Vince and I were keen for him to take over the Guest House business. D. L. Joyce and Joyce were the Company accountants previously and were well respected by the family. Ron took over our business in 1966 and we relied on his advice and guidance as we took on building projects and improved facilities over the years. Ron's son Brian is now our accountant and adviser so the Ramsey family has been handling our business for over forty years.

Vince O'Reilly held the post of company chairman till 1995. The business is now in the hands of the next generation and an external chairman runs the meetings and there are external directors as well. Apart from Vince and me, Rhelma, (Bernard's daughter) was the only other member from our generation of the Guest House O'Reillys. Rhelma was born and bred on the mountain but she was not involved in the running of the Guest House once we took over. She unselfishly relinquished her shares and now they are all controlled by Mick and Annie's descendents. They don't own the shares personally because they are held in two family trusts and the members have control over the trusts. Both the Vince and Lona trust and the Peter and Karma trust can appoint two representatives to the National Park Pty. Ltd. board.

The company has experienced a series of highs and lows during its history but the commitment of the family never wavered. We experienced a difficult time in the 1970s when we were slow to adjust to the steep rise in the inflation rate. The inflation rate had been minimal for a long time and our tariff was kept in an affordable range because people in those days were aware of costs and we wanted to give them value for money. Wages rose in response to inflation but three weeks would elapse before we were notified and would have to make up the difference in back pay. A raft of changes to the awards that came in at the time added considerably to our costs so we had to make major adjustments.

The variations in the award were impossible to adhere to if you were running a resort in an isolated location with a live-in staff. The Federal Government did some plain talking at the time saying that the books of every employer in the country would be inspected and any business not adhering to the award would feel the full weight of the law.

Mick was keeping an eye on things at the time and the difficult situation really worried him. What normally happened at the Guest House was that staff would work in the morning up till lunch. They would have time off in the afternoon and then return for dinner duties that night. This suited everyone because the staff were all 'live-in' and generally did not own cars.

There was a limit on the spread of hours a staff member could work in the new awards which meant the present working hours were not valid. Also if a person worked earlier in the morning or after six of a night they were to receive time and a half. It made the whole system complex and almost unworkable. Time and a half also had to be paid for weekend work and this caused some disquiet among staff. In those days it was not convenient to shop at weekends and staff were happy to work then and have days off through the week. The extra money for weekend work appealed to everyone and created competition for the weekend jobs, which was not good for staff harmony.

We were talking to the *Binna Burra* management about the difficult situation and John, the manager at the time, had some experience in industrial affairs and approached the relevant union and told them about the difficulties both businesses were having given their remote location and live-in staff. They could see we had a genuine problem and adjusted the award to suit the situation at both *Binna Burra* and *O'Reillys*. The spread of hours was increased so staff could work through the whole day and the overtime commitments removed in return for a higher base salary. The staff was represented at the negotiations and we were all happy with the outcome. None of our staff were in a union at the time but they were required to join. We were asked by the union not to spread the word about our agreement so we kept it to ourselves.

Time to Settle Down

In the late 1950s Vince and I were courting two Brisbane girls. That was not a surprising development as the Guest House seemed to have an attraction for young females at the time and many came from Brisbane. The attraction had nothing to do with us; boys seemed to go to the coast and the girls to the mountains. Also girls made up their minds and booked earlier while boys would try to book in later when it was often booked out. To remedy the situation when the place was filling up for short breaks like long weekends or Easter the office staff would not take any more bookings for girls and leave the vacancies open for boys so we would have a more even crowd for dances and outings.

So you can see the Guest House was a good place to be for a single lad in those days. We both married Brisbane girls that we had met at the Guest House, Karma England was my bride while Vince married Lona Murphy. I thought I was very lucky to marry the beautiful redhead Karma and I believe Karma's parents agreed with me and wondered about her choice of this fellow from the hills who was a bit rough around the edges. I did not think much about it at the time but it must have been a culture shock for our young brides when they arrived on the mountain. We were still milking cows, collecting eggs, killing our own beef, generating our own power and relying on firewood to heat water and to keep warm. Our house was sitting on an exposed windy spot and the cold wind would whistle past in winter.

Fortunately, I had married a good cook and housekeeper who over a period of time proceeded to knock the rough spots off her husband. Karma had an outgoing personality; she made friends easily and fitted into the Guest House scene as if it was made for her. She loved people and they loved her. Children started arriving in both families and another generation of O'Reillys was on the way. Our son Shane was the first to arrive and five days later Vince and Lona's first girl Kerry was born. We seemed to do things in unison, every one of our children had a twin in the Vince and Lona family and the children grew up as one big family. The real difference was we gave up after five children and they ended up with ten.

Karma in our courting days

O'Reillys Guest House was a great place to raise children and I don't think they would have swapped their way of life with the Royal family or anyone else for that matter. In a sense they were isolated, confined to the mountain for their primary school education but their horizons were broadened by the continuous stream of people flowing through the place. They came from many areas of Australia and countries of the world with varying lifestyles and cultures. The young O'Reillys joined in the dances on Saturday night, went to our campfire nights at Lukes Bluff and had plenty of opportunities to meet and talk with the guests in a relaxed and friendly setting.

They were also exposed to the natural world of rainforest and wildlife and their appreciation of nature would have been stimulated by the daily Guest House routine that concentrated so much on it. Walks to waterfalls and lookouts with the guests were so much part of their lives as well. Some families came regularly to the Guest House during school holidays and their children formed close bonds with the O'Reilly children and some of these friendships still exist today.

We would take the kids with us at times when we were out working and one afternoon I took Pete and Mary with me as we hauled some lignum vitae logs out of the scrub near Moonlight Crag. The timber was broad-axed and used in the Guest House dining room. Pete and Mary were quite young at the time and we had some drama that I remember well. I got Reg to tow the Land Rover I was driving up the very steep hill to Moonlight Crag with the bulldozer so we would have our tools on the job. It was a slow process extracting the logs from the scrub and it was about dark when Reg hauled them down the hill from Moonlight Crag.

I had Pete and Mary in the Land Rover with me as I followed Reg down the steep hill. I got a real shock when the Rover rapidly gained speed even though I had my foot on the brake. I did not realize what was happening at first but the logs had crushed the lush green grass and exposed the greasy sap. The Land Rover was skiing over it and rapidly gaining speed as it went. I told the kids to jump out, which they did, and Mary said the back wheel just missed her foot. More by good luck than good management I slewed the Rover off Reg's track as I aimed it towards some trees around the side of the hill. The wheels gained traction on the undisturbed grass and the vehicle gradually slowed. I ended up across the steep side of the hill with the Land Rover in some danger of rolling over.

It all ended well. Mary was Vince and Lona's daughter and when we arrived back she went off home. I said to my son Pete or Little Pete as we called him then, that Mum worries about things especially when we get home late and what happened on the other hill can be our secret. The whole drama was too much for Little Pete, he walked in ahead of me and announced to his mother, "Something terrible happened on Moonlight Crag Hill but I am not allowed to tell you." Well, I had to confess my sins on the spot.

When Shane and Kerry reached school age a governess was employed to supervise their correspondence lessons. Her responsibilities increased as more children came of school age and at one stage there were five children at school. One of the old army huts was converted into a school room but during school holidays, in true O'Reilly fashion, it became accommodation again and the guests were entertained by the children's works of art and their scholastic efforts on the walls. Even former Deputy Prime Minister, Tim Fischer had the honour of sleeping in the schoolroom at an earlier time.

The children attended school at regular hours and were dressed in a school uniform. A bell was rung each morning by the teacher to remind them that school was starting. The daily ritual was of interest to many guests and turned out to be a mini tourist attraction in itself. *O'Reillys* little school was invited by the Canungra school principal to send a team to the Canungra district school sports day each year. The *O'Reillys* Correspondence School Team would march around proudly in their sports uniform and that was good for the morale of the children. The invitation to take part in the sports was greatly appreciated.

The children had a pet calf they called Simon who was one of twins and he made a lasting impression about the place. His mother accepted the first born but rejected Simon, which showed some good sense on her part. My son, 'Little Pete' was in charge of feeding him and Simon was smart enough to head up to the school hut around three o'clock and wait for the children to come out. He received his education around the Guest House away from other cattle and he became incredibly smart and developed into a real rogue.

He would go down to the camping area and raid the tents and help himself to bread or anything else that took his fancy. If he couldn't get in the front entrance he would put his stubby little horn under the tent flap and lift the pegs out of the ground and get in that way. Ismey, our receptionist, replaced many a loaf of bread that went missing and I can remember a young lad with tears in his eyes saying 'a bull ate our bread'. He would raid the rubbish bins at the Guest House and make a general nuisance of himself. Vince always liked things to look neat around the place and one day he was walking past and noticed Simon lying down on the carpet in front of the open fire in the new lounge. Vince had him out of there in no time but thought later that he should have taken a photo first.

The children boarded away for their secondary education and their correspondence schooling seemed to prepare them well for it and they were not disadvantaged in any way. The older ones spent the last year of their primary education at Beaudesert Convent to give them a taste of a real school before going away to boarding school. During that year they boarded with Tom and Josie Dunne at Kerry and travelled to Beaudesert in the school bus.

The Duck Creek Road was pushed through in 1980. It linked us to the Kerry Valley and shortened the distance to Beaudesert to thirty-nine kilometres. This meant that a few years later our little school could be closed down and the remaining children travelled to Beaudesert for their education. It was a long day for them but they seemed to accept it well. It was Reg Cullen's job to run the children nineteen kilometres down the Duck Creek Road to Kerry to meet the school bus that took them on to Beaudesert.

Karma and I had an exceptional little boy who became an intimate part of our lives.

Having children seems like a miracle to young parents and our hearts were bursting with pride as we brought our second child the newborn Daniel Patrick O'Reilly home up the winding mountain road for the first time. Danny's birth was not a difficult one and he had a pleasant little face and as the weeks went by he would greet us with a beautiful smile. As months slipped past he seemed slow to develop and as parents are apt to do we would compare him with other babies of around his age. It was a painful experience, as parents of handicapped children will tell you. Danny's progress seemed very slow. At six or even nine months he couldn't sit up or even hold his head up.

We took him to various doctors while he was still young and were told that children develop at their own pace and to give him more time. Even a small improvement would be greeted with great excitement and give us fresh heart but generally we waited in vain for any real progress. It was a very stressful time especially for his mother but Karma never lost faith in Danny and our capacity to do something for him.

When Danny was in his second year we had a referral to a specialist on the 'Terrace' in Brisbane and he examined him thoroughly. He was rather gruff and sat us down and told us that Danny would never do any more in his life than he is doing now and that was virtually nothing. He couldn't feed himself, he couldn't talk, and his actions were those of a young baby. The doctor was right of course but we did not want to hear it. We still hung on to our dream that we may find someone who could help Danny to at least care for himself. Karma was particularly upset and so was I as we sat in the car outside the surgery and talked over what the doctor had said and what we should do next. We were soon bought back to earth when a parking attendant told us our meter had expired and he would book us if we didn't move on.

We did persist with Danny. We took him to the Spastic Centre over a period of time and came home with exercises for him but in spite of their good efforts and ours too he did not improve. We were told at one stage that as Danny showed no signs of improvement and that we had other children to consider we would be best to put him in a home and forget that we had him. We put him in Xavier Home for two weeks of specialized treatment but he would cry as we left him. He lost weight and showed no improvement so we took him home and cared for him till he passed away in 1982 at eighteen years of age.

Danny never progressed physically and had to be fed and changed and bathed all his life. Feeding him was an acquired skill: food had to be mashed finely with no lumps. It did not always go down well and it took at least a half hour to feed him. I would normally get up first, change Danny, mash up Weet-Bix in hot milk and feed him while I talked to him and listened to the news. Danny couldn't speak but his bright little face would light up when I spoke to him. It was a relaxing way to start the day before I went over to the Guest House. Karma bore the brunt of caring for Danny as well as looking after the other children.

He had his likes and dislikes and would let you know what he wanted. Karma played records for him every day and when the Kenny Rogers album came out it would be greeted with a big smile but there was a different reaction when Nana Mouskouri was given some airtime. He didn't like her at all. Danny had a winning smile and was quite a personality in his own right. Quite often people who were on holidays at the Guest House would drop in to see Karma and have the traditional drink before dinner, they all knew Danny and treated him like an old friend.

He was not the easiest to feed and look after but there were two ladies who could handle the situation very well and Danny loved them both just as we did. One was my cousin Karleen O'Reilly and the other was our receptionist of long standing at the Guest House Ismey Hoffmann. If we wanted to go away for the night either Karleen or Ismey would come and look after Danny and our other children seemed to enjoy the change of command.

Danny's influence was an inspiration to Karma and being always a positive person she contacted the parents of handicapped children in Beaudesert and between them they formed a support group. Karma's original idea was for the group to be a support for the mothers of handicapped children who could often feel isolated. As she was well aware it is quite often difficult for mothers to get away when there is a handicapped child in the house and it is not always easy to talk over their problems with mothers of healthy children. The group rented premises where mothers could bring their children and talk over their difficulties in a relaxed way with people who understood their problems. The local Beaudesert community gave them wonderful support and raised money that allowed them to get professional help and buy equipment that would benefit the children.

There have been changes over the years but it is wonderful to see a group still operating in Beaudesert that had its origin with Karma and some friends years ago. A few of the 'originals' are still in the group today. The RLO is run professionally and receives support from both the local community and from Government. The work they do is a tribute to the dedication and love of the people involved and I have great admiration for them.

Their Mission Statement is worth recording:

Rural Lifestyle Options Assoc. Inc is committed to integrating people with a disability who reside in the Beaudesert Shire, into the community, where their human worth and dignity will be realized for the purpose of achieving a reasonable quality of life in their own rural locality.

Karma's effort in helping the handicapped children in Beaudesert was rewarded when she received the Citizen of the Year Award for the Beaudesert Shire in the Australia Day Honours in 1982. Clyde and Irene who were good friends of ours were minding Danny on the night Karma and I went to Beaudesert for her to receive her award. The really uncanny thing was that almost to the minute that Karma was on stage receiving her award Danny's little body gave up its struggle for life at home and he died peacefully in Clyde's arms. It was as if Danny had focused Karma on the welfare of handicapped children that she pursued with her usual vigour and now the job was done.

We arrived home to be told that Danny had died and a hearse was already there to take his body away. It was a great shock for us. He did have an infection and his lungs were congested as they often were because of his lack of movement but we did not think that he was in any danger. His heart just gave out. It was a sad time for us, he had been so much a part of our lives for so long, and the house was empty without him. We missed him most at meal times when feeding him had been part of an eighteen year ritual. But life goes on and in a sense we were free to spend more time with our other children and to enjoy more of life together.

Karma's reaction to Danny's condition taught me just how precious a human life is, a life that was completely dependent on us, a life that was the source of many tears as well as lots of smiles. It also illustrated just how much a mother is prepared to give of herself to a child. But I believe we all contributed and I hope and trust that I am a better person because of Danny. Well meaning people would tell us at times that a handicapped child brings a family together. I suppose it can have that effect but the stresses of caring for a handicapped child on the parents can put a strain on the whole family. It means you have less time with your other children. Certainly all the family is affected and must make adjustments. I know that whenever I see parents with a handicapped child my heart goes out to them.

Above: Tim and Danny O'Reilly.

Left: Shane, Tim and Pete.

The National Park Workers

We had the guests for company every day and that was generally a rewarding part of our lives. It was also good to have the National Park boys to yarn to on occasions when we needed a break. The isolation of earlier times drew us together, we were neighbours and permanent residents on the mountain and developed close friendships. They were respected members of our mountain community and we relied on each other for assistance in times of need. They came into the Guest House to pick up their mail and supplies and their meat was put into the refrigerator till they arrived.

The upkeep of National Parks was the responsibility of the Forestry Dept. until 1975. They showed great enthusiasm and commitment in the 1930s when they developed an extensive track system in Lamington National Park. They made the rugged gorges, the tumbling waterfalls, the lookouts and the magnificent rainforests accessible to the people. The pride the Forestry Department members showed in the track system and in the National Park generally came right from the top. We at *O'Reillys* also realized what a great asset the excellent track system was and like many of our visitors we were proud of our National Park.

The tracks themselves were constructed by men with hand tools who were skilled at their trade. They are of an easy grade and are often supported by rock walls in the difficult terrain and I cannot help but admire the skilled work that went into them. When the tracks were being constructed camps were established in many isolated areas in the rainforest and no doubt the track workers had a tough time of it in the wet conditions.

The track gangs were disbanded when World War II broke out so that towards the end of the war the only worker in our area was Lou Wellish who came from Canungra. Lou's camp was located where the loop track past the gardens joins the main border track about seven hundred metres south of the Guest House. A powder box was hidden in the rainforest behind his camp where explosives were kept. This box came into the Guest House when the camp was disbanded and was used as the wood box for years. After the war a working gang was reformed made up of ex-servicemen who were really tough characters. They sang colourful army songs that we kids thought were great but I imagine that we only heard the censored versions.

A decision was made at that time to establish the Forestry Camp for the workers on Norb O'Reilly's old selection that had been reclaimed by the Government when he was killed in World War I. Much of the land was cleared so it was good from that point of view for a camp. The drawback was that it was isolated being two miles south of the Guest House and generally only accessed by a walking track, although the old horse track along the top of the range was still open.

The Forestry Dept. bought quite a number of ex-army huts as accommodation for the camp and these had to be carried on to the site. It was backbreaking work in the extreme. The floor of each hut was divided into two sections. They were heavy, being constructed of hardwood timber, and it would take two men to carry each section along a narrow walking track. They were suspended from long poles so the men could take the weight of each section on their shoulders. The walls and roof were also divided into sections and carried the same way. You can imagine the time and effort and the miles of walking that was necessary just to carry one hut to the clearing. From memory I would say that there were six huts built there.

Beds, chairs, cooking equipment and a hundred other items had to be carried out as well. There would have been many arduous journeys but they were tough lads and the job was finally done and a mountain village blossomed in Norb's old clearing. Food items were brought in twice a week on packhorses along the original riding track by Vince in the early stages but kerosene for heating and lighting had to be carried in by hand and was treated like gold.

Tents were erected beside each hut. The tented areas also had floors in them and served as the living quarters where people spent their leisure time. An individual galley close by was where the meals were cooked. It was made of stone grouted together with concrete and was housed in a building of galvanised iron construction. Cooking was done over an open fire. Meals were eaten in the tents and the huts were considered to be the sleeping quarters. These grandiose structures were in demand and were generally reserved as married quarters while the single men lived on the western side of Morans Creek in single huts.

The gang consisted of five or six men in the early stages and three of them had their wives billeted there as well. Jack Clancy was the boss at the time and he and his wife Jean reared their daughter Kerry at the camp. Kerry has visited the Guest House in more recent times and related her mother's story of the difficulties she experienced raising a child out there. The camp was two hundred and fifty feet higher than the Guest House and appreciably colder. The frost would lie on the ground for days at a time during the winter.

I remember hearing earlier that Kerry had a little blue toy car that proved to be irresistible to a male satin bowerbird close by. Blue is the bowerbird's favourite colour and it would regularly disappear and turn up in his bower along with other trophies. Kerry's father would retrieve the car to restore calm on the homefront and when they left the little blue car remained behind. Some members of the family returned to the old camp later and found the car – still a treasured item in a bower. They left it with the bowerbird and possibly it is still doing the rounds. Male satin bowerbirds are competitive creatures and stealing trophies from a rival is considered fair game. It may help to entice those elusive females to their bower.

The southeasters brought regular showers to the high country so the wet conditions also posed a problem for the camp dwellers. Water had to be carried from Morans Creek for washing nappies or anything else for that matter or drawn from a well when the creek was low. Getting clothes dry in the damp conditions would have been a real problem. Water was heated over an open fire and the rainforest

Ladies at the Forestry Camp doing their washing with daughter Kerry in the stroller

timber did not produce good firewood. I know the women would come into the Guest House at times and be invited by Molly to have a shower.

The women established a garden and grew flowers and vegetables but they had to be there early to beat the bandicoots and birds to the produce. Foxgloves did well for they were one of the few plants that the pademelons would not eat. The ladies were glad of the company and it was always a welcoming place for our guests to visit. A walk to Lyrebird Lookout generally included a visit to the Forestry Camp.

I remember an incident at the time that caused an upset at the camp. The forestry workers were working at Pat's Bluff and they walked up the hill past Pat O'Reilly's hut on their way home. Now Pat was a hospitable character and asked them in for a drink. They were invited to sample his latest batch of home brew that he had just finished bottling. Mountain residents were, however, always wary of Pat's home brew because its strength varied widely from one batch to the next. Sometimes it was quite mild while at other times it would blow the top off your head. Well Pat must have been heavy-handed with this particular batch because the workers did not arrive home that night and some distraught wives arrived at the Guest House after dark looking for their husbands.

The camp lingered on till the early 1970s well after mains power arrived at the Guest House and new quarters were built where the National Park buildings are now. A tragic event occurred at the old camp not long before it was moved, with the disappearance of the head ranger, Eric Johnson. The rest of the gang came in to the Guest House to say they were worried because Eric had disappeared and they couldn't find him. The police were notified and Vince and I went out and after searching found his body under the cliff at Lyrebird Lookout. When the police arrived we retrieved his body and it was a sad time for all concerned. Eric had been at the camp for many years. He was a good friend of the National Park movement and the O'Reilly family.

The new barracks were more convenient in every way and having power connected would have seemed like a luxury after life in the old camp. They still had a wood stove to do the cooking and to provide warmth and the workers borrowed O'Reilly's truck on occasions to go out for a load of firewood from our property at 17V. Over the years we maintained a good relationship with the National Park workers and even enjoyed mutual Christmas parties. They were good people and took pride in their work and the tracks were well maintained.

My thoughts go back to Norbert O'Reilly who originally cleared the country that was the site of the old Forestry Camp. He built a hut and made his home there. In fact a couple of his peach trees survived beside the camp but the possums considered that they were entitled to have first pick of the fruit. It would have been isolated for him as well. Norb's land was too far away from the other blocks to be used as part of their dairy, unless they had plans to keep their dry cows there. It would entail much work to establish another dairy but that may have been Norb's plan. I never knew him. He died before I was born but photos of him tell me that he was a tall, big-framed man who towered over his siblings. I have read his diary from World War I and I see him as a gentle kind soul whose personality would have blended well with the isolation of his land.

I believe we should remember Norbert O'Reilly and the contribution he made when he cleared his land a hundred years ago. We should also remember the Forestry Dept workers and their families who lived there and the contribution they made to the track system in the National Park and to life on the mountain. They are all part of the history of Norb's isolated Portion 47 that is now being reclaimed by the rainforest.

The walking tracks that were the pride and joy of the whole National Park movement have been allowed to deteriorate in recent years and some tracks have been closed. It is still a wonderful track system and a valuable asset to the community and must be preserved. We as a community should encourage our politicians and bureaucrats to rekindle the pride and the positive attitude that was evident in the early days of the National Park. As Romeo Lahey appreciated, people are important to the future of the National Park, they should be encouraged to learn about it, to enjoy it and they will be there to help protect it. That is what the track system he designed is all about. I would like to see his dream live on and be a guiding light for the National Park Movement today.

Three of the Forestry workers with Vince O'Reilly second from right

Traditions

Life at the Guest House in those early years would have developed a certain rhythm with guests riding in on horses and outings and entertainment being arranged for them. That rhythm would have received a jolt in February 1937 when Bernard O'Reilly found the wreck of the Stinson airliner. This event resulted in enormous publicity for the Guest House and the family responded, possibly after answering a thousand questions, by putting together the Stinson Slides. The showing of these slides is a weekly ritual that has become a tradition over the last 70 years and they are still popular today.

The originals were a collection of dramatic photos depicting the Stinson drama accompanied by a commentary that led you on a search for the lost plane. The presentation also included photos of early O'Reilly history on the mountain recorded on large glass magic-lantern slides. Rose or Viola showing these slides are among my early memories of the mountain. The slides were shown in order accompanied by a very personal commentary while the guests sat enthralled as they walked with Bernard on his journey and the occasion was given real atmosphere as the commentary emerged through a haze of tobacco smoke. Vince took over showing the Stinson slides when the older members faded out, I had my turn and then Rhelma showed them for years with a very personal commentary in the same tradition as her mother and aunts.

Vince and I were aware that people came to *O'Reillys* because they liked the place and the traditions that have developed around it. We were keen to retain those traditions. They also appreciated the hands-on involvement of the O'Reillys and the concern the family showed for their wellbeing and enjoyment. The interest of the family in the rainforest and wildlife that they shared with their guests was something special that had to continue.

Nature slides have been part of our program for many years and they effectively introduce people to the different rainforest communities from the temperate Antarctic Beech Forest on the crest of the range to the warm-subtropical rainforest in the valleys. It was a wide-ranging presentation that covered different aspects from the geological make up of these mountains to the wildlife and insects. The presentation hopefully opened the eyes of our guests to better appreciate our magnificent National Park. The expertise of Glen Trelfo with a camera meant that the quality of our transparencies rose to a higher level when he joined *O'Reillys'* staff and everyone was impressed by the excellence of his six-projector audio-visual.

A walk after dinner of a night to see glow-worms and the occasional luminous fungus is an activity that has stood the test of time. In my younger days it was considered the romantic thing to do to take a girl you were keen on down to see the glow-worms and the walk proved quite popular with the younger generation. In those earlier times we walked to Box Forest two miles away and I can remember groups of thirty or forty young people hiking down there. If we saw a ringtail possum or a leaf-tailed gecko in the torch light it was a highlight.

Another activity that has been around since the early days of the Guest House and was popular during our time was the sing-a-longs. In earlier times there was quite often a pianist staying in the Guest House who accompanied the singers. Back then people really loved to sing. We even sang as we walked along the tracks or rode on horses. Later on I would get people to sing as I drove the bus home from an outing but it was usually the older ones who responded.

Fred Walgate on violin accompanies the piano for a sing-a-long

Our generation seems to be the last who loved to sing. The art of enjoying life in a spontaneous and natural way seems to have eluded later generations.

The dances on Saturday night were popular and in earlier times we relied on a pianist for them too. We entered the era of records to supply music for the dances later and the same records seemed to be played every Saturday. A Forestry worker, Freddie Walgate, would play the violin for the dances when Rhelma and I were young and if we didn't get straight up and dance when Freddie started to play we would be 'encouraged' to do so without delay. There were quite often a good percentage of young people in the Guest House around that time and the dances would go till midnight and later.

People who visited the Guest House in earlier times were prepared to walk. The system of communicating with the guests and organising their day seemed to be written in the statutes of O'Reilly law for it did not change for over sixty years. Going around the tables at breakfast to inform people what the suggested walk for the day was or finding out where else people would like to go was a time honoured ritual that stems from the first days of the Guest House. The number of lunches that were required was written down and the packs gang stood by ready for action. Supplying guests with lunch packs that were assembled in the traditional O'Reilly way was another custom that remained unchanged for decades.

During a busy time the packs, as we called them, had to be organised for fifty or sixty people – some in large groups some just couples. They had to be put together in a very short time so the guests could pick them up by 9:30am. The list of items that went into packs was extensive and included: bread, butter, meat, cheese, tomato, onion, salt, pepper, honey, jam, billy, tea, milk, sugar, mugs, cutlery, fruit and kindling. These items were wrapped in paper to withstand movement as they were carried along and then placed in haversacks. In earlier times we never put matches in the packs as there were always smokers in the party but as the years went by and the number of smokers decreased matches went into the packs as well.

There was nothing pre-cut or pre-packaged as there is today. The bread had to be cut by hand and the cheese was carved off a large round block by someone with a strong arm. Meat was carved too while the honey, jam and milk were all put into bottles or jars and the tea and sugar had to be placed into containers as well. It was a real madhouse while the packs were being assembled and in spite of our efforts to organize it effectively it wasn't unusual for something to be left out or to end up in the wrong pack. When the Guest House was busy extra staff were roped in to help and the more people on the job the more potential for mistakes.

If the weather was cooperating we would suggest a Border Walk as we called it – a walk to the interstate border on the crest of the McPherson Range. It is an enchanted area dominated by ancient Antarctic beech trees in a mossy damp

In earlier times hikers carried their enamel mug on their belt

A rather hairy trip to Lower Morans
Photo: Jack Justins.

Lightning and Thunder Falls at
Black Canyon Photo: Max Upham.

environment. There are impressive views from the border lookouts into the Tweed River Valley of NSW. You could walk there directly the short way or, as most people did, follow the creek up past the waterfalls that would make it a rewarding round trip. There were two Border Walks: one of eighteen kilometres that followed Toolona Creek and the other of twenty-one kilometres that followed the Albert River. Both walks involved quite a bit of climbing so people usually had a good appetite by the time they reached the lunch spot.

The guests would respond to the walk that we suggested and we may end up with twelve or more in the group that normally included some regulars who knew the ropes. We packed their lunch, gave them a track map and directions, wished them luck and away they'd go. The walkers were instructed where to fill their billy at the last water at the top of the creek and to carry the water to the lunch spot near one of the lookouts. With a bit of luck the billy was boiled in spite of damp wood and the inexperience of the fire makers. While this was going on bread was buttered, tomatoes and onions sliced and meat and cheese added to make up the sandwiches.

When you think about what had to be done it was quite an undertaking but the guests took it on cheerfully and generally treated it as an adventure and often that's what it turned out to be. The inexperience of the walkers or maybe just plain bad luck contributed to the occasional mix-up or drama happening along the way. They usually sorted it out in the end and the incident would be a talking point at dinner that night. Often cloud settled down on the top of the range and there would be no view from the lookouts but at least the Antarctic Beech Forest looked its best in the mist. Leeches were another hazard that was encountered on the track and people were advised to take repellent if the weather was damp.

There is nothing like a day out, an adventure with a group of people you have just met, to cement lasting friendships. You may have tired limbs but you have earned that meal together in the Beech Forest. You have boiled the billy and shared an exhilarating experience and now you have something unique in common that you will always remember. I know of many friendships that originated around O'Reillys that blossomed into lasting romances and of course I can include my own.

The method of 'doing the packs' was streamlined to some extent but generally stayed with us for another thirty years. I was in charge of the packs for most of that time and must accept the credit or the blame for resisting change for so long. You see I loved those lunches. I loved boiling the billy and cutting up the tomato and onion and adding meat and cheese to a sandwich and getting stuck into it. It tasted so good. I agree with Bernard that some freshly cut onion adds so much to a sandwich in the bush.

In the earlier times we would put five slices of bread each in the packs. Now they are flat-out eating three. Tea had to be strong then but that has changed too. Today people are fussier about what they eat and individual lunches are the order of the day with fruit juice to drink. Groups of people from the Guest House now must have a guide with them. Fires are not permitted in the National Park any more so the challenge of boiling the billy in the rain and groups of adventurous guests heading to the border under their own steam are a thing of the past.

Other destinations that were popular included Blue Pool and Stairway Falls where people liked to swim in the summer. The waterfalls on the shorter Box Forest circuit were an attraction as well. Short walks to the lookouts along the western cliffs were popular too.

When the O'Reillys were still living in the old slab hut they would often take their visitors to Lower Morans. It was still a popular destination during my time at the Guest House. The trip provided people with a challenge as well as an exhilarating experience. It is my favourite 'off-the-beaten-track' walk and I would often take groups down the Commando Track and follow Morans Creek back up to the Guest House. It is a beautiful creek with some impressive lowland rainforest and waterfalls as well as a half-mile long water race. There are a couple of caves there as well where you could still see the charcoal of Aboriginal cooking fires. There are no tracks along the creek so rock hopping is the only way to travel.

In earlier times the walk ended with a rather hairy climb up the cliff near Morans Falls. The Forestry Dept. put in an excellent track up the cliff in the 1950s with steps on the steep sections. The track was damaged in a vicious storm in 1983 and unfortunately a 'no entry' sign went up and nothing has been done to repair the track since. If people shaped up well on the Lower Morans walk I would take them to Black Canyon. This rugged and beautiful area on the

Albert River was more physically demanding but to my mind was well worth the effort.

Another walk we did regularly was along the top of the McPherson Range to the Stinson crash site following Bernard's trail when he was searching for the lost Stinson. I remember well the first walk I did out there. Vince had been there once before and he led a party of thirty people in 1968. We did it over a weekend and left the Guest House around 10pm on Friday night after the bus arrived and walked the five miles to The Valley of Echoes. It was winter and we camped on a level spot in a saddle on the top of the range above Echo with the gorge on the southern side directing the cold wind straight at us.

The group camped the second night at the Stinson campsite close to the spot where the Stinson crashed. They walked out along the stretcher track the next day, which was the original route that was put through to carry the survivors out. We took a tape recorder and in the darkness of the campsite played a recording of an ABC dramatization of the Stinson story. It was quite effective. We supplied the food for the group and it wasn't the dehydrated stuff you take today. It is a tough walk with plenty of steep climbs and we were labouring along like packhorses. Later, we shortened the journey by avoiding the stretcher track and going down Christmas Creek past Westray's grave. It is still a tough walk but the track has improved to what it was and we now do the thirty-two kilometres walk in one day.

An event we organised regularly that brings back a host of pleasant memories was the popular Campfire Nights and barbecues on the cliff edge at Lukes Bluff. These events belonged more to our generation and I think after arranging them for thirty years we had them fairly well organised and people responded well to them. We had logs arranged in a circle with a fire in the centre and we brought mattresses that were past their used-by date, and the guests sat on them with their backs against the logs and were waited on by the staff.

We quite often catered for 80 to 100 people who had to be fed in a short time and we had the food preparation down to a fine art. The sausages were parboiled before we left home and even the potatoes that were thrown into the coals spent some time in the steamer along with the onions that were given the last rites on the hot plate. I chose good quality rib fillet steak and cut slices that were on the thin side and it was cooked quickly on our heavy barbecue plate.

Getting there in the back of the cattle truck was the original mode of transport and was part of the adventure especially for the children. We used to clean the truck up before it was used as a people mover and I didn't receive any complaints, not from the cattle anyway. When the buses came on line we used them but our truck, not the cattle truck any more, was popular for many years. There was always a ladder taken along for the convenience of patrons climbing aboard.

Exuberant children ready for the campfire night at Lukes Bluff

When we arrived at Lukes Bluff we admired the view and if it was spring we looked for the peregrine falcon nesting in the Pats Bluff cliff opposite. The guests would be admiring the sunset from the cliff edge while we set things up and lit the fires. People would then settle down around the fire and the catering exercise would start. The staff would proceed in a line the first with a serviette next with bread then steak then onions plus tomato sauce and salt if needed. Every course was served in this way and even with the potatoes every spud was cut open and butter and salt applied. The last course was apple pie and after everyone had eaten and had a mug of tea we gave out songbooks with large print and had a rousing sing-a-long. Aussie ballads and well-known songs that were easy to sing were featured which was just as well because I led the singing. People were invited to contribute items and they usually did and we enjoyed some great nights. It gave me a good feeling when things went well and we had a good time. We would end up singing in the bus on the way home.

The campfire nights were my baby and I would try to have one each week. The first day that the weather was okay I would have the gang at Lukes Bluff cooking the steaks and the rest of the activities programme for the week would slot in around it. It meant that every week was different and that suited me because that's the way I liked it. The weather was always a risk and we had the occasional disaster and ended up eating our steaks in Lukes dairy sitting on hay bales one night.

The decision on whether to have a campfire night during the storm season could be a difficult one that had to be made early in the afternoon so the cook could get organised. I was always keen to go for it and followed the principal that fortune favours the brave but I found on quite a few occasions that it has no sympathy for the stupid. I remember one night we were eating our apple pie in the drizzling rain and a lady came over and said with a smile, 'I enjoy this kind of madness.' I found no ready reply and just smiled but I knew what she meant. These nights were unpredictable and that is what I liked about them.

Bernard O'Reilly and I both loved and supported the Campfire Nights and he would give a talk that was always entertaining and appreciated by the guests. He came out one night after he had suffered a stroke and had some difficulty in expressing himself. I asked him if he would still like to talk to the people. He got up and spoke and it was a struggle for him but he persisted. There was not a sound as we listened in silence to every word. It was a moving experience for all of us and I think that both Bernard and I realised that it would be the last time that he would do it.

Home Grown Beef

Vince and I realised that we would have to get the place going well before the bank would consider supporting us in a positive way that would allow us to make real plans for the future. Well we couldn't build without money and one way to save it was to have plenty of our own beef and the other was to make every effort to make the place pay. Involving ourselves in the work and keeping staff numbers down would help. We certainly put our hearts into it.

Using home grown beef was a necessary part of life when the long haul up the Stockyard Creek Track by horse made it difficult to transport fresh meat to the mountain. For many years after that using our own beef proved to be a valuable saving. The method of processing our beef could be described as a bit rough during our early days at the Guest House but became more sophisticated to accommodate the demands of the governing bodies and with the added experience of the operators.

During my early working life at the Guest House I still had a bit to learn about the butchering business. It was a busy holiday period and meat was running short so Neil Walker and I were commissioned to go out to our paddock 17V about four miles away and find a suitable killer. None of the cattle at the Guest House were in good enough condition. We set off with a half-draft pack mare in tow and armed with knives, steel, saw, axe, clean bags and rifle – the trusty 310.

The packhorse did not lead all that well along the narrow winding track through the rainforest so on the way out I decided to relieve Neil of the job of leading her for a while. I rode up beside the packhorse unfortunately on her blind side, in other words on that side her sight was not good. She lashed out and kicked me just above the knee and when I felt the groove in my thigh muscle, that I still have today, I thought my leg was broken. It took me some time to recover and realise that my leg wasn't broken so we continued on our way.

We found the cattle near Rocky Creek and selected a bullock and I lined it up with the 310 and soon we were taking the hide off him. It wasn't in an ideal spot for butchering. It was on the slope of a hill and naturally we couldn't string it up, which would have made the job easier. We laid the bullock on its side and skinned one side then rolled him over and skinned the other side. While we had him there I thought it would be easier if we took the hide right off him and just let him lay on it instead of trying to do it later. You could almost guess what happened, the carcass slid off the greasy hide down the hill into the kangaroo grass. We had no choice but to work on it there and it ended up with a liberal coating of grass.

We battled on regardless. With no more dramas we packed all the meat back to the Guest House arriving with the final load at 9:30pm on a beautiful moonlit night. I thought I would be able to remove the grass from the carcass once we were back in the meat house but the spiky kangaroo grass really penetrated the fat lining the meat and it was impossible to remove it all. One of the guests asked me about the grass in the lining of his sirloin steak and of course I couldn't tell him the awful truth. All I said was, "He must have had a big feed of grass before I shot him." If it happened today the chef would have given the dish a fancy name or added that it was embellished with kangaroo grass grown on the southern side of Rocky Creek and everyone would have been happy.

A project Mick took on in the early 1950s was building another set of gallows in the yard on the southern side of Morans Creek. We hauled logs down from the open forest country on top of the hill in the Balancing Rock area with the Blitz-buggy. We would load the Blitz up well but always dragged a log behind us down the steep side of the mountain because one could never be sure if the brakes were up to the task. Mud at times would seep in around the brake drums and make them ineffective. Mick always walked down the hill behind the Blitz because as he said, "Good men are scarce."

We had the Jeep to transport the meat up the hill which made that part of the job more convenient and also the cattle were easier to yard down there. Even so we had some wild musters and a few times we shot bullocks in the paddock with the 310 and dragged the carcass over the kikuku grass to the gallows. A nasty Jersey bullock, one of a mob that had gone wild at 17V, had sharp horns and would put his head down and have a go at our horses when we tried to yard him. He gored the horse I was riding one day and ripped the stirrup off Frank's saddle while he took evasive action. The bullock was impossible to yard so he had to be shot in the paddock.

The value of using our own beef was obvious when you consider how much we ate at the time. I was generally handling the meat and we had steak for breakfast every morning as well as bacon and eggs. We had mutton (not lamb) twice a week and pork on Sundays. We had chicken on festive occasions that were usually the unlucky hens that were not laying any more. Other than that we ate beef that was prepared in various ways and I imagine vegetarians were an endangered species at *O'Reillys* at the time. Catholics did not eat meat on Friday then so smoked haddock was the highlight of their dinner menu. I was a hard working lad at the time and didn't appreciate the Friday menu. As a result we loved the taste of fresh fish, which we ate any time we left the mountain.

The fact that we were feeding the general public meant that using the gallows wasn't acceptable any more and work commenced on a slaughterhouse in 1952 that was built to government specifications. Bill Wyeth who was our architect, and Neil who was an apprentice carpenter at the time also gave us a hand. It was a solid job and of course the structure is still standing after fifty-six years. It was used as a slaughterhouse for about twenty-five years.

The floor of the slaughterhouse had to be concreted and this was done on the cheap first by filling the base up with local rocks that we picked up along the road and belted into place with a heavy hammer. We poured a fine and very wet concrete mix into the rock base until it was filled. A sand mix was used to finish off the floor and slope it to drain off blood or water that was caught in buckets. We used Canungra Creek gravel for some of the rougher jobs. We shovelled it into bags at Frank Adkin's dairy at the bottom of the mountain and bought it home in the Blitz. An endless chain was used to lift the carcass as we dressed it and the whole building was well designed and did a good job over the years.

A hole had to be dug by hand to bury the intestines and the blood, and all the remains were loaded on a slide and dragged to the gravesite by the jeep. There are many gravesites on the hill nearby. The killing was done late afternoon and the carcass left to hang overnight in the slaughterhouse where dingoes and other wildlife couldn't get at it. We would break it down into six portions early next morning and line the back of the Jeep with clean sheets to take the meat up to the Guest House. Other odds and sods like the tail, the tongue, the liver and heart and also the neck would be added to the load. The meat would set beautifully overnight and keep well in the cool mountain climate and people would comment on how tender and flavoursome it was.

In earlier times the meat was left to hang in quarters in the meat-house and only broken down when it was needed. When the meat was cut up it was stored in three household kerosene refrigerators in the staff dining room. They did a good job over the years and kerosene had to be kept up to them. If the wick was turned up too high black smoke would issue from the flue that was supposed to be a fire hazard but in spite of it all the place never burnt down.

As the 1950s drifted past a series of improvements were carried out to streamline meat production. A larger meat-house was built in Ann's vegie garden near the kitchen to replace the small one that was in use. A large refrigerator running on 110volt power was installed and we started the motor up for an hour or two during the day to keep the meat cool. In 1970 we installed a cold-room that made the job so much easier.

There was a different attitude to the whole process in those days. At times we would ask people in the Guest House if they would like to come and see how the dressing of a carcass was carried out. Many of the young people including the girls would come down and watch. The demise of the beast took place in a killing pen with hinged doors and was shielded from the eyes of our visitors but even so we didn't put on a show in a tourism friendly manner as is the trend today. If people decided to come down they saw the lot and at times we took some pleasure in their adverse reactions. On reflection I think our Public Relations or PR skills as they are termed today could have done with some refining.

It was a full day's work breaking down the carcass, boning out sections of it, salting, mincing, rolling roasts and cutting up stewing meat. We had it well organised so that all the different cuts of meat ran out around the same time. I would tell the cook what meat was available and we would decide on the menu for the day. We usually killed once a week but more often in holiday times.

Before each killing Mick would sharpen the knives and he did a great job. It was noticeable when he was away and I had to touch up the knives myself, they were never as good. When we cut up the carcass there were certain cuts of meat that had to be put aside for Mick. He was one of the old brigade and did not ask for the choice cuts of steak but had a taste for both ends of the beast, the oxtail and the corned tongue. He liked corned brisket as well which he said had more flavour than corned silverside.

We would clean the hide in a little waterfall on Morans Creek, the washing machine the O'Reilly boys used to wash their clothes when they first came to the mountain. The slaughterhouse was built quite close to the site of the old slab hut. In those days they would tie a rope around the clothes and hang them in the waterfall for a time to wash the sweat and dirt out of them. Bernard writes in *Green Mountains*, referring to a time when he first came up to the slab hut, of hearing the little waterfall bubbling along from his bed at night. We put it to a more practical use.

The hide after it was cleaned was taken up and salted and stored under the church. We found it difficult to store them anywhere else because brine would run out and tended to rust any tools or equipment around and besides we never really had a shed to store them in anyway. A disadvantage was that the local cattle had a craving for salt and the calves that were small enough to fit under the church would go in and lick the hides.

Monsignor Steele was the Parish Priest from Beaudesert at the time and wondered what the bumping noise was on the church floor when he was saying mass. When he investigated he found the calves and O'Reilly's store of hides. He let me know with a bit of authority that he didn't think that under the church was the place to store hides. Mick suggested I should move them but I had nowhere else to store them so they stayed there. It was accepted after a time and became something of a joke and even Mons Steele had a laugh about it. By the way, hides do get a smell about them when they have been stored for a while and that didn't help the situation.

Today the slaughterhouse has been enlarged. Photographs of O'Reilly's memorabilia grace the walls to add atmosphere for groups of Japanese tourists who come up each night to enjoy a barbecue dinner and a walk to view glow-worms. I have some graphic photographs of the slaughterhouse taken during its glory days or maybe gory days that have not been included in the presentation. They would not be conducive to enjoying a barbecue for the visitors.

The Telephone

We knew that something would have to be done with the Stockyard Creek telephone line before too long and that it was approaching the end of its useful life. It was now thirty-two years old and many a tree had fallen over that single wire that swung from tree to tree on its journey down the mountain. There were also countless joins where the wire had been broken and repaired and some of these were more effective than others. It was still our link with the outside world and was of great importance to the Guest House.

The telephone was a necessity for the Guest House right from the very beginning. In earlier times it was needed not only to allow prospective guests to inquire and book a room but there had to be horses waiting for them at the foot of the mountain when they arrived. Supplies, equipment and a hundred other items needed to keep the Guest House running had to be ordered and there was no doubt that if the business was to run with any semblance of order it had to have a telephone.

The first move to construct a telephone line that I could find was the following letter written by Mick for the O'Reilly Brothers to the Director of Forests in 1924.

It was written two years before the Guest House opened but the groundwork was already underway and Mick's letter would have been part of the forward planning. The family was seeking permission to put a telephone line through the National Park. It was to go around the side of the mountain below Castle Crag and then follow a steep ridge as it descended into the valley. The proposed line would cross the left branch of the Albert River and rise up over the range below the Lost World. It would then join a party line at Darlington that was connected to the Hillview exchange.

An amazing thing by today's standards anyway was that the letter was dated the 11th of February and permission was granted on the 16th of February, yes the same year! Mick's letter would have taken at least two days to arrive in Brisbane after travelling by horseback, the Kerry Coach, and then the train to reach Brisbane. And to think the Director would have made the decision off his

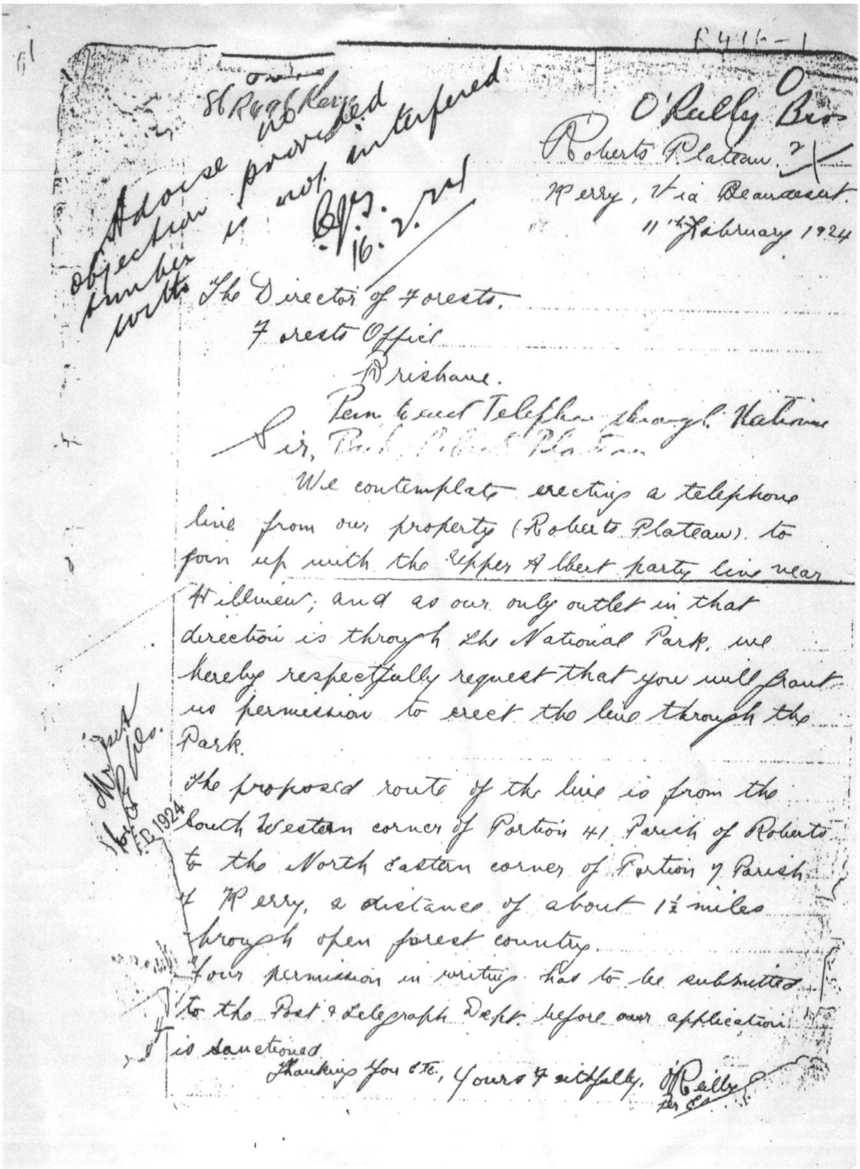

Handwritten letter:

[marginal annotations: A house provided objection is not interfered with timber / Reregistered / BJ? 16.2.24]

O'Reilly Bros
Roberts Plateau.
Kerry, Via Beaudesert.
11th February 1924

The Director of Forests.
Forests Office
Brisbane.

Sir, Re erect Telephone through National Park, Roberts Plateau

We contemplate erecting a telephone line from our property (Roberts Plateau) to join up with the Upper Albert party line near Hillview; and as our only outlet in that direction is through the National Park, we hereby respectfully request that you will grant us permission to erect the line through the Park.

The proposed route of the line is from the South Western corner of Portion 41 Parish of Roberts to the North eastern corner of Portion 9 Parish of Kerry, a distance of about 1½ miles through open forest country.

Your permission in writing has to be submitted to the Post & Telegraph Dept. before our application is sanctioned.

Thanking you etc., Yours faithfully, O'Reilly Bros

own bat and not been advised by an army of bureaucrats.

The first part of the proposed route would have traversed some really rugged country over cliffs and steep gullies. Just following the direction of the line would have been difficult while constructing and maintaining it would have been a real challenge. The thing in its favour was that it was a considerably shorter distance than constructing a line to the Kerry exchange.

The fact that they considered the Darlington line at all would have been a reaction to a disagreement with their cousin, Luke O'Reilly, over the line.

Following the Stockyard Creek Track was the obvious route for the line to go but it had to pass through Luke's property. That would not normally have been a problem as it was the route everyone used to travel to the mountain and both families had been involved in constructing the track. The thing was that Luke did not want the line and was not prepared to put any time or money into it. There seemed to be some ill feeling over the matter.

It must have been sorted out to some extent because the telephone line was eventually constructed down Stockyard Creek beside the well-used track that made it more convenient to check on and maintain. The first twelve kilometres section traversed rugged mountain country as well as a considerable area of rainforest so it was this section where most of the problems occurred. After cyclones or wild storms there was often days of work removing fallen trees and generally restoring the line.

The fifteen kilometres of line to the Kerry Valley was not the end of the story. It had to be extended to the Kerry exchange that was a further nine kilometres away. The line down the side of the mountain and through the rainforest was run through insulators that were attached to trees but poles had to be erected in the open country for the rest of the distance along the valley. It represented quite a commitment by the family both in man-hours and money but it was a necessity for the fledgling Guest House. *O'Reillys* had to construct and maintain it at their own expense.

Many of the farms in the valley were not connected to the telephone at the time and five of the local families joined the *O'Reillys* 14 line. They no doubt paid for the privilege and that would have helped the O'Reillys recoup some of the expense of setting it up. I imagine the newcomers assisted with the maintenance of the line in their areas as well. The whole exercise would have helped cement the friendship and goodwill that existed over the years between the O'Reillys and the people of Kerry.

Later on in the 1930s the 14 line had a new subscriber on the mountain. When Luke married, his wife Marie naturally wanted a phone. A company had been formed by this time to oversee the management of the Guest House and Luke was granted permission to join the line by the external Chairman of the board Mr Dare Lea. I heard there were a few rumblings from the Guest House O'Reillys when they found out. Still there was always a good relationship between the O'Reilly families on the mountain even though they had taken different paths.

The *O'Reillys* 14 line was a party line and each subscriber had a letter after the 14. The code for the letter was rung to call that particular number. The Guest House number was 14S and three short rings for S meant that the call was for the Guest House. For instance the ring for 14D was a long and two shorts. It was not the done thing but anyone on the line could pick up the receiver and listen in on a neighbour's conversation

Mrs. Nelly Johnston was the telephonist for many years and would have been doing the job when the O'Reillys joined the line. The exchange was operated from the home of the person responsible for it at the time. It all looked rather frightening to an outsider with shutters, cords and plugs and it took some skill to operate but the telephonists then seemed to stay at the job for a long time. When my grandfather, Peter O'Reilly died in Brisbane in 1917, in the days before the O'Reillys had the phone connected, Nelly Johnston's husband Bob rode twenty-four kilometres up to the mountain to tell the boys. The people who operated the exchanges were dedicated and took on extra responsibilities. If there was an urgent message for someone without a phone connection the nearest neighbour was rung and would deliver the message.

Laurel Keppel took over in 1950 when Nelly retired and she was the exchange lady for twenty-five years. The hours of service on weekdays were from 7am till 1pm and from 2pm till 9pm. On Saturday the hours were from 8am till 1pm and on Sunday from 9am till 10am. An opening fee could be paid to open the exchange at other times in case of an emergency or an important call. When more lines were added between Kerry and Beaudesert. Mrs Keppel would plug us through to Beaudesert if she was going away in case there was an emergency on the mountain.

Moving the exchange from one house to another was quite an expense and the Dept. was reluctant to do it. According to Laurel's son Ross, when the exchange was moved to Keppel's, three guarantors were required to post a bond of one hundred pounds each. Laurel took over at 6pm in May 1950 and they waited an hour for the first call. Eventually two technicians arrived from Beaudesert and found that the exchange had not been connected.

Ringing up was quite a business in those days. To ring Brisbane from the

Guest House for instance, you had to wait till the line was free, then ring Mrs Keppel at the Kerry exchange and ask for trunkline. She would put you through to the Beaudesert exchange and you asked the telephonist there for trunkline. When you were put through to trunkline you gave them the Brisbane number you wanted and waited while they rang the Brisbane exchange who raised the number and made the connection. If you wanted a number in Charleville for instance it could take quite some time to connect the exchanges along the way. The telephonist would interrupt your call every three minutes and ask if you were extending and if you were it would add to the cost of the call. At the end of your call you rang-off, by giving a short ring to let the exchange know that you had finished.

For most of the time Mrs Keppel was at Kerry there was just one line between Kerry and Beaudesert. In-coming calls had precedence over other calls and as you could imagine the Guest House would have a line up of calls coming in and would often monopolize the line. Anyone who wanted to ring out had to wait. The O'Reillys had many friends at Kerry but they must have thought at times that they would be better off without us.

Mrs. Keppel, as we called her, was the telephonist at Kerry during my time working at the Guest House and she was a real saint. Quite often while we were on the 14 service the line would blow down or be touching wet leaves or lantana in the rainforest, which made it difficult to hear. Mrs Keppel could hear both the caller and the O'Reillys and she would relay the conversation in both directions. Over a period of time she became so conversant with our business that when we were cut off completely she would take bookings for us. No doubt we at the Guest House would have tried her patience many times but she was always polite and helpful.

In 1946 when I was still a lad, Rose sent me down the Stockyard Creek Track with a horse for Ped who was working on the telephone line. The horse I was leading did not appreciate going down the rocky track and kept lugging back so I got off my horse and led them both. As I walked along I heard a sound overhead and saw rocks hurtling through the air from the cliff above me. The horses wheeled as I dived in to hug the cliff beside the track. Rocks the size of footballs landed on the track beside me but soon all was quiet again. I walked to the edge of the track and watched the rocks on their journey to Stockyard

Creek hundreds of feet below. A fire had burnt up the mountain recently and the country was black and often rocks roll in steep country during and after a fire. I had to go back to the top of the mountain to find the horses and then went on down to meet Ped. He was not a horse lover and told me he was quite happy walking but I was pleased to see that he did get on it.

In 1954 many of the Kerry phone subscribers decided to combine their efforts and put in a new pole line with a cross arm that would take all their individual lines down the valley to connect with the PMG line. The Guest House was in on the deal so Frank Young and I went down to work on the new line with the Kerry boys. It was an enjoyable week. We stayed with my uncle Herb O'Reilly and enjoyed the break away from the mountain. We had sharp axes in contrast to the farm axes that the Kerry lads had on show and I did some lopping of branches in trees that were hanging over the line. Most of this work did not benefit us due to a decision made in 1959 to build a new O'Reilly line down Duck Creek that would join the PMG line further down the valley.

When the Canungra road was constructed it meant that the Stockyard Creek Track was not used very much so the line became difficult to check on and maintain. After a good blow it would go 'dead' and it meant a long trip down the mountain and back to find the cause. It was not always convenient to ride a horse because of all the equipment that had to be carried. As well as an axe and brush-hook, pliers and wire, a ladder was needed as well. The insulators were fastened to trees and if a tree fell and broke the wire it would often pull through a number of these insulators. A ladder was necessary to feed the wire back through them. I often took our jeep to the top of the track and walked down. I remember walking back up the mountain with the usual load and being spurred on in my endeavour to stay ahead of the shadow of the setting sun that was creeping up behind me.

The decision to put a new line down Duck Creek was influenced by the construction of a road to our property 17V that was about eight kilometres along the route that the line would take. Duck Creek heads on 17V so to construct the new line down that valley was the obvious way to go. Work began in early 1960 and the road made it easier to erect and maintain the first section of line. From 17V the line followed a ridge down the steep side of the mountain to the Duck Creek Valley and then along the creek to Dunne's house.

Tom and Michael Dunne allowed us to attach our line to their poles for the rest of the journey from their house to the PMG line at Kerry. The 14 line had been a lifeline for the Guest House for the last thirty-five years and it was sad in a way to see it go but I couldn't say I missed the walk down Stockyard Creek.

Spikes and insulators were bought from the PMG Dept. at a reasonable cost and were used when attaching the wire to trees through the rainforest and our own property at 17V. We used an extension ladder and fastened a rope around the tree to hold me as I leaned back to bore the holes for the spikes with a brace and bit. We fastened the wire high on the trees but kept it reasonably loose to avoid it breaking if a tree fell over it.

Poles were used down the side of the mountain and for the rest of the journey. I used a draught horse from Luke's farm to haul poles into position down the steep side of the mountain. Running the wire was a bit of a challenge but between Frank Young and me we managed it. When I tightened up the wire it ended up well above two of the poles so I had done some unnecessary work along the way.

The new line was still a party line but this time there were only four O'Reilly phones on it. It was called the 8 line now and the Guest House letter was D so our new number was 8D. It was a big improvement on the 14 line but it was still far from perfect. The crackling was so loud during a storm that sometimes it was almost impossible to hear. The exchange was eventually converted to automatic and so ended the role of the telephonist at Kerry. The telephonists were an unselfish breed and contributed to the community in so many ways. If someone needed help or was sick or there was a death in the family the telephonist was relied upon to spread the word in the district and people were only too willing to help.

The Guest House entered a new era in 1978 when a radiotelephone link was established to *O'Reillys* from Tamborine Mountain. We had continuous service at last and you could ring anywhere by just dialling a number. Being able to hear the person on the other end of the line clearly was a new experience. It is hard to imagine that the Guest House relied on the old party line for the first fifty years of its existence and still survived.

Stock - Cattle and Horses

There were a good number of both cattle and horses on the mountain when we returned to the Guest House and as we saw it they represented a real asset. Riding parties were still part of the weekly programme and cattle were needed for milk and meat. Horses were the life-blood of the O'Reillys in earlier times and it is hard to imagine how the Guest House could have existed without them. They were the only means of transport for the family and the early Guest House relied very much on horses till the road arrived in 1947. They transported essential goods and supplies as well as bringing in the paying customers who were an essential ingredient if the place was to have a future.

Most people went out walking at the Guest House around that time but if they wanted to give their legs a rest or were just keen on horses they joined a riding party. These parties involved a dozen or more people and there was quite a bit of work to be done before they rode off along the ridges. The horses were rounded up and saddled and everyone was allotted a horse. Stirrup-leathers were adjusted and people climbed aboard quite often with some assistance. The horses were generally quiet and well-behaved and this was just as well because many people had little or no experience with horses. Lunches were put into sugarbags that had a hole cut near the top so that the stirrup and leather would pass through to suspend the bag that was thrown over the saddle to hang on the opposite side. Boiling the billy was a lunchtime ritual and the whole outing had something of an adventure about it and people enjoyed the whole experience.

Originally riding parties had a wide choice of destinations, even out to Mt Bithongabel on the crest of the Range along the old riding track. When I became involved with the riding parties we rode regularly to scenic spots on the northern side of the Guest House to places such as Cainbable Falls, Kerry Lookout and Blue Creek. We also went to closer destinations like Snake Ridge and West Cliff on occasions. It was a pleasant experience riding through the rainforest and being able to look up at the ferns and orchids in the trees without having to watch your step on the rough track. People were warned about prickly vines such as the raspberries with the hooked wait-a-while thorns and the infamous stinging trees that could inflict a very severe sting. The burning

Above: Two regulars help with the milking, my sympathy is with the cow Photo: Frank Young

Left: Horses at Morans Creek
Above: Peter doing the milking –
there were no bails in those days

vines, as we called them, did not look threatening. They had no prickles but gripped on to your skin and if they dragged across your throat as your horse moved forward they left a red mark and a sharp stinging sensation.

Everyone who lived on the mountain had an encounter with the leaves of the stinging trees sooner or later. I remember Rhelma and I as kids were endeavouring to burden Nibs, a rather cranky old packhorse, with a packsaddle that he objected to. We had him tied to a stinging tree and he sat back on his halter and pulled the tree down on top of us all. Horses are susceptible to the stings as well and Nibs took off over the hill dragging the tree behind him. I was not wearing a shirt at the time and we both suffered badly. It took a while to calm us down and that included the horse.

Horses were also needed to round up the cattle in the rough country on the mountain. The cattle were an important element too as they supplied milk and meat and so were a valuable asset to life on the mountain. Also, they were the reason the boys came in the first place – to establish dairy farms. Cows were milked daily until 1969 to supply milk for the Guest House.

Keeping up the supply of beef cattle for the Guest House meant that a lot of fat cattle were needed and it was not always easy to supply them. We made use of the other property that was owned by the family, 17V. Some of the cattle had grown up on 17V and were real scrubbers and almost impossible to yard. It was a difficult paddock to muster because the country was rough with rainforest on two sides and cliffs or steep country on the other boundaries. The adjoining rainforest bordered on the National Park that was endless. Cattle do not live in the rainforest, they are grass eaters, but would nevertheless head for it as soon as we arrived on the scene. The difficulty with rainforest is that cattle can race through it but it is impossible to ride a horse after them. You have to get off your horse, tie it up and try to get around them on foot. Generally if you could not get between the cattle and the rainforest and keep them out of it you could wave them goodbye.

The cattle were not used to dogs and generally they were no help but one day we had Fred Williams to help us muster. He had a reputation for yarding scrubbers further west and had two dogs with him. We managed to herd a mixed mob of rather nervous cattle away from the scrub when a young bull, about eighteen months old, broke away and took off down a steep ridge and into the rainforest on Rocky Creek. My only thought was to let him go and hold on to the rest of them but Fred said his dogs would bring it back. I was doubtful as we could hear the dogs barking and the bull roaring in the scrub below. Then they appeared; one dog hanging on to his nose and the other one nipping at his heels. They brought him back to the mob and he did not attempt to break away again. If you did happen to get cattle on to the track home you still had to drive them along a narrow rainforest track for four miles to the home paddocks.

Tom Dunne, our neighbour from Duck Creek in the Kerry Valley, was always part of the action when we had a muster. Tom had plenty of experience working cattle in mountain country and we felt we couldn't have a muster without him. We would plan our tactics and set off and although we had some success it never went according to plan. We even tried approaching the paddock from the eastern side leading our horses in over Cainbable Creek so we would approach them through the rainforest. When we pushed a vehicle track through to 17V from the Guest House in 1957 the job was made easier but generally the odds were still in favour of the cattle. I fenced a wing from the first road cutting in the rainforest out into the open forest and we did have some success. We managed to get a mixed mob into the Guest House at one time. The cattle were generally in good condition and the slaughterhouse was humming along for weeks afterwards with beef in plentiful supply.

Later we drove a lively bunch of bullocks down the mountain to Tom Dunne's place at Kerry. They were big rangy Jersey bullocks that had only been yarded once in their lives. They were not really suited for the Guest House menu. We were disappointed with the price we were offered by the meatworks for them, the reason being that they were jerseys and their yellow fat was not in demand. Other breeds of cattle have white fat. We had no real option but to accept the price, well we were not going to let them go back up the mountain and these wild creatures wouldn't go too well in a sale yard. Tom and I drove them to Tancred's meatworks the next day arriving there after dark. We had a job driving these nervous big brutes towards the bright lights around the yards and were on edge ourselves and it was a good feeling when we closed the gate behind them.

I shot a few of the remaining wild cattle but could not get near the last one, a cunning old cow that was a real scrubber. We had already built a yard out there and this day we intended to poke her along quietly with other more docile cattle into the yard. She was too cunning for that and took off by herself across Belsens Ridge heading for the rainforest below. I was riding a mare that had been recently broken and instead of turning the cow we somehow collided with her and we all came crashing down on the rocks along the ridge. I was the first to my feet and grabbed the cow by the head and held her down. I didn't quite know what to do with her but I was not going to let her go because she would have the other cattle as bad as she was after a time. Frank was following me and we agreed the only practical thing to do was knock her on the head. We did not have a gun or even an axe to do the job and I hadn't the stamina to hold her down for too long. Frank used a large rock, which did the job quickly. It isn't a pretty story but it was at a time when the Guest House relied on the savings our own beef gave us. We needed to be able to yard the cattle when we wanted them. They were tough times.

We found that we had to buy cattle to keep up with demand for beef at the Guest House. When we gave up milking we went out of jerseys and concentrated on the beef breeds. I bought fat cattle from Tom Dunne to augment our beef supply for the Guest House and we would drive them up the steep spur out of Duck Creek and through to the Guest House. We lost a beautiful Angus cow over a mini cliff one day and had to sit on our horses and watch her die. Any cattle I bought in from outside had to be dipped because our country was generally clean of ticks. If we brought in ticky cattle there was a danger of an outbreak of tick fever in our cattle that were not resistant to it. After the road was put through to 17V I built a yard there with a loading ramp and could truck cattle into the Guest House. That made the job a lot easier.

When you live on top of a mountain blessed with a good outlook and a high rainfall, life will be difficult for handling cattle. You will be surrounded by steep country and have lots of showery weather. If you wanted to take cattle away it would be raining for sure. The external boundaries of the Guest House property were either rainforest or cliff-face and that was good because there were no boundary fences to maintain. When we stopped using our own beef we would sell our fat cattle and on this particular day I yarded some bullocks that we were going to sell and Reg was bringing the cattle truck down. Our cattle truck was also a tip truck that we used to maintain the road. When we had cattle to move we would attach the stock crate and chain the back down around the chassis. We loaded the cattle and as I was driving off I asked Reg, "You've chained down the back?" He replied, "It won't need it."

I should have stopped then but went down a slight incline on to the Red Road. As we did I felt the back going over and next thing we were all going over and landed on our side. I could see Reg falling onto me from what seemed like a great height. The cattle were sprayed out on to the ground and I suppose they couldn't believe their luck as they took off. I let them go. We would try again another day. The truck had no real damage and we soon had it back on its wheels.

Another time we had the local carrier, Jim Salisbury, arrive to take cattle away. As it was raining his truck was left near the main road on top of the hill and we used our International to ferry our cattle up to it. The Red Road at that stage was a steep, greasy track and any gravel that was applied seemed to have disappeared into the red dirt. Our truck was being towed up the Red Road by the bulldozer so there we were with Reg on the dozer and me driving the truck that was sliding around as we made slow progress. Bulldozers are not what you would call gentle machines and the truck was being jerked and pulled rather violently as we progressed up the steep hill and all the weight of the cattle was on the back of the stock-crate.

The result was the welds along the bottom of the frame at the back of the truck gave away and as we went around the back to have a look there was a bullock with his two hind legs hanging out under the frame and almost touching the ground. The situation looked grim. We couldn't keep going like this with the bullock half out of the truck. We couldn't get him out and with the slope of the hill and the weight of the cattle on him we couldn't get him back in. I thought what the hell are we going to do. Jim was unfazed by the situation and we eventually eased the weight of the other cattle off him and with a big effort on our part and the bullock we had him back in. We quickly chained the frame together and arrived without further mishap. We didn't attempt another load and I said to Jim you wouldn't strike anything worse than this and he replied that he had seen a lot worse. Well, I would like to know what it was. Maybe Jim should write a book!

In the 1960s we went through a tragic period that saw the demise of many of our horses. When you think about it horses made it possible for the O'Reillys to exist on the mountain and now they were dying not quickly, but singly, over weeks and months. They died of pneumonia and the local vets would treat them with drugs but it was to no avail, they died regardless. Another vet was called in and he inquired over the border in the Tweed River Valley where they gave him the answer. The condition was caused by crofton weed that the horses soon developed a liking for. The weed effected their lungs over a period of time till eventually they had very little lung left to use and pneumonia set in.

This garden escapee was new to Queensland for the wind-blown seed had recently arrived on the southeast wind from over the border. It grows well in 'scrub country' with good rainfall and our mountain really suited it. When they get a taste for it horses go looking for the weed but cattle never touch it. The invasion of crofton weed brought to an end the riding parties, which were an important part of our weekly programme. I kept a couple of horses to work the cattle but try as I might to avoid it the crofton weed would get them in the end. There are no horses or cattle on our property now so an important era of O'Reilly history has come to an end.

Rose leading a riding party on a day's excursion

The Necessities - Firewood, Power and Water

When we were generating our own electrical power we had limited output and relied on wood for cooking, room heating and for hot water. Firewood was in demand and keeping up the supply took up much of our time. There were two large stoves in the kitchen, an open fireplace in the dining room and later a chip heater as well. Water for showers was heated in a large boiler that consumed great chunks of wood and a smaller boiler was used to heat water for the kitchen. Up until 1957 all the wood for the Guest House was cut with a crosscut saw and split with wedges or an axe. I had my first lessons from Mick on the fine art of using a crosscut saw and he told me I was a natural, which was good for my morale because there seemed to be lots of things I wasn't good at.

Mick and Vince did their share on the crosscut in earlier times but once Frank Young came to work at the Guest House it was he and I who were the woodmen. The crosscut saw that we used now adorns the dining room wall at the Guest House and people viewing it would have little appreciation of what was achieved with it. Many tons of firewood was cut and the sweating bodies on either end received some healthy exercise.

We had virtually no access to eucalypt forest at the time so we relied on dead rainforest hardwood logs that did not rot when they fell and lay on the forest floor. These were collected from O'Reilly property or from along the road that accessed the Guest House. Most of the rainforest species are softwoods that decay in a short time after they fall so there were a limited number of trees that we could use. Penta ash or penteceras as we called it was the most common hardwood that burnt well but we also used lignum-vitae and saffron-heart. We did not use crows-ash as the oil it contained burnt with black smoke that gummed up the flue and so it did more harm than good. Mararie, a common rainforest tree, was used in earlier times because it burnt when it was still green but our generation never used it.

Some preparation was needed before setting out to bring in a load of wood. If the teeth of the Cross-cut saw were getting rounded off Mick was told and he would put his glasses on and attack it with file in hand and the saw set up in a sharpening frame. It would take him quite some time but it was a great feeling when we started cutting to see the saw biting into the wood and the sawdust ribboning out of the log. It made the job so much easier.

Before we started, petrol was siphoned from a forty-four gallon drum and the Blitz-buggy was topped up, lunch was cut and placed on board along with the tools for the job in hand. The tools included two axes, a brush hook for cutting a track and clearing an area around the log, a maul and wedges for splitting the logs and also to stop the saw jamming as it cut through the log. A wallaby jack and of course the crosscut saw were all added to the list of equipment.

We set off along the road and when we found a suitable log a track was cut into it and the log was lifted off the ground with the wallaby jack and chocked. This made the job easier on our backs and negated any danger of the saw hitting a rock that would take the edge off it. The log was cut into six-foot lengths. It was then split into post size sections with the maul and wedges making the timber light enough for two people to carry and then it was loaded on to the Blitz. From the sawing at ground level till it was all loaded on the truck you would have to say it was all good exercise and I believe we must have been fit in those days.

We made up our lunch similar to the lunches that went out in the packs for the guests at the time. Bread, butter, tomatoes, onions, meat and cheese were all included and the ingredients cut up as we made our sandwiches on the spot. The billy was also boiled because a mug of tea was a necessity. Guests used to come out with us occasionally and on this day a lad about our own age who we knew fairly well came along to give us a hand. We admired the meticulous way he cut up the filling for his sandwich into small, neat pieces using my pocket-knife. When he had finished Frank told him that the blade he was using was the one I used to castrate the bull calves. His reaction was immediate; he sent the sandwich flying off into the bush much to our amusement.

Next day at the wood-heap we spent all the morning lifting the six-foot lengths on to a sawhorse and cutting them with the crosscut saw into short sections that would suit the stove. All that had to be done then was to split the blocks into usable pieces that would fit into the stove or wherever else they had to be used and deliver them to the various wood-boxes. The whole process took up much of our time, such was the demand for firewood, but I enjoyed the work.

The crosscut saw was pensioned off in 1957 when we modernised our wood gathering activities and entered the era of the chainsaw. The first chainsaws were not user friendly and I remember being more fatigued after operating the great heavy thing for a day then I was after a day on the crosscut saw but I did cut more wood with it. I was unaware of the effect a noisy chainsaw was having on my hearing at the time and would have better hearing today if I kept using the crosscut. Also we cut the wood into short lengths in the paddock with the chainsaw. That saved double handling and made the firewood easier to load. High sides were erected on the Blitz so more blocks of wood could be loaded.

When the road was pushed through to our property 17V, we had access to our own eucalypt forest seven kilometres away and a plentiful supply of good wood. Supplying wood for Guest House needs was still a big commitment until external power arrived in 1968 and then, would you believe, O'Reillys bought a gas stove. Some of our regular guests held this up as an example of O'Reilly logic but it was the prospect of a prolonged blackout that influenced our decision. We also bought electric hot water systems and these savings cut the demand for firewood by something like ninety percent.

The lighting plant that was in operation when we arrived back was a 32-volt system that was powered by a single cylinder Lister diesel engine. Reg Cullen, who worked at the Guest House before the war, said that when he returned from the conflict he went to change the oil in the Lister. When he unscrewed the drain plug the oil wouldn't run out because it had congealed in the sump. The important thing was that the motor still ran. Reg's stories should always be treated with some suspicion but it was a wonderful old motor that was easy to start and gave us many years of faithful service.

The 32-volt lighting plant that was supplying power when I first worked at the Guest House was certainly way ahead of kerosene lamps that were used originally. One good thing about it was that there was no danger of being electrocuted – the 32-volts would not do you any harm. The same could be said for the 110-volt plant that followed it. Dot, who was a guest during that time, was hanging out her washing and these rather low slung power lines were handy so that's where Dot's washing ended up. The electrical system shorted out and she remembers that Mick was not at all happy when he found her washing draped across the power lines and earthing down on to the clothesline. The black patches on her washing would not have added to its appeal either.

It was 1952 when Mick bought another Lister diesel 8 horsepower faster revving motor that was needed to drive the 110-volt generator. The Guest House had to be rewired and new light fittings installed and the old wiring in metal conduit was scrapped. We built a shed on what was once the old tennis court to house the new lighting plant. The motor was closer to sleeping quarters and a bit noisy but people didn't complain. The lights went out at about 10pm at night as they had always done. When guest numbers increased we bought an ex-army Ford V8 motor coupled to a 240-volt generator as an auxiliary with a transformer in reverse to knock the volts down to 110.

One holiday weekend when people started arriving about 9pm the diesel was labouring so Vince and I decided to start the V8. It was slow to fire and the six volt battery had a heavy load and was running low so I primed the V8 from a bottle as it was turning over – not very smart. I was a bit generous with the fuel and it fired back through the carburettor and ignited the bottle, which burst in my hand. My face was on fire, which was frightening for both of us but we soon had the flames extinguished and I came out of it fairly well. Vince ran me to Beaudesert Hospital where I spent the night. He picked me up next day and we drove to Beenleigh to pick up a carcass of beef because I wasn't in any condition to kill a beast the next day as we had planned.

The diesel with the occasional help of the V8 was the source of power for the Guest House till the eventual arrival of mains power in 1968. We invested in an auxiliary power plant to help us survive the blackouts. Over the years these power plants were replaced by larger outfits as our demand for power grew. Our present backup plant now has the capacity to generate 5KVA of power.

Water is a necessity wherever you live and particularly for the O'Reillys when they built a Guest House on top of a range well above the nearest permanent water. Tanks were used to supply water to the early Guest House and the tank iron had to be carried up the track by manpower and the tanks made on site. As the Guest House expanded these tanks proved to be inadequate and Tom put his divining skills to work and declared that there was water about seventy feet below ground on the hill above the complex. A well was dug before the war and a stream was located at roughly the level that Tom predicted. The Lister diesel engine that provided power for the lighting plant was also harnessed to drive a pump that lifted the water from the well into a holding tank.

The well was still supplying water for Guest House needs when I first worked there but it was struggling to keep up with demand during periods of low rainfall. Morans Creek was the answer but the Guest House was five hundred feet elevation above the creek. Bill Wyeth, our practical architect and general all-rounder, was advising Mick on a plan of action to remedy the situation. It was decided to make use of a hydraulic ram at Morans Creek to lift the water three hundred feet up the hill. A windmill would be used to pump it up the remaining two hundred feet to the Guest House.

Providing a system to supply water to the hydraulic ram was a complex undertaking. We had to divert Morans Creek while we built a three-foot high weir across it that would give us enough head so the water would flow one hundred metres to a holding tank that was well above the hydraulic ram. A smaller pipe dipped sharply from this tank to the hydraulic ram that forced the water three hundred feet up the hill to another tank near the windmill. The hydraulic ram did the job till mains power arrived fifteen years later. The windmill was a different story. We thought we were in the windiest spot in Queensland but there was not enough wind to keep the Guest House supplied with water. It was a disappointment after going to the trouble of digging holes for the foundations and setting the mill up. We replaced it with a power kerosene motor and pump that did the job.

The biggest headache with the hydraulic ram was that a deposit of very hard material would build up in the two and a half inch galvanised pipe that brought the water from the weir to the first holding tank. There was very little fall in this section of pipe and the deposit built up in the gently flowing water. It was a bloody awful job unscrewing these heavy pipes and getting rid of the hard material inside by sliding a smaller G.I. pipe with a round scraper attached up and down for minutes to free it up. We did this with the rather cold Morans Creek water flowing through the pipe to take the sediment away. This had to be done at regular intervals otherwise there was not enough water arriving in the holding tank to keep the ram going. We were pleased when power arrived in 1968 and an electric motor and pump replaced the hydraulic ram and the power kerosene motor.

The electric pump that was installed when power arrived did not require much maintenance. To avoid the trip down to the creek to start the motor Vince installed a float in the tank at the Guest House and strung a heavily insulated copper wire along a fence line to the pump that automatically started when the water level dropped in the tank. It worked well on the first day but on the second day nothing happened. Vince investigated and found that our rather aggressive rainforest rodents had made short work of the wire that we had strung and it laid on the ground in a number of pieces.

The only thing to do to remedy the situation was to attach an insulated wire to the power poles on their way to the pump well above rodent level and this is what Vince did. Of course it had to happen, one day the SEQEB man arrived and saw the offending wire and said it was illegal to attach another wire to their power poles and it would have to be removed. Vince who could be relied on to be cool under pressure said quite innocently that he couldn't see any wire. The response was a waving of hands pointing out the wire and in spite of his efforts Vince still couldn't see it. This went on for a while till the exasperated rep. finally admitted defeat and said, "Okay, I can't see it either."

O'Reillys had always supplied water to the National Park barracks and it was suggested that they would like to be independent and obtain water from Canungra Creek. *O'Reillys* was invited to be part of the scheme and it sounded good to us. Water could be gravitated from the creek down to our clearing. Three miles of PVC pipe was laid and the fall in elevation from the creek to the clearing is three hundred feet. It was laid through some wild country and floods at the intake, tree-falls that squash the pipe and airlocks that develop at times on the ridges, were all hazards that had to be overcome.

Once we were troubled with a diminishing water supply over a lengthy period and after an extensive search undid a pipe to release a fair-sized blue spiny-cray. It would have entered the pipe when it was quite small so it could make it through the screen and had been living happily in the pipe with a supply of food flowing past him. The bigger he became the less water arrived at our tank. When we released the culprit it looked rather disappointed as it scrambled off in the direction of the creek. Another pipe has been installed since and the quality of the water is excellent.

O'Reillys Staff

We had a great staff in the period when Vince and I returned to the Guest House and they were real personalities. The isolation of the place at the time seemed to attract these people who were a different breed from the average and they added humour and some real colour to our lives. They were not perfect by any means but showed great dedication to the work that had to be done. Cooks particularly stand out as hard working but generally were not easy to get along with. Bernard said that if a cook was good tempered and easygoing he was usually not much of a cook. After Molly had given away the cooking role at the Guest House we relied on cooks to keep up the standard that Molly had set and I think it would be fair to say it was with varying degrees of success.

A chef was a title that was never used at the Guest House after the war when they were all cooks. They were generally without qualifications but most were experienced and did a good job. They were a dedicated breed and worked long hours and in a way the smooth running of the operation depended on them. If the food was good everyone from the guests to the boss was happy. There was often a down side to them. They were usually cranky, drank too much and quite often made life unpleasant for the rest of the staff. Even if you owned the place you made sure that you did not upset the cook. A cook had to be versatile at that time too because we killed our own beef and poultry, milked cows and collected eggs that were all added to the menu. The chefs of today might be a little nonplussed if we presented them with a carcass of beef and told them to use every bit of it. The frowning old wood stove would have been a challenge for some of them too.

In those earlier times the cook produced three meals a day, so it was a long day but they had time off in the afternoon. During the fifties and early sixties Tibby was our cook and Hughie, (Mrs Hughes) was the wash up lady and they were a great combination. Tibby made no secret of ducking down to her room for her first rum of the day about mid morning 'to keep her going' while Hughie kept an eye on things in the kitchen. Mrs Hughes was a dairy farmer's wife from Killarney, Queensland and although she was of slight build she was a well-organized energetic worker who had the stamina to handle the washing up job at the Guest House. She organised the whole kitchen and things usually ran smoothly when Hughie was in charge. Tibby and Hughie were a pair of characters and were always telling yarns. Tibby had a great laugh and a good voice too and would sing 'Paddy McGinty's Goat' at *O'Reillys* concerts. Hughie retired when mains power was connected and we bought a dishwasher.

We had a staff of around ten in the late 1950s and they were all live-in, which meant they were naturally part of the family and became our good friends. We worked with them in those days and they were a great crew. They were versatile too and applied their skills to keep the Guest House running smoothly. Pam and Bernie from the dining room would help service the rooms after they cleared the tables. The sheets were washed and dried between showers of rain and a hundred other jobs had to be done. Even Vince B the yardman would come into the kitchen and help wash the pots at times.

Freda, a little Aboriginal girl whose parents were having a tough time on a share dairy near Canungra came up to work. She told me later she was only thirteen and my mother put her age up to fourteen when she employed her. She was a great little worker and when she was paid two pounds seven and six a week plus her board and keep she would not open the pay-envelope but give it to Vince J the bus-driver to take down to her parents at Canungra who needed the money. She was only small and would stand on a Tristram's soft-drink box so she could stir the porridge in the Guest House kitchen.

Another cook who left his mark on the place was Jack. He was an economical and excellent cook who had the welfare of the Guest House at heart. He did not waste a thing. He became a good friend and worked for us for over ten years. He liked a few drinks but would never let you down. Sometimes he would have a beer in the kitchen while cooking but would drink it out of a cup and people would think he was having a cup of tea.

Jack was not a good driver and the road was rough and narrow at the time so he would have a beer or two or three in Canungra to fortify him for the trip up the mountain. He did not like the pyramid rock corner that was a very tight bend in earlier times with a big drop below the road. It was usually at night as he returned and when he made it around the corner he would say, "Beat you again you bastard." Another night he hit a tree on the way home and Reg said to him later I've seen plenty of cars that have hit trees before but never one to climb six foot up a bank to do it. Jack thought for a minute then smiled and admitted that it was not a bad effort.

We had another cook Tom who went over the side of the mountain while coming back to cook for a ball we were having that night. Tom was lucky not to have been killed but ended up in hospital. Jack had a catering contract at a golf club in Brisbane at the time but when we informed him that we were in trouble he got someone to take his place and came up and helped us out. Wally cooked for us at a later date. He was a good cook but did not carve the meat well and either Vince or I was usually on hand to carve at dinner and it suited us to keep an eye on the meals as they went out.

Another time we were desperate for a cook and I rang an employment agency in Brisbane. They said they had a cook who had a girlfriend and that she wanted a job as well. We employed them both and they came up in the bus and settled into the job. Two days later I came back from Brisbane about 9pm and Karma came up whispering in great secrecy to tell me to take the keys out of the car and to lock it – a thing we never did at the time. She told me the police had rung and were chasing the cook and his girlfriend who were wanted for murder.

The police arrived at six the next morning, young fellows dressed in jeans and casual clothes and I took them up to the kitchen. The thought occurred to me to ask them to wait till after breakfast was cooked but it was a serious business so I said nothing. They took them both away and I went in to console the kitchen staff and when I asked about the cook Heather said some friends of his had come in and he went out with them. The police were smooth operators. I told Heather what had happened and that she would be cooking breakfast. The couple the police took away were convicted and served jail terms. As time went by the cooks or chefs became more professional and there was less involvement of the O'Reilly family in the kitchen.

Miss Beattie, a woman of indeterminate age but not young, worked in the dining room at the Guest House for many years. She would be remembered by our guests as a typically old-fashioned lady with an air about her that belonged to a bygone era. She organized the dining room well and was a stable influence because she never seemed to change in appearance or manner or anything else in all the years she worked for us. When she rang the gong to announce that meals were being served she did it with great flare and people would stop and listen. Unlike Miss Beattie, Kathy belongs to a later generation. She was a local from Biddaddaba Creek when she first worked at the Guest House on leaving school. She spent some time away but returned later to take up a management position. She is typical of the staff today that we employ locally from the Beaudesert and Canungra districts, who continue to play a valuable role at the Guest House.

We've had so many great staff over the years and plenty of staff dramas as well that I could not possibly have room enough to record in this book. One thing is for sure they didn't come any better then Ismey or Esmay as we called her. She was our receptionist for nineteen years and saw many changes during that time. She hailed from Jamestown in South Australia and in the early 1970s she worked with my father Mick in the original old office. She also had to battle the crackly old party line during storms and wet weather. While she was with us we went from the party line to a radio telephone with all the modern equipment but she retired before computers and emails took over which was probably just as well.

She had an interest in botany and birdlife and the rainforest fascinated her and she could spend a day by herself in the forest and be completely absorbed by it all. It was an interest we shared and we would put our heads together to identify rainforest fruits or leaves that Guests brought in to be identified. Esmay was neat and meticulous and put together a laminated botanical collection of rainforest plants that the guests could access. I collected many of the specimens for this mini herbarium and we enjoyed working on it. Many of the guests who visited O'Reillys during the 1970s and 80s would remember Esmay as a genteel lady who was always well dressed and had a generous caring nature. Her generosity hid to some extent her inner strength and dedication, qualities that we appreciated. She became a good friend and support to the O'Reilly families, she would mind our children at times and was always there when she was needed.

Glen Trelfo is another one who has been part of the landscape at the Guest House for a long time and has been a great asset to us. In earlier times he would come up and camp and he always had his camera handy. Our birder friend, Roy Wheeler struck up a friendship with him in 1978, when I ran my first Bird Week. Roy invited him up from the campground to be part of the event. Roy could see his potential and introduced him to me and that introduction initiated a productive and close relationship with the O'Reilly family that has benefited us both. Like Roy I could see he was abounding with enthusiasm and talent so I offered him a job. Thirty years later he is still working for us.

During the first Bird Week we both saw broad-format six projector audio-visuals for the first time put on by Peter Slater and Steve Parish and we were blown away by them. Glen produced one for *O'Reillys* that I thought was a classic. It was accompanied by music and flowed along beautifully and the audience was enthralled by it. He also filmed documentaries for us. His excellent camera work and creative ability is such that the finished product is outstanding. The DVD of the secretive Albert lyrebird is my favourite. I work with Glen on the background story and the script for the documentaries that are still being produced today and we have a great time doing it. Glen is a good communicator as well as an enthusiastic naturalist and is very much in demand as a guide at *O'Reillys*.

Another person who left an impression on the place was Col Harmon. Col had a broad interest in botany but native orchids were his real love. He originally worked in Brisbane but came up with a few mates at weekends to give us a hand. About this time rainforest was being cleared on land that was to be used for grazing cattle further out along the mountain. We were told that we could take the orchids from the debris before it was burnt. This sounded good but where could we put them so they would not be eaten by the hungry pademelons? An enclosure was built with the help of volunteers to keep these rainforest wallabies at bay. Col moved up to the mountain and it was his baby for the next thirty years. He ended up planting other species so there would be something flowering all year round.

It went well for years but as Col aged it all became too much for him and the gardens became very congested. There is no doubt we have a lot to thank Col for. He really loved those gardens and towards the end of his tenure his aim seemed to be to protect them from the visitors, which was not always done in a polite way. Col has since passed away and the Natural History Association share the responsibility for the gardens with *O'Reillys*.

Keith Woolley was another one who left a job in Brisbane to come up and work for us. He became a good friend and a valued employee over the next twenty years. He had knowledge that was invaluable of where the underground water pipes and power cables were located or where to find material or equipment that was needed. We really missed Keith when he retired.

Clockwise from above: Esmay; Tibby; Miss Beattie; and Glen Trelfo with tour group.

Upgrading the Old Building

When Vince and I returned we were aware that the expectations of guests who stepped out of a bus at the front door were different now to the days of the horses. To us it seemed to accentuate the rather tired appearance of some of our old buildings. We were keen to give the old place a facelift and make certain areas of it more user-friendly.

There was a good deal of repair work to be done as well that included an upgrade of the old shower and toilet block. The building was the original that was used from the start and was made to look more presentable with some tiling and sheeting to give it some resemblance of a modern appearance. Vince O'Reilly, who had stocks and dyes, did the plumbing. It is difficult to work on a building that has drifted out of shape over the years or maybe it was never in shape in the first place. It meant that the finished product was only temporary till a new block could be built.

The dining room had to be enlarged and we did this by annexing a couple of adjacent bedrooms. The noisy table tennis activities were moved out of the dining room into a narrow room at the front of the building that became known as the ping-pong room. There were a few bedrooms at the time that opened on to either the dining room or the ping-pong room and they would have been incredibly noisy so we were glad to do away with a couple of them. We played table tennis on two long narrow tables that were pushed together, nothing like the conventional table tennis table but I was practically unbeatable on it. We played progressive ping-pong there as well and had a great time.

Another problem that was obvious when we had a dance was how the dining room floor would pulsate up and down with the rhythm of the dance. We crawled under the house and found that quite a number of posts had rotted through and the rest had been driven into the ground by the force of the energetic dancers. The original posts were all of rainforest timbers and did not stand the test of time, especially when there were liberal amounts of water thrown on the floor every Friday when the dining room was scrubbed. We brought posts in from the eucalypt forest to replace the rotted ones.

It was a difficult job digging holes and replacing the posts under a low dining room floor but we ended up replacing the wide hoop pine flooring boards with brush box timber. This had to be done in two sections so the guests would have somewhere to eat. During the second stage access to the kitchen was over a walkway with the wind whistling up through the non-existent floor and flapping the tarpaulins erected to protect the guests from the elements. The elements were making their presence felt as rain fell making it a difficult situation for management, staff and guests. Fortunately, things soon got back to normal and the impact of sixty dancers all doing 'Little Brown Jug' at the same time drove the new posts into the ground. We once again had our sprung floor back that felt so good to dance on.

The first architect involved at the Guest House was a good friend, Bill Wyeth, who had spent many weeks exploring the more inaccessible areas of Lamington National Park. He, with two National Park workers, opened up the walking track through to the Stinson Wreck in about 1950. Their track is still there and has been used ever since literally by thousands of people who have made the historic journey to the Stinson crash-site. They would have followed the original route, which was a track put through in 1905 by John Buchanan who worked under the direction of Robert Collins. Collins was the person who first conceived the idea that these beautiful mountains should be protected by a National Park and the purpose for the track was to interest people in his ideal. We have much to thank him for. Bernard O'Reilly would have fought his way through the dense lawyer vine along approximately the same route when searching for the lost Stinson Airliner thirty-two years later in 1937.

Bill Wyeth was a 'hands on' architect who made a positive contribution to the Guest House over many years. He drew up plans for a future Guest House in the early fifties that really impressed us, although we thought it did seem to be a bit grand for *O'Reillys*. It was of the style that was in vogue at the time in hotel accommodation with a passageway down the middle of the building with rooms on both sides and a toilet block down at one end. If we succeeded in implementing Bill's plans we would have ended up with a smaller version of the Hydro Majestic in the Blue Mountains. It would have been a mistake although we didn't realise it at the time. The user-friendly self-contained style of accommodation would supersede the more formal hotel building over the next twenty years. We approached the bank with the design and they did us a favour by knocking us back.

Even so by 1958 we built the first new guest accommodation of our era: a block of eight bedrooms in the old hotel design. Two years later we added a modern toilet block close by. These buildings were constructed by a meticulous Brisbane builder, Bob Plattern, and were of good quality and considered to be a bit flash at the time. They were part of Bill Wyeth's grand plan and were designed to carry another floor above. It was the last of the old design that was constructed as part of the Guest House although when Vince and I both married in 1961 each of our houses were designed by Bill Wyeth and built by Bob Plattern.

We anticipated that we would be doing more building in the future but were not sure what our next move should be. We thought it wise to have a look at comparable resorts in Victoria to help us make the right decision when the time came. It was May 1966 when Vince and I left on a drive south and the decision to do so showed some enterprise on our part and illustrated our desire to enter the real world.

We enjoyed the drive and visited five resorts and were most impressed with Mt Buffalo Chalet. We were thrilled to see snow for the first time in our lives. We visited resorts that were of a similar age and style to our own and did not see any self-contained units that would be in demand in the future. Nevertheless the whole experience gave us many good ideas. We had just entered the era of using Land Rovers as people movers ourselves and inspected a fleet of Land Rovers that were fitted out to carry skiers to the Mt Buller snowfields. We were impressed too with the magnificent fireplace at Mt Buller Ski Resort with its copper canopy and flue and copied the idea on a much smaller scale when we built our new lounge. It still survives forty years later.

What was very obvious to us on our return was that we needed a lounge. I can almost hear you say, "Surely you didn't have to go to Victoria to find that out." I suppose we realised that we would add a lounge at some stage but to us it didn't seem to be a priority. Even in 1966 everything happened in the dining room. The big old fireplace was there that everyone migrated to. It brought the guests and the family together – they sat there and yarned and had a cup of tea. All the indoor entertainment took place there. The dining room was where it all happened and it seemed to keep our mountain community together as a family. We realized though when we were at the Chalet at Mt Buffalo that it was nice to retreat to a quiet lounge with a log fire burning and read a newspaper or a book. Yes, a lounge would be an essential part of the Guest House but I do believe we lost something because of it.

We were determined to proceed with the concept of a new lounge. We inspected the scene with our local builder, Ted Tomkins, to see what could be done in a practical sense with the old building. We decided to virtually build a new building and tack it on to the existing old one. A new roofline was constructed that would blend with the dining room when it was eventually renovated and the result was a comfortable, well-lit lounge. It served us well for eleven years before its prominent position demanded that it be converted into the guest reception area.

The dining room had to wait nine years before it was renovated. This time we put in concrete stumps and a crows ash floor. We cut some of our own timber for the walls including blackwood, rosewood and red cedar. I also cut some lignum vitae off my own property. We broad-axed the lignum vitae into posts and beams to support the ceiling of the dining room. We were given some valuable lessons on how to square off the posts with a broadaxe by some of the experienced National Parks workers who came over to give us a hand after they had knocked off. We needed the broad-axed timber in the dining room because we wanted to retain some semblance of the original dining room. It was a lot of work but we believed it was worth it.

Later, when we extended the dining room the Robert Collins birdbath was in the way. Instead of moving this large rock we came up with the idea of building a concaved section around it to make it blend with the dining room and it created a real feature. The birds coming in to drink or eat during the day as well as the mammals at night can be seen by guests during mealtime.

It was a great era for doing things. We worked out what we wanted and what we could afford and talked it over with the builders, the Tomkins family and between us worked out a practical way of doing it. There was no architect involved at this stage. State government did not have the regulations that make life difficult today and we found Beaudesert Shire Council to be co-operative in working with us to iron out any difficulties.

The new lounge was a well-lit welcoming room, a good place to read during the day and it proved popular from the start. We erected a concrete wall at the front that allowed people to sit in the sun protected from the wind. It was all very practical but not aesthetically pleasing by today's standards but I think it reflected the practical tone of the time when we made use of new material and ideas without apology. When we built another lounge ten years later it was architect designed and the building was of a mountain style with smaller windows and more subdued lighting and was not as well lit.

Our next building, constructed in 1972, did not have much of a resemblance to the old slab hut on Morans Creek or any other building at *O'Reillys* for that matter. They were motel style units with shower and toilet, constructed of concrete blocks that did not blend all that well with the mountain environment. Nevertheless, they had the amenities people appreciated and were popular with the guests and of course they were streets ahead of any other accommodation that we had. They were built near the church by Ted Tomkins of Beaudesert with son Vince as an apprentice and are still in service thirty-five years later.

We didn't know how well off we were. Everything seemed straightforward to us. Ted Tomkin's wife, Joyce, drew up the plans and took them to council and they were approved and away we went. We didn't realise it then but there were hordes of bureaucrats waiting in the wings with reams of red tape and restrictions in the guise of fire safety regulations when we tackled our next building project in 1977. We were confused by the complexity of it all and council officers themselves seemed to have trouble interpreting the controls under which we had to build. We realised at this stage that we needed an architect to advise us and to gain the necessary approvals. We hired Maurice Hurst from Noosa who guided our many building projects over the next twenty years. The Tomkins family were our builders during that period and it was a happy relationship based on friendship and trust.

Certainly, the decade of the seventies was a time of change for the Guest House and now that we had mains power we were keen to upgrade our buildings and facilities to a standard people looked for. The place was no gold mine but at least it had its head above water and was making a modest profit. Big changes were in the wind and it was pleasing that banks were displaying a more co-operative attitude towards the tourist industry now and in particular that place way up in the hills called *O'Reillys*.

We were told by the authorities we should prepare for radiotelephone and that it would be a reality before long. This meant that the old office off the dining room, which had been used since the beginning of time, would be annexed into the kitchen and the lounge would be converted into the new office and reception area. The old office had served us well but that's all it was, an office, and we needed a more welcoming environment in a prominent position. As well as a reception desk and booking office, a room was needed for the electrical equipment required for the radiotelephone. We also planned to build a new lounge and games room on two levels so it ended up being quite a big undertaking.

We went to the bank with our hats in our hands and were eventually told, to our surprise, that they would not approve the loan as it stood unless we built units as well – thereby creating some return from the outlay. Our accountant and financial adviser, Ron Ramsey, added up the figures and said that we could do it so we went ahead with the biggest project we had ever undertaken. We had confidence in Ron and if he said it was OK we would accept that and concentrate on getting the job done. I know Mick was concerned about the amount of money we borrowed but he need not have worried because inflation skyrocketed at that time and those big repayments we were committed to, shrunk as the months went by. Three years later we were building again.

We put quite a bit of our own timber into the new buildings. A magnificent tallow-wood tree on the Moonlight Crag ridge had been struck by lightning so I fell it and used it for the wall between the lounge and the games room. The log was cut into slabs five inches thick and we adzed both sides which certainly made a rugged wall. Timber is a serviceable material in areas used by the public because it does not show marks. We lined both ends of the new units with our own blackwood timber.

We built a block of single units in 1982-83. People mixed well at *O'Reillys* and as a result the place attracted a good number of single people who could feel part of the crowd. We felt we should cater for them. We revamped the kitchen with a cold-room and freezer-room and installed new equipment that gave it a fresh, almost modern appearance. It was an expensive exercise, which we thought would last us for ages but it seems to be an ongoing process and we've had a couple of revamps since then. 1982-83 saw the arrival of a new office block and *O'Reillys* first bar: the original 'Rainforest Room'. The Guest House had been operating for about fifty years before it acquired a licence.

In 1985-86 we built ten more units, and added an audio-visual room with sophisticated equipment installed for showing documentaries and slide presentations. A new shop was built on the site of the old Green Mountains Store that was Mick and Annie's old home. Their house was moved up into the staff village and converted into staff quarters. The older accommodation buildings were all in prime positions and Possums Playground, the Mustard Club and the Intermediate Building were all moved at different times, generally to the staff village to make way for new buildings. All the original buildings that were constructed of rainforest timber could not be moved. After giving service for fifty years and more they had deteriorated to a great extent and were pulled down.

1990-91 saw thirteen new units as well as a new bar and an extension to the shop. The renovations and construction of new buildings continues today. The improvements since the start of the 1970s have been consistent rather than spectacular. We did not take risks in that we had one loan under control before we embarked on our next project. Vince and Lona, Karma and I put our lives into it. We continued the personal service that had become synonymous with *O'Reillys*. We lived there and were part of it every day and we showed the dedication that was needed and I believe we can be proud of what we achieved.

In the early part of our reign people did not have much money to spend and would notice it if the tariff rose, even by a modest amount. From the start the O'Reillys had run the Guest House in a very much hands-on way and Mick did the same so we just followed their example. It was necessary when money was scarce and buildings needed upgrading. We applied ourselves to anything that had to be done and kept staff numbers down. It allowed us to keep our tariff at an affordable rate and our occupancy consistent. We relied very much on the local market and the Tourist Bureau personnel would comment that we seemed to be immune from the lows that affected many others in the tourism industry. It allowed us to consistently upgrade our buildings and facilities over the years.

Bernard O'Reilly at Pats Bluff with the helicopter that bought the first line over the gorge

Mains Power Comes to *O'Reillys*

The year was 1967 and we still had a lot of work to do at the Guest House to improve the standard of our accommodation to meet the demands of a changing world. If we were going to make a real impact we realised that we needed to be connected to mains power. Our principal competition at the time, Binna Burra, had already been connected and that was a handy lever to get outside power ourselves. Connecting power to *O'Reillys* was a more difficult undertaking but the government of the day was right behind us and the electricity authority, SEQEB, tackled the project in a positive way.

Surveying the route the line would take was complex and took months to complete because the country was rugged and the Guest House was surrounded by National Park. Both these factors presented difficulties: the main one being there could be no clearing under the line through a national park. It meant the poles had to be located on high points and the lines would be strung from crag to crag to keep them above the trees. There was much discussion between SEQEB and the National Park Authority and many options were considered. The eventual route that was chosen took advantage of an easement along the cliff-edge at Pats Bluff and also the O'Reilly property near Balancing Rock where poles were positioned.

The electricity authority brought a cannon that could fire rockets with a rope attached for a distance of a kilometre or more. This would work if the area under the line is cleared otherwise the rope would get tangled in the trees so it was of no use in our situation. Rightly or wrongly the cannon was left at *O'Reillys* for a time and firing a couple of rockets became part of out New Year celebrations for the next few years. A decision was made to use a helicopter to assist in running the lines. It would carry a light nylon rope over the rough country and this method was used on three spans through the National Park. Using a helicopter was considered to be an enterprising move back in the 1960s.

Much of the work necessary to construct the line had been done: the postholes were dug by a private contractor and the experienced SEQEB workers skilfully erected the poles in some rather precarious places. The poles were stayed, cross-arms and insulators attached, and then they were ready for the next stage. A rather light helicopter had to come from Sydney to do the job and the mountain was abuzz with excitement.

On the day before the big event some of the experts from SEQEB made a detailed inspection of the route and decided some trees growing on the side of the cliff on the Pats Bluff end of the span to Balancing Rock were in danger of fouling the rope as the helicopter dragged it across the gorge. After discussion with National Parks I was commissioned to do some clearing on the steep side of the mountain. It was late in the day when we started and there was a wind blowing at the time. I had a rope around my waist with Frank Young on the other end holding the rope that had been wrapped around a tree for safety. He altered the length of the rope as I needed it.

The side was just about perpendicular and as I fell the trees they dropped down into space never to be seen again, not by me anyway. I was crawling around the steep side like a spider, relying on the rope as I went from tree to tree. It was a bit scary but I trusted Frank. He did a good job and we finished as darkness was setting in, without mishap.

A directive from the SEQEB authority advised us that dragging a rope over the gorge by helicopter was a delicate operation and that they didn't want any publicity on the day – only after the event. I think it is fair to say that the Guest House was lagging behind the accepted standards of the day and being connected to outside power was just the publicity we needed to let the world know that we were moving ahead. Well, as you could imagine, it was too good a chance for *O'Reillys* to miss and, as they say in political circles, a statement was leaked to the press and they just happened to be there on the day.

It all took place early the next morning before the wind could get up. The first run of the helicopter, trailing a light nylon rope like a giant spider, could be seen coming from the Balancing Rock side towards Pats Bluff. As the helicopter flew over the gorge the nylon rope had to be released from a reel while retaining a certain tension to stop it falling and getting tangled in the trees. We were watching from the Pats Bluff side and were alarmed to see the helicopter losing elevation. Too much tension was being applied to the rope as it left the reel and the helicopter pilot was about to jettison the rope when the ground crew realized what was happening and freed it up.

When the helicopter landed the SEQEB workers took the weight of the rope and tied it off around the pole. The first part of the operation was completed with some sighs of relief all around. A photograph of Bernard O'Reilly sitting on a rock with the helicopter still in the air coming in behind him appeared in the newspaper the next day. It was just the publicity we needed.

The pilot said the next span from Pats Bluff over the cliff to the valley was more difficult because of the thousand feet vertical drop between the two poles. He said that the helicopter had less pulling power while descending and there was more danger of the craft getting entangled by the rope. Anyhow, it all went to plan as did the next span back over Morans Creek but this time at a lower elevation. We watched from the grandstand that was Pats Bluff as it all happened below us. What a memorable day it was for *O'Reillys*.

Well it was a great day but that wasn't the end of the story: much work had to be done before we could be connected to the power. The sequence of events that had to take place before the power lines spanned the gorge was:

1. The nylon rope that the helicopter brought across the valley would pull a steel rope across the gorge
2. Next the steel rope would pull one electricity cable at a time across while also taking the nylon rope back with it.
3. The nylon rope would drag the steel line back again ready to pull the next cable across.

The nylon rope, the steel rope and the electricity cable were all fed from reels with brakes attached to keep the lines above the trees. It was a delicate operation.

I was over on the Pats Bluff side and watched the nylon rope drag the steel rope one and a half kilometres over the gorge for the first time without mishap. The electricity cable was attached to the steel rope and the nylon rope was also joined for its return journey back across the gorge. The reel feeding out the cable had a conventional brake drum attached with a metre long bar as a handle to apply pressure to the drum.

All went well and the cable was over half way across the gorge when a heavy shower of rain brought a stop to proceedings. When work got underway again it wasn't long before the reel feeding out the electricity cable started spinning too quickly because the brakes were wet and were not operating effectively. The man on the end of the bar that operated the brake applied extra pressure to try and slow the reel and stop the cable from falling. The extra pressure ruptured the connections and in a second the reel was spinning out of control as the cable fell to the bottom of the gorge.

After it left the reel the electricity cable was being fed through a pulley on top of the pole to give it clearance above the trees and there was someone there keeping an eye on it. I can still see him on top of the pole leaning back as the cable whistled past him. It was just as well for him that the cable didn't tangle or he would have been in real trouble. It didn't take long for the reel to stop spinning as the electricity cable settled into the trees fifteen hundred feet below.

No one said a word for a while as the enormity of the situation sank in. It was the first cable that was being taken over so it looked as if the link across the gorge had been lost. If that were the case it would mean getting the helicopter back from Sydney at considerable expense. It was soon realised that all might not be lost because the cool gent who was feeding out the nylon rope let it go when the brake drum failed on the electricity cable reel but applied the brake on the nylon reel again when it slowed as it reached the bottom of the gorge. This meant the nylon rope was still attached to the steel rope and possibly hung just above the trees but of course it had a kilometre of electricity cable attached to it.

We had a night to think it over and the only solution that seemed feasible was to cut the cable as close as possible to where it joined to the other ropes to avoid the loose end tangling in the trees and then winch it up carefully and start again. I volunteered to lead a small group of men down into the Morans Creek Gorge as I had often taken groups of hikers down there and knew the area well.

I decided to go over the edge near the power-pole on the Balancing Rock ridge so I could keep an eye on the steel rope that was hanging just above the tree line. This would take us to the spot where the cable was attached to the steel rope. From the top we could see the cable lying across and through the trees way down below. The country was pretty steep and we had to scale around a couple of cliffs on the way down. That didn't please everyone but we managed to reach Morans Creek in one piece guided by the wire rope overhead. We crossed the cascading stream and could soon see the cable tangled in the tall rainforest trees and we located where it joined the steel rope.

One thing I had always enjoyed doing when I was a kid was climbing trees. I could see one of the trees close to the join in the steel rope had enough vine on it that would allow me to scale up the trunk so that once I was into the branches it looked as if I would be able to climb higher, hopefully to the very top. I set off with a rope attached to my belt that would allow me to drag up a set of bolt cutters once I had reached the safety of the branches. I dragged the bolt cutters up and did not have a great deal of difficulty climbing up through the head of the tree and I selected a branch that would take me close to where the cable joined the steel rope. Considering everything, I was fortunate to be able to get there without putting myself in any real danger. In other words I had enough solid branch to support me as I reached for the cable with the bolt cutters. It was a relief when I succeeded in cutting the cable only about six metres from the join.

I called out to the men below that the job was done and they radioed the word to the crews above the cliff. Before we left the gorge we received the welcome news by radio that they had succeeded in winching the nylon rope in on the Pats Bluff side. This was done ever so gently over the trees with the steel rope still attached. They were ready to start the process all over again.

I suppose we arrived back like conquering heroes and the relief was evident at a quiet celebration at the Guest House that night. We felt that mains power was a step closer to *O'Reillys*. With the brake drum repaired and no more rain to interfere with the delicate operation the complex procedure of connecting *O'Reillys* Guest House to outside power was achieved without any other major hitch. There were five long spans of over a kilometre from the valley at Darlington to the mountain and when you look over the country I think the surveyors could not have done it any better. They chose the most practical route.

A major upgrade of the electrical system was carried out in preparation for 240-volt power. After what seemed a long wait the time came when mains power was switched on at the Guest House. It was a night to remember, we didn't have to start the engine, a routine that had been part of Guest House life for over thirty years. It is marvellous what you get used to and we found there was something comforting about the throb of a diesel motor and when it wasn't there it left an uneasy feeling. The silence was unreal.

It didn't take long to get used to it and we gathered for a celebration dinner in the Guest House dining room. The O'Reillys and the invited guests lined up for the meal with candles on the table and after some fanfare the candles were put out and the lights were switched on to the general applause of all present. These days candles have a romantic aura but we were at the end of an era when they were an inconvenient necessity.

Getting the power connected didn't break the bank as far as *O'Reillys* was concerned. We were not charged for the installation of nine poles on our own property, which would have been costly. All we had to do was guarantee a certain usage figure each year. SEQEB treated us well. We changed all our hot water heating over to electricity, which reduced the quantity of firewood used and made life much easier for us.

Looking back at the evolution of the Guest House since it opened in 1926 there are certain events that altered its course and gave the place a lift and I believe getting mains power was one of these. It inspired us with a more positive attitude and an ambition to raise the standard of the Guest House to a more acceptable level. The business was more viable now and the bank more inclined to lend us money. New buildings were added at regular intervals over the next twenty years and it allowed us to update facilities and provide some of the comforts people appreciated.

Natural Events

When you are sitting high on the crest of a mountain range the effects of the weather are more extreme and your appreciation of it is heightened. The weather was so much more part of our lives in earlier times. It was considered when advising people on where they should walk that day and was a crucial element when accessing the likelihood of the service car or bus arriving. We seemed to enjoy the rain when we were children; we never wore raincoats but made use of a corn bag each that was folded in half to make a pointed pixie-like hat over our heads and the rest of the bag hung down to cover our back and arms. It was our normal gear while rounding up the cows for milking when the weather was wet.

Hessian bags were popular wet weather gear in earlier times

Local weather forecasters were much in demand at a time when communication with the outside world was limited and people relied on them to a great extent. Guests who were due to leave would take a great interest in a report from Canungra to say that the service car had left but that was no guarantee that it would arrive. I remember my uncles particularly, who seemed to be custodians of the weather, looking over the ranges to the west and south for indications of some influence that would herald a change coming through. Local signs were looked for too like the currawongs singing with great enthusiasm to announce the impending arrival of a cold change or the scrub turkeys scratching up their mounds because they knew that rain was coming. Nature offers us many highlights that can enrich our lives if we just open our eyes to them.

Normally, we wouldn't send people out to the high country if the southeasters were blowing because it was often showery and low cloud made seeing the view from the lookouts a matter of chance. From the local forecasters' perspective they were often inconsistent and difficult to predict. Just when you had predicted a dull, showery day the cloud would lift and prove you wrong. I remember my uncle Pete's answer in response to a query about the weather at the border saying, "It might rain and it might not, and I should know – I've been here for years." My uncle Tom responded to the fact it seemed to rain every Friday to add some uncertainty as to whether the 9pm bus would arrive that night saying, "I would normally say it will be fine today but seeing it is Friday it will probably rain."

Life at the Guest House was never what you would call predictable but would breeze along comfortably enough and dealing with the odd minor crises was all in a day's work. Natural events like cyclones could completely disrupt this routine and guests and staff were forced to adapt to a new situation. Cyclones in 1947, 1954 and again in 1974 isolated the Guest House and consequently trapped holidaymakers. The situation forced the *O'Reillys* and staff to be somewhat creative when deciding on the menu during their time of isolation. Fortunately, we were still killing our own cattle for beef in those days. The 1954 cyclone passed close by and the resultant destruction closed many of our walking tracks.

An event that stands out in my mind is a severe cold snap that was the coldest time on the mountain that I can remember. I am not sure of the year but it was the early 1950s and at the time I wore shorts and no shoes, even in the winter! That made me appreciate just how cold it was. We had a forty-four gallon drum on the roof above the hot water boiler for the kitchen to ensure a continuous flow of water to the boiler if the supply was interrupted. This heavy gauge drum was sealed and by 9pm that night it froze and burst and feet long stalactites of ice hung down from the tank. Next morning Mick went around the water pipes at 9am with a blowtorch to melt the ice. The pipes were freezing up again even at that time of day and there was ice on the back steps of the kitchen for three days afterwards.

We experienced another traumatic event on Easter Monday night in 1970 that disrupted the Guest House routine for a time. Fortunately, the Easter campers had left during the day and that night a severe gale blew-up. I doubt if there would have been a tent left standing. I drove down and picked up the one lone camper. Mike Hopkins was sheltering in his car and I ferried him up to our lounge for the night. Vince and I were checking on how the Guest House was standing up to it when the lights blinked a few times and went out. The power lines on the one and half kilometres span over Morans Creek had blown into trees on the side of the mountain and one had burnt through and dropped into the gorge. We had only been connected to outside power for a couple of years so it was not a big effort to switch back to auxiliary power for two weeks and get back into the old routine again. It was quite a job replacing one line and checking the others for damage. The lines were tightened to the maximum tension allowed as a result and we've had no trouble since.

The wildest storm, or tornado perhaps, that hit the mountain since the O'Reillys arrived over seventy years earlier flattened strips of rainforest. The year was 1983 and luckily the Guest House was not in the direct path of the storm. The damage was restricted mainly to windows. It took four men three days to repair all the windows and Vince and Lona's house was the hardest hit. It was dinnertime when the storm hit the Guest House. The lights went out and the glass skylights in the kitchen smashed and cascaded down amongst the staff serving dinner to the accompaniment of some screaming that all added atmosphere to the occasion.

The wind funnelled down into the gorges and spiralled up the eastern side of the next mountain in a series of strips that broadened as they rose and then did the same in the next gorge. It was just as well the storm hit late in the day. If people had been out in it they may have been killed. It certainly would have been impossible for them to find their way home as some of the tracks disappeared under a sea of fallen trees. The National Park workers did a sterling job reopening the tracks.

Research was carried out into a portion of the devastated area by Dr Mike

Olsen and later by my son Peter, and it is interesting to see the plants that can take advantage of the situation and are part of the recovery process. Generally the vines survive the storm so they get a flying start and the situation suits the colonisers – the species of trees that germinate in a more open environment and do not live to a great age. They are replaced later by more permanent species that is all part of a process to restore the rainforest. There are more birds in the storm damaged areas than there are in the surrounding rainforest and as Mike said, "This event adds dynamics to the system and the rainforest will be going through a series of changes in floristic makeup for maybe two hundred years."

Snow on the ground at Mt Bithongabel

The following year was marked by another unusual event for our area, a fall of snow that was heavy enough to lie on the ground around the Guest House. Snow is not a big deal in cooler climates but my son Shane sent home a cutting from a newspaper in England with the heading 'Snow in Subtropical Queensland'. I had the opportunity of flying over the area in a helicopter soon afterwards and could see a wide brown strip along the top of the McPherson Range where snow had rested on the leaves of the trees. The Antarctic beech trees were unaffected.

There was big rain in 1989 that really drenched the National Park around *O'Reillys*. It was noticeable that large areas of the rainforest floor had been swept clean of leaf-litter and much of it could be seen later as it covered the Albert River flats at Kerry. Three bridges over the Albert River at Kerry were washed away. We did not know at the time but that was the last big rain before a prolonged dry spell during the 1990s and early 2000s. When it comes to the weather it is the extremes that we remember when Mother Nature overplays her hand and we all feel it.

Transport and Roads

The service cars did a great job

The road arrived at the Guest House in 1947 and bought with it the era of wheeled transport. The Blitz and the Jeep were bought and were the first vehicles that we drove on the mountain and they served us well for many years. The Blitz and the Jeep were eventually replaced by later model vehicles as the roads improved. There was always a need for a 4WD around the hills; a Land Rover replaced the Jeep and did its tour of duty.

We realized that a road to 17V would be of tremendous value to us as a source of good firewood because it was getting scarce closer to home. A road seemed like an impossible dream to us when Rose and Joe O'Reilly retired and expressed a desire to have a house built at 17V beside Duck Creek. We thought how much easier it would be if we had a road there. We were aware that it would be a difficult undertaking considering the roughness of the country and the rainforest that grew along the route it would take. Also there was little money available in the 1950s to fund such a project.

The Dunne family in the neighbouring property were taking timber out of their top paddock just below 17V at the time and I approached the bulldozer driver to see if he would haul a bullock wagon loaded with timber and building material up from the valley. He said he could do it and I even had a wagon lined up to do the job. It looked like a solution to the problem. We spoke to our local council member, Archie Stephens, about it and he said that we were entitled to a road to our property and should investigate if it was feasible. He promised some council funding if we decided to go ahead with it that would allow us to hire a bulldozer. There was already a road surveyed from the main road to our property that was a distance of 3.5 kilometres and the proposed route followed a ridge through mature subtropical rainforest. To avoid going over two sharp hills it was necessary to take the road around the steep side of these hills and that would be a job for the bulldozer. The road had to be extended past our boundary down to Duck Creek where Rose and Joe's house was to be built.

Mick was calling the shots at the time and in order to cut down on the expense and save the bulldozer for the steep country he decided to buy a tree winch, which meant that we could work on the first 1.7 kilometres at our leisure. It was doubtful also if the small bulldozer that was within our price range would make much impression on the mature rainforest trees. It also meant that we could do the job with a minimum of disturbance. The National Park authority was notified and gave us guidelines to work by.

Frank Young was my work mate on this section of road clearing and we used an extension ladder to attach a steel rope well up the trunk of the tree to be taken out. The winch itself was attached to the base of another tree. My arms were longer than Franks and I supplied the power for the long-handled winch. Mick was the surveyor and I was his assistant and we avoided large trees and generally took the line of least resistance. Setting up the winch, the wire ropes and pullies was heavy work that kept us in good shape. I would wield the winch handle and apply pressure to the tree. If the strain on the winch rope and on the sweating individual applying the pressure were too great I would have a spell while Frank cut a root or two of the tree to be removed to relieve the strain. We soon developed a routine to get the job done and it was satisfying to see our road creep slowly along the ridge.

It took us some time and a gallon or two of sweat to push our road through but it is marvellous what can be done with a tree winch and a couple of willing hands. When we arrived at the area where the land fell away to the left around the first hill we stopped because it was bulldozer country from now on. Mick and I ran a line around both hills with Mick's clinometer and although the country was steep in places the survey worked out well. A horse track that connected 17V to the Guest House climbed up over both these hills and Mick decided that it would be more convenient for us and the horses if we put a horse track in around the hills following the survey line. We constructed a kilometre of track similar to the graded walking tracks in the National Park and the horses loved it. This was done with a mattock and shovel as well as an axe for cutting the network of roots. The whole project was hard work but it was a rewarding job that we appreciated.

The road was a way off yet and we needed a hut at 17V where we could stay while we were fencing and yard building. Also the builders would have somewhere to stay when they were working on the house. I carted galvanised iron out to the end of our hand-winch-road in the Blitz and carried it around the hills to the edge of the rainforest. I made a slide there by splitting the runners from a bolly-gum log and trimming them up with the axe. A draft horse supplied the power for the slide as we took the iron down to Duck Creek where our hut was to be built. It was an interesting exercise as we had to lay poles along the side of the hill to stop the slide tobogganing sideways on the slippery kangaroo grass.

We built the hut with round timber wired together and nailed the iron on to it. Frank and I camped out there for a few weeks while we did some fencing. He put some corned-beef on to boil in the camp-oven one day and left it boiling while we went off to work. He returned to the hut midmorning to add water to it and stoke up the fire. What he found was that the fire had cooled off enough to allow a goanna to knock the top off the camp-oven and pinch our precious corned-beef. The goanna had crawled up a tree nearby to safety and it was just as well he did. He looked rather contented with a belly full of corned beef but Frank was really mad and if he'd had a gun the goanna would have had a short life expectancy.

Mick Lee and the bulldozer eventually arrived from Canungra and considering it was on the small side (only a D4) it did a great job. Mick O'Reilly was the powder monkey when we struck hard rock and explosives were required. Drilling the rock to insert the gelignite was done by hand. Mick heated the drills in his portable forge and sharpened them by hitting them with a heavy hammer. A large stump on the steep side, with massive roots covering the ground, presented a problem for the dozer. A difficulty with these shallow rooted trees is that the dozer is sitting on the roots holding them down as it applies pressure to the stump. Mick was called in and buried a big charge of gelignite under the stump, then inserted the detonator and fuse and sealed it off with soil that was compressed around it. We watched from a distance as the charge lifted the huge stump out of the ground and down the hill out of the way. Mick was treated like a hero for his effort. The road was completed and a track pushed down to Duck Creek. Now work could start on the house.

The road very soon turned into a quagmire in places and the Blitz became bogged in the deep mud while I was taking a load of timber out for the new house. We applied many loads of gravel to the bad spots and it seemed to be a constant job keeping the road trafficable. The road proved invaluable over time for it not only gave us access to a valuable source of good firewood but it also allowed us to truck cattle from 17V to the Guest House to avoid the difficult job of driving them through the rainforest. The spectacular lookouts from 17V also proved to be a popular destination for our 4WD buses years later. When the Duck Creek Road was constructed our road through the rainforest became part of it but no one would ever realise that a section of it was put through by two fellows with a tree winch.

Keeping the Guest House supplied with stores was a big job. When mains power arrived and brought us into the age of cold-rooms and freezers it increased the scope and variety of goods that were required. What didn't arrive in the bus Vince brought up from Brisbane. Originally we bought a VW Kombi van that Vince would drive to Brisbane and come back loaded to the hilt with grocery items and anything else that was needed. The Big Hill, about a mile from the Guest House, was rough and steep at that time and the VW could not always make the climb. The reverse gear was lower than first gear so Vince would attack the hill in reverse with the motor roaring, usually in the dark of night. It was no wonder it developed a few faults and was a tired old bus by the time we sold it.

Obviously a truck was needed and that was next on the shopping list. Vince would leave in the truck for Brisbane while it was still dark to get to the markets early for fruit and vegetables. Then he went to Tickles for the wholesale grocery items, and it was always a big order. Tickles was like a giant wholesale supermarket at the time and trolleys had to be loaded with bulk items. It was slow work and took ages for everything to be checked out and loaded on the truck. I hated the job when Vince was on holidays because I could never find what I wanted. Then the bottled gas for the stoves was next on the list followed by ice-cream packed in dry ice from South Brisbane and there were usually many other items on his list. As time went by the demand for goods increased and that made Vince's day in town a hectic one. The original truck was a second-hand International and it proved to be a versatile old truck. When it finished its life carrying stores I had a stock crate made for it and would truck cattle home that would eventually add to our meat supply.

There was a growing number of older people coming to the mountain and we realised they were important to us. Retired people are more flexible and could visit us during the quieter periods between the major holiday breaks when we were often low in numbers. We were well aware that they did not want to walk everywhere and would appreciate being taken to scenic spots in a vehicle. A move into wheeled transport did seem an obvious one to us for we had some scenic lookouts and interesting and attractive places on our own property that were accessible to 4WD vehicles.

We started off modestly with a Land Rover station wagon bought second-hand and it proved to be an immediate success. We bought a second one and even with the extra space there was still never enough room. People would sit on the bonnet at times for we never had a great distance to travel and would poke along quietly on the bush tracks. If we were really stuck the cattle truck was called into action, especially for the campfire nights at Lukes Bluff. It had high sides and kids especially loved to ride in it. As time passed we made use of a later model truck that Vince drove to Brisbane to collect stores.

We soon realized that a 4WD bus was needed but at that stage there was none available. When we inquired about buying a motor and chassis and building a body on it we were told there was none available because the government grabbed them all. The only thing to do was buy a 4WD truck that they were finished with and build a bus body on that. We approached two leading coach-building companies but they said it could not be done because the 4WD mechanism meant the centre of gravity of the bus was too high and the Transport Department would not approve them as roadworthy. They spoke with such authority that we believed them but later we heard that a truck repair crowd, Recar, was about to build a 4WD bus that would operate on the beach north of Noosa. We approached Recar and they agreed to build one for us as well. They also told us they would not have a problem with the Transport Department regulations.

The body was eventually built on an International truck chassis that in its previous life was a gravel truck. It was registered to carry twenty-three passengers and went into service in 1977. We christened her 'Bertha' and she was part of the O'Reilly family for almost twenty years and wasn't she a great old bus. We also bought a 2WD bus as a back-up for Bertha that was used on the more moderate going.

Bertha did such a good job that it was not until 1987 when we bought our next 4WD bus. The Guest House was more affluent by this time and we bought a new Mercedes engine and chassis and had a twenty-eight passenger body built on it. It had no bonnet and the front had a bulky square look and when we first went for a drive along our road it gave the impression that it wouldn't fit between the trees. It had the ability to frighten hell out of anyone you met on our rather narrow road. In the early 1990s Vince proved to be the big bus buyer when he went to an auction at an open-cut coal mine in WA that was closing down. He bought three Mercedes 4WD buses at a reasonable price and had them trucked back to Queensland where they were refitted. They were a good investment and were kept busy for many years.

We had some really good destinations for our 4WD buses on our property close to the Guest House as well as at Lukes farm. Certainly a road to 17V, that was put through years before, added some interesting destinations for them. There were some beautiful lookouts on the edge of the escarpment at 17V.

Carting our own goods to the mountain has well and truly come to an end now with delivery trucks and buses arriving each day at the Guest House. The road up the mountain to *O'Reillys* from Canungra is all sealed and follows the same alignment as it always has with many turns and hairpin bends. The drive along the top through some beautiful rainforest is a rewarding experience. The nicest part of the road is the last six kilometres that follows what was once *O'Reillys'* old horse track.

O'Reillys enter the four-wheel drive era

The Duck Creek Road

The Duck Creek Road had been talked about for almost as long as the O'Reillys have been on the mountain. The Government's original idea was that the high country along the Sarabah Range would be opened up to establish dairy farms just as the Beechmont Plateau to the east had been. Naturally a road would be put through to access them. There were a few possible routes further along the range suitable for a road but the most accessible was via Duck Creek. The plan to build a road was dropped when a national park was proposed and the rest of the land was withdrawn from selection.

Herb O'Reilly was at the forefront of a fight for a road to take the O'Reilly's cream out and generally make life easier for the settlers on the mountain. When his efforts proved fruitless a horse track was constructed down Stockyard Creek to the Kerry Valley and that track remained their access for twenty years. Herb had been relentless in his pressure on authorities to build the Duck Creek Road and at one stage the surveys were completed and the council was almost ready to commence construction and only some local opposition prevented it becoming a reality. When Laheys Ltd., saw-millers of Canungra, constructed a timber road up the Sarabah Range to terminate six kilometres from the Guest House it would have relieved pressure on Government to construct a road up Duck Creek.

Road or track building seemed to be in Herb's blood and earlier he constructed an elaborate horse track up a ridge above Duck Creek that was known as the Zig-Zag. He believed the Duck Creek route was the best way to access the Guest House. When Herb was getting on in years he said to me one day that he wanted to show me where he thought the Duck Creek Road should go. We meticulously followed his route down the Mt Alexander spur into the valley. I had Mick's clinometer and checked on the grades. When we arrived at his house he gave me photographs taken from the range opposite with the position of the road marked on it.

I stayed with Herb that night. His wife had died years earlier and Herb had slipped back into bachelor mode. The bread was not in a cupboard but was tied up in a sugar bag that hung from the ceiling. It reminded me of Bernard's yarn about Herb in the slab hut on Morans Creek in their early days on the mountain. To keep the rather aggressive native rodents at bay he would wrap the bread in a sugar-bag and tie it up firmly and then hang it from the ceiling. Herb was tall and had long arms and if Bernard, who was only a lad at the time, wanted some bread during the day he had to stand on his toes and his arms ached as he tried to untie Herb's knots while stretching at full length. It was good to see that Herb still had a bit of the old slab hut in him. At Kerry he always insisted on travelling the two and a half kilometres to mass on Sunday on his Ferguson tractor.

The Duck Creek Road became a reality but it was not until 1980, well after Herb's death, that the first vehicles travelled on it. The seed was sown during a conversation between Vince O'Reilly and Beaudesert Chamber of Commerce member, Wilf Moss. Vince pointed out the benefits to Beaudesert that the Duck Creek Road would have from a tourism perspective. Wilf was an enthusiast who liked what he heard and took the idea back to a meeting of the Chamber. Luckily, there were members present who had the vision to see the future benefits of a road and did not baulk at a challenge, because that's what it certainly was. It was a compliment to the members who backed the project that they received good support from local businesses and people generally. They were achievers in their own right and their standing in the community was high.

Much of the road would pass through Tom and Michael Dunne's country and the rest through O'Reilly property. It then entered the rainforest along the existing 4WD track that accessed our property 17V. There was already a road surveyed up the mountain but it was not a practical route to follow in the steep country. Without the co-operation of the Dunne Family the road would not be there today and we are indebted to them for their generosity. Tom was a good friend and we had often driven cattle up these ridges so I knew the country well. I offered to run a line where I thought the road would go and put Mick's clinometer to work again. Mick had died the year before so I guess I inherited the clinometer.

We armed ourselves with brush-hooks to do battle with the lantana and tackled the survey with enthusiasm. It was done with great precision. Keith Woolley, who was about my height, was my partner in the project. He put some red tape in his hatband and I would set the clinometer at a grade I estimated was needed to negotiate a section of the proposed road. I looked through the clinometer and then directed Keith to the right spot and he would mark the ground where he stood and that was where I had to stand for the next shot. We tried to avoid any really steep sections and kept the grade as moderate as the country would allow. I became skilled at selecting the correct grade and generally it worked really well. We would tie red tape around a bush or a sapling to indicate where the line went and Brian and Rob Fechner followed that line later with their bulldozers. We ran the line around the steep Heartbreaker spur that dives down into Cainbable Creek. It was the route the O'Reilly boys used when they first came to the mountain. We spared a thought for my father and uncles toiling up this ridge carrying their heavy loads seventy years before.

I found it difficult to pick out the red tape on Keith's hat on a dull day while looking through a sea of lantana and checking on the bubble in the clinometer. John Pforr, a friend from Brisbane, offered me a gadget – an optical reading clinometer by name that did the same job. Once I became used to looking along the side of it and not through it I found it easy to operate. I could pick out objects I was looking for much easier. I used it for the rest of the road and extensively over the years on various projects including the Tree Top Walk and surveying the Wishing Tree and Python Rock tracks. Ten years later John asked for it back to use in some project he was working on and I told him that after ten years I thought it was mine. He is a good fellow though and when he had finished with it he gave it back to me for good.

I knew the country well and my knowledge of its topography allowed me to follow ridges and make use of ledges wide enough for hairpin bends to change the direction of the road. It was hot work brushing a line through the lantana but our line eventually arrived at Dunne's house following an acceptable grade. I did not follow Herb O'Reilly's suggested survey because it went through a section of National Park. The route I chose passed by some spectacular lookouts that I believed were important for a future tourist road. The section of road to be constructed would descend five hundred and sixty metres into the valley and that meant wandering around a bit to get an acceptable grade. The mountain section was just over five kilometres and with a bit of luck constructing it would not present any great difficulties. Some time later with the Chamber of Commerce members, the Fechner brothers and Jack Hurley of Kyogle, who was involved in constructing the Lions Road, we walked down the line I had surveyed and agreed that it was the most practical route.

Fechner's pushed the road through without any real trouble, although explosives were needed in a big way to penetrate the hard rock on the first cutting on the way down. Terry Dunne drove his Land Rover up to be the first visitor to use the road and I bought 'Bertha' our 4WD bus up from Kerry a few days later with some adventurous guests who chose to be the first bus passengers to use the road. We were down at Kerry on an excursion and I gave them a choice of coming home the long way or the short way up the new road. The road was narrow, just wide enough for the bus, and we were clipping the end of roots protruding from the bank that often had small rocks sitting on them. These rocks cascaded off the side of the bus with great sound effects and all in all it was an exciting trip. It was also an exciting time for us all and we thought of Herb. His dream of a Duck Creek Road had finally come to fruition.

The Duck Creek road was a private road and it was the responsibility of the Duck Creek Road 'true believers' in the Chamber of Commerce and the O'Reilly family to raise the cash to maintain it. The Chamber members Don, Ric and Co displayed flair and imagination in their efforts to raise the money and it was a pleasure to be involved with such positive people. They had various money raising schemes that we were also involved in and some of them were legal.

Selling spots along the road at auction proved to be a financial windfall. People did not buy the real estate but the naming rights and it was up to them to select the name. Lookouts, inclines, corners, gullies, ledges, picnic spots, sticky dips in the road and even prominent trees and rocks were sold as well. After some serious consideration we decided not to sell the occasional wallaby or carpet snake beside the road but bidding was so brisk on the day I think we might have got away with it. The various spots along the road were marked with numbers and I drew a rough map of the road with the accompanying numbers as well as a brief description and the saleable features of each spot. These maps were distributed at the bottom so people could make their selection on the way up. The day attracted plenty of publicity and many locals turned up as well as 4WD club members and O'Reilly guests who all contributed to a crowd of over five hundred people.

The auction was held at a picnic spot on top of the mountain and started quietly under the guidance of a local auctioneer. Lots at the bottom of the mountain were sold for a moderate price but as proceedings moved up to the higher levels the bidding became really brisk. The road fund ended up $12,500 richer at the end of the day, far in excess of what we anticipated. Last lot to sell was a picnic area at the top of the mountain that I bought for the Guest House but the top price was paid for the beautiful lookout close by that was bought by John Shepherd for $2,250 and is now known as Shepherds Lookout. We've called the picnic spot 'Herb's Dream' and it is a regular destination for our 4WD buses to visit as well as a popular picnic spot for day visitors.

A Duck Creek Road picnic day was held there regularly with a bush band providing the entertainment. Money making events were organized as well, featuring two-up and shanghai competitions. Visitors were 'encouraged' to donate to the road fund one year by a couple of bushrangers riding horses and threatening them with guns. There was a 'body' hanging grotesquely from a tree close by to illustrate what would happen if they did not donate generously. The bushrangers turned out to be Terry Dunne and my son Pete. The local people supported these events very well and they were really good fun.

The Ducky-Doo Dinners, first held in Beaudesert in 1981, were also successful money raising events. With *duck 'a l'orange* to eat and Cold Duck to drink who could resist. After that you could try to win some money at the races with wooden horses that were operated by the customers and there were bookmakers and a tote present if you fancied a bet. The climax was viewing the Marx Brothers' film *Duck Soup* in the theatre next door.

A donation box that was placed near the gate at the bottom of the mountain was well patronised. Machinery was brought in on occasions to maintain the road but Chamber of Commerce members and the O'Reillys also played their part. *O'Reillys'* rather ancient bulldozer and grader were used with Reg Cullen at the helm. Both operator and machinery had the same antiquated look about them that perhaps they had seen better days. The grader disappeared over the side of the mountain one day and Reg did well to bail out in time. We had another grader that was used for spare parts so it was put to good use.

The Beaudesert Shire Council now has responsibility for the Duck Creek Road so the days of home-grown maintenance have ended. The road has not been improved to any extent but is still popular as a 4WD track.

Green Mountains Natural History Association

Natural history associations were new to Australia when John Luscombe, the manager of *Binna Burra* at the time, visited the USA and saw how they operated successfully over there. They were attached to various national parks and their members were volunteer naturalists who assisted by increasing community awareness of the national park. They generally served as a link between the national park and the people. John was a 'mover and shaker' and soon had Lamington Natural History Association up and running. *Binna Burra* CEO, Tony Groom, was also conversant with them in the States and took an active role in setting it up.

I was part of the organization representing the O'Reilly area on the committee, which met at *Binna Burra* and we certainly achieved some good things. John was a real zealot and it was due to his enthusiasm that the Lamington NHA moved along so well in the early stages. Interpretive programmes were formulated for day visitors and guests over holiday periods that we were all part of and there was an active junior ranger programme that was well supported. It was not always convenient for me to go to Binna Burra for the meetings and, I suppose, I did not fit all that comfortably under John's direction. Anyway, a decision was made to start our own natural history association on our side of the mountain and so the Green Mountains Natural History Association was born in 1977.

For better or for worse I was elected chairman, a position I held for twenty-three years. We were still involved with interpretive programs that John Luscombe had printed in conjunction with the *Binna Burra* programme. The local National Park staff as well as people from the Guest House, myself included, all contributed and we took out walks and gave talks that were open to guests, staff, campers and day visitors. Junior Ranger Certificates were awarded in the Guest House dining room after dinner of a night and children from the campground would visit to accept their awards. The National Park Service supported and encouraged natural history associations at that time and between us there was much enthusiasm and contact with the general public through enlightening interpretive programmes.

I did find it difficult to devote enough time to the Green Mountains NHA programme while being involved with a busy Guest House. We might have had a shaky start but over the years with the support of an enthusiastic committee and members we went from strength to strength. I organised our first Bird Week in 1978 and a Forest Week the following year, both through our Natural History Association. It gave our organization a sense of purpose and made some money for us as well.

I had developed an interest in birds and rainforest botany over the years and it has always been a great pleasure for me sharing that interest with visitors to the mountain. People who had an interest in either subject or both could come and learn more about them and gain a greater appreciation of the rainforest flora and birdlife. I did not realize at the time that it would be the start of a tradition that, even after thirty years, both events are still bowling along really well.

Bird Week particularly developed into something of almost religious significance where many people would return each year not so much to see new birds but to share the beauty of the rainforest and wildlife with their friends. There is no doubt in my mind that the pure beauty of the natural world has no equal in our man-made creations. The whole experience, the people and the birds became an important part of my life. The regulars returning each year added exuberance to the occasion and an atmosphere that was special. It is still unique to Bird Week.

I would hire top leaders for Bird Week from around Australia to show off our birds. One of these was Roy Wheeler from the Bird Observers Club in Victoria who was a great friend of the O'Reilly family. He gave me moral support and encouragement that first year and in the early Bird Weeks. I needed it all because I had never organized such a week before but the people present were tolerant and showed loads of enthusiasm that really encouraged me. I remember we did some birding standing on the back of *O'Reillys'* cattle truck with our esteemed group leader, Peter Slater pointing out the birds. Later, Graham Pizzey was also a leader for a long period and both Peter and Graham produced well-known bird guides. Glen Trelfo also made an outstanding contribution to Bird Week over the years.

Bird Week was amazingly successful and we would book the place out for the week each year. It was like a reunion when the regulars greeted each other and a light-hearted atmosphere prevailed over all. We enjoyed seeing the common birds but accepted the challenge of tracking down the rare or difficult species in more rugged terrain. It developed into a tradition and each year we walked out to the Antarctic Beech Forest to look for the shy rufous scrub-bird and down the historic Stockyard Creek Track to observe the birds in the valley.

It was my baby for twenty-five years. Every Bird Week we followed an easygoing programme that included the birds of the lagoons and seashores that totalled two hundred and sixty species overall. The week would end with a campfire night at Lukes Bluff where we had a barbecue followed by singing and concert items and poems about all the highlights and lowlights of the week. A prize was awarded for the best spotter of the week. People would enter into the spirit of it all and we had a great time.

After my twenty-fifth Bird Week I handed the reins over to my son, Tim who now runs it. I made many friends through Bird Week who are numbered amongst my closest friends. I produced a booklet for the twenty-fifth event and I will enclose my concluding lines because they summed up my feelings:

Memories can be such pleasant things when you look back on a part of your life that has given such fulfilment. As I gathered material for this booklet memories smiled at me from around every corner. People whose friendship I treasure put out their hand to greet me once again. They have lifted my spirits when I needed it most and showed me life's true values.

I thank them all.

Forest Week does not have the exuberance of Bird Week. To gain some knowledge of the complex rainforest flora you had to concentrate on the job at hand so it is by nature a more studious week. It is nevertheless an enjoyable experience getting to know the plants that make up the different rainforest communities and appreciating the hidden qualities and great complexity of these forests. I know I have been absorbed for many hours sorting out the different species of trees and vines, maybe finding an owner for some fruit lying on the forest floor and looking to see what birds may be eating that fruit. The rainforest has been part of my life for so long but I know that if I lived for three lifetimes I still would not know all its secrets.

Even though we put plenty of variety into the programme we soon realized that a week was too long and that after three days your brain was rather cluttered with the knowledge you had gained and that you needed some time to absorb it all. We shortened the week to a weekend and that has worked very well. One person who has been involved with Forest Week since it started and has been a guiding force behind it ever since is Dr Bill McDonald. Bill works at the Queensland Herbarium and has an unsurpassed knowledge of the rainforests of Southern Queensland. I have less involvement in Forest Weekend now as Bill and Tim O'Reilly organize and run the show. We have a loyal following that appreciate getting to know a little more about our beautiful rainforests.

I believe any place or programme that introduces people, especially children, to the natural world is doing the whole community a service. I don't think it is good for young people to grow up in a completely urbanised environment where their judgements are influenced by a materialistic world that could lead them in the wrong direction. Young children have a natural affinity with wildlife and every child should be given the opportunity to experience the thrill that contact with our native birds or mammals can give them. I have seen it many times, the look of wonder in a child's eyes when they see a beautiful bird for the first time. That experience will create a lasting impression that I believe will be an influence for good in their lives. It is crucial that we give our children that experience.

The rainforest was something of a mystery to me when I arrived on the mountain and it took a few years before a desire arose within me to get to know it better. W.D. Francis' *Australian Rainforest Trees,* first published in 1929, was my bible at that stage and it was a great book for its time. The problem was there were no publications to follow it for many years. The book identified the common large trees but it was not all that comprehensive.

It wasn't till Mike Hopkins arrived to research rainforest regeneration areas around *O'Reillys* that my knowledge of rainforest flora was increased. I developed a friendship with Mike. He would send specimens away to be identified and we enjoyed expanding our knowledge of the rainforest together.

Rainforest botany is highly complex and one has to work hard to gain a general knowledge of it. When you think about it I was lucky to have it all at my doorstep and then to have people like Bill McDonald who I could call on to identify any plants that had me stumped. The visitors who kept asking me questions and bringing in fruits to be identified kept me on the ball and finding answers to their questions naturally increased my knowledge. It was exciting for me finding and identifying a new tree or vine that I had never seen before.

There has been many research projects focused on the rainforest of the National Park around *O'Reillys* but one that stands out was the original under the direction of Professor Joe Connell. The year was 1965 and it seemed a long way for a Professor from the University of California to come to virtually initiate rainforest research in Australia. Joe, with the assistance of two Australian scientists, Len Webb and Geoff Tracy, selected about a hectare of rainforest just north of the Guest House and identified and tagged every tree above two inches in diameter on the plot. The composition of rainforest is constantly changing and Joe's ambition was to monitor these changes over the years. Joe was quite a personality and he would come out each year and round up a group of volunteers to check on and record what was happening on the plot. Deaths and tree-falls were recorded and seedlings were tagged and counted. Joe added another plot not far away as well as one on the Atherton Tableland. He also monitors a patch of coral at Heron Island.

One year there was a carpet of *Doryphora sassafras* seedlings on the rainforest floor and Joe knew that when he returned the following year there would be only a few remaining. He put gauze over one group of seedlings to prevent insect attack and over another group he placed wire netting. Both groups of sassafras seedlings survived en masse when Joe returned next year while the ground outside was almost bare. It seems that the principal culprits were not insects but birds like logrunners, lyrebirds and turkeys who scratch vigorously as they search for food in the leaf litter and the delicate rainforest seedlings are cast aside. The grazing mammals such as pademelons would also have an effect on the survival rate of the seedlings.

The responsibility for the research now rests with some Australian scientists but now that Joe has retired money for the research has dried up and it is very much in need of financial backing. Joe asked me to check on the flowering and fruiting of selected species on the plot, which I have been doing once a month for ten years. Bill McDonald assists with these observations. Considering that this research has been carried out for forty-three years there is valuable information to be gained from it especially now that we are concerned about the effect of climate change.

These two photographs are of the same booyong tree with an accompanying fig taken in 1916 and 2008. In rainforest strangler figs germinate high in the branches of host trees and send their roots to the ground. It is a slow process and the fig in the top image is over fifty years old. Ninety years later the fig has made good progress but the host tree is still alive. These photographs give us some idea of the time it takes before the fig stands there alone.

Tree Top Walk

The Green Mountains Natural History Association took on its first project in 1982, which was a track to the Wishing Tree down by Morans Creek. It all started when I took my daughter Woo camping down near the Wishing Tree one January when she was just a little girl. It was the time of year when it usually rained and I suggested we keep out of the damp rainforest and camp in the open eucalypt forest at 17V where there was plenty of firewood. That was not acceptable, Woo had been to the Wishing Tree earlier and that is where she wanted to camp. Little girls have a way of getting around their fathers so we pitched our tent beside the creek at the Wishing Tree and as darkness closed in the glow-worms lit up like stars on the bank of the creek. Next morning the calls of the rose-crowned and wompoo fruit doves greeted us as we awoke. At that time *O'Reillys'* guests and campers walked seven kilometres return trip to a spot near Picnic Rock to see glow-worms. I found it a real drag having to take guests there after dinner of a night and the two kilometre return walk to the Wishing Tree site really appealed to me.

We started taking guests down the old track to the Wishing Tree but it became wet and slippery with use. We rigged up a rope on a steep section so people could pull themselves up however it was dicey. The demise of an enormous brush box tree, which had fallen across the track, made the route impassable and the building of a new track a matter of urgency if the Wishing Tree glow-worms were to be a regular feature. We discussed the possibility of constructing a track with a more acceptable grade at a Natural History meeting. A few of our members who were blissfully ignorant of the amount of work involved were enthusiastic in their support. I put the clinometer to work and set about surveying a new route. I was disappointed that I would miss out on an attractive lower section of the old track that ran along a ridge between two gullies that were lined with tree ferns. Keith Woolley came up with the idea of building a suspension bridge across a steep gully to access the area. I thought it was a great idea so we started planning for it.

We had some 800 metres of track to construct before we arrived at the proposed bridge site. We had help from quite a few generous volunteers with much of the work being done by Chris Mead, Mike Kent, Keith and myself. Peter Main, an engineer friend, drew up plans for the suspension bridge. We cut a track to the bridge site along an old logging track for Keith's 4WD tractor and he bought in tallow-wood poles to support the wire ropes that took the weight of the bridge and the sand and gravel for the foundations. Bernie Moloney, the National Parks head ranger who was a good axeman, sapped our tallow-wood poles for us after his knockoff time and some of Chris's army mates dug the excavations for the concrete foundations, which was a big job. John Shaw supplied the wire ropes and his expertise, while students from Qld. University at Gatton supplied plenteous labour and enthusiasm for the project. The Wishing Tree track and suspension bridge was officially opened by Tony Elliot, the Government Minister at the time, and the bridge has been in use ever since.

The completion of our first suspension bridge seemed to lead naturally to think of bigger things. The idea of building some sort of suspended walkway where the general public could view the rainforest canopy had been with me for some time and we discussed it at our Natural History meetings. We could go on talking about it forever but if it was going to become a reality now was the time for action.

I have a keen interest in rainforest botany and would sometimes climb trees to see what was flowering and fruiting in the canopy. Most of the action in the rainforest takes place up in the sunlight where there is a continuing battle for dominance. The canopy is an area of great interest as trees and vines flower and fruit, attracting many species of birds and insects. I have always been fascinated by suspension bridges and the vision of having a series of them wandering through the rainforest canopy really sounded exciting.

I collected a small group of practical people who had a history of building things with the hope that we would come up with a plan to build a Tree Top Walk. Peter Main, our engineer, was one of the group and I chose an area of rainforest to look at which was accessible and hopefully suitable for a canopy walkway. I had the idea that perhaps we could use trees to support the structure, which could be linked by suspension bridges that would give people a very natural experience. The more we looked the more we realised that the idea was not practical. First of all the trees that were large enough to support a bridge were not positioned to allow a continuous walkway. I was also doubtful if our soft-wooded rainforest trees would cope with having a bridge tacked on to them. It was decided to scrap the tree idea and support the walkway on poles.

I chose a mararie, which is a common rainforest tree, as our destination. It was a large erect tree that stood firmly in the ground and did not have any obvious faults. It had survived the big blow of 1983 while many of its mates lay rotting on the forest floor. It was of interest too because it had ferns and orchids growing on its branches and a strangler fig wrapped around its trunk. Figs progress slowly and this one had perhaps a hundred years to go before it replaced its host so that would not be a worry. Peter Main took some levels and decided three suspension bridges would get us there with the fall of the land allowing us to attain the height that we wanted. Peter designed a platform at the end of the walkway that would sit on poles. He drew up plans and now we were ready to get down to the details of how it would all come together. I enquired of our guests, many of whom were well travelled, if they had come across a canopy walkway anywhere but no one had. It meant really that we were the first. We did not have another walkway to copy or anyone to advise us on the best way to go about it.

Finding a firm that sold poles over twenty metres in length took me some time and then I had the idea that a timber jinker would be needed to bring them up the mountain. I had trouble getting someone to commit to the job and was advised to contact the local carriers. Dale Farmers of Beaudesert brought the poles up on a semi with a minimum of fuss. He came up early in the morning to dodge the traffic and it was exciting to see them arrive. Barry Backhoe, as we called him, would drag the poles in for us with his backhoe but standing them up would be another challenge. I discussed with Bob Beeton, a lecturer from Qld. University at Gatton, the possibility of erecting them the way power poles were stood up when power arrived at the Guest House. We discussed the prospect of using large numbers of students to supply the power to lift the poles instead of using mechanical power.

I could see that it would be an extremely difficult operation considering the length of the poles and the overhanging rainforest. I received some more advice and that was to use Gerry who erected power poles locally and he could dig the holes and stand up the poles in one operation. We had to have Barry

Backhoe in there to position the poles and it would not take much more effort to get Gerry's equipment in there as well. The process of lifting the poles that would often contact overhead vines and branches provided difficulties that had to be overcome. Barry and Gerry worked well together and eventually the poles were erected and positioned, stayed and concreted in the ground.

The poles leaned in at a slight angle and positioning them apart so they would be the width of the proposed walkway while looking up many metres into the branches of trees required some guess work. It was not all that hard because the poles are quite flexible at that height and we had no trouble adjusting them to attach the heavy cross members that supported and governed the width of the walkway.

Now that the poles were erected they had to be drilled to secure the suspension and walkway ropes and that proved to be a difficult task. We eventually erected scaffolding so we had a platform to stand on and that proved the best way to go. I hired a power drill from Beaudesert and never realised until I used it that there was no reverse gear and once it started into the hardwood poles no matter how I tried I couldn't pull it out. It just went on till it jammed. Then I would detach the motor and wind the bit out with a heavy Stillson wrench while my arms ached. Dismantling and re-erecting the scaffolding was a tedious job in itself and I found this early part of the construction to be the most difficult and frustrating of the whole operation. We were on a steep learning curve and I certainly did many things the hard way. When we extended the walkway the following year we had learnt a lot and bought a chainsaw with a drilling attachment. It had more power and a reverse gear that made drilling holes in the posts so much easier.

Eventually, all the drilling was done and I had a list of fittings from Peter Main that were required so I went shopping. John Shaw bought us some wire rope and Peter Main was on hand the first weekend of construction to offer help and advice. All the fittings I bought had to be stamped with the correct strength rating and we became conversant with shackles and turnbuckles and other items that we handled every day. We were advised by Peter Main and John Shaw on the correct procedure when attaching the wire rope to fittings. We realised that people's safety was in our hands and that everything had to be done thoroughly. It was slow work but eventually the cables were attached and we wound up the turnbuckles to tighten the cables ready for the decking.

Each individual board had to be drilled and attached to two wire ropes with U bolts to form the deck. The deck then had to be supported by suspension cables above and attached to them with chains. The length of the chains was adjusted so they all took some of the load. It was slow and painstaking work but eventually it all came together and the job was done. Scaffolding was also used to erect the deck at the end of the walkway. That was a tricky job. Climbing up twenty metres of scaffolding was not to everyone's liking but eventually it was finished and looked pretty good to us. Barry Backhoe excavated the holes and carried in the concrete for the foundations that would anchor the walkway at each end and when it all dried and settled down we attached the anchor ropes and wound the turnbuckles up to tighten the whole system and it was ready for use.

The Tree Top Walk, being the first of its kind, received plenty of publicity and we were surprised at the number of people who came up to see it. As you could imagine it became congested with people walking in and out along the same three suspension bridges and it was difficult to limit the numbers on each span as we were advised to do. It was not long before I was looking at the possibility of extending the walkway to make it a one-way experience. I walked around with my clinometer and took levels and decided that it could be done. Six more spans could be added and the first four would traverse the ridge at a high elevation affording views of the rainforest down the slope towards Morans Creek. The final two spans would return up the slope to ground level. There would have to be four concrete foundations put into place to anchor the walkway as it changed direction and some were in difficult places.

Well, I did the best I could and sent my deliberations and levels to Peter Main who must be about the most patient man in the world. Peter drew up some more plans and we were ready to roll but with more confidence than we had the first time. I knew whom to approach to get things done and a bit more about the construction of a Tree Top Walk this time round. The project was made more difficult because the ground was wet from recent rain. Barry Backhoe worked well with Gerry to position his equipment for the crucial work. I have great respect for both men who took valuable equipment into impossible places and did a job that had to be done if this exciting project was to proceed.

There were many volunteers who helped and they included *O'Reillys* staff, University students from Gatton, and some retired electricity linesmen who really knew their stuff. We also were offered wire rope at a bargain price and really, considering what an asset we ended up with, it was not a big outlay for us. The dearest items were the poles and the decking for the walkway. We received a $2,000 Bicentenary grant, which did not go far, and we were strapped for cash when it was all over. The Guest House paid their share in cash, as well as physically supporting the project in many ways.

Six suspension bridges had to be constructed this time and the poles erected to support them. It was a much bigger project than the first stage but the job proceeded smoothly although the rainforest did its best to make life difficult for us. I had to crawl up to the top of a scentless rosewood to lop a few limbs that grew in the path of the walkway but the rosewood was covered by a climbing raspberry, a vigorous climber that was armed with thorns. By the time I had finished I looked as if I had been to the war. Barry dug the foundations and carried in the concrete to anchor the walkway and it was certainly a difficult operation in rough country. We set the steel anchors into the concrete and when it dried attached the ropes. There is a lot of fiddling around adjusting six extra suspension bridges ready for people to walk over in safety but it all came together by late 1987.

I told our guests in the morning that we should be finished the work by lunchtime and I would conduct the first walk around the nine suspension bridges after lunch. We worked on the ramp at the far end of the walkway in the pouring rain while sliding around in the mud. When we had finished the job I cleaned myself up and went into the dining room to tell the guests what time I would meet them for the walk. Many were surprised that the walk was still on but I told them if they wanted to be on the inaugural walk they had to brave the pouring rain. I was really proud of our effort and in spite of the rain enjoyed escorting the guests around the walkway pointing out the different trees. Morry, who was a regular guest and a good friend, said with a grin, 'stuff the trees', and kept walking back to the comfort of the Guest House.

I had been over to Western Australia earlier in the year and climbed the Gloucester Tree, which is very tall and I did feel rather exposed climbing up the

Above: O'Reillys famous
Tree Top Walk
Photo: Glen Trelfo

Left: Lorries deliver the
poles

Below: Securing the
rigging

spiralling ladder around the bare trunk. The idea came to me that it would add some excitement and a beautiful view over the rainforest if we erected a ladder so people could climb up the mararie from the deck of the walkway. I believed that we could make it feel safer than the Gloucester Tree. Tony Kelly, a National Parks employee, had climbing gear and together with another employee, Rob, he attached a rope to the tree. That allowed us to work out if it was practical to go ahead and just what were the possibilities. A ladder was lashed to the tree to make access easier. After a thorough inspection and due consideration I decided that we could construct two observation decks. The top deck would be about thirty metres above ground with a view overlooking the rainforest to the south. It really looked good to me. The decks would be accessed by climbing permanent ladders that would have a safety cage attached to protect the climbers.

We were keen for the project to proceed as soon as possible and started work on the lower deck. At that level the trunk of the tree was large and 'bumpy' because of the fig roots growing on it. I had some No. 8 wire that I worked into the shape of the tree trunk with the intention that the wire would be a pattern for a heavy steel band that had to be made to fit snugly around the tree. It would be attached to the fig rather than the host tree. Figs are really tough and durable trees and this one would be considerably younger than the host tree and would presumably have a longer life.

I attached sticky tape tags marked with a 'H' on them where I wanted holes drilled for the stainless steel coach-screws that would attach the band to the tree. I had other sticky tape tags attached and marked with an 'S' to indicate where I wanted steel members attached that would support the deck for people to stand on. Stays had to be positioned to support these steel cross members and angled down and attached to the tree with coach-screws to stabilise the deck. Provisions had also to be made for vertical struts to support a fence to enclose the deck. The size of the deck was calculated and measurements taken. This work had to be done while scrambling around the tree about twenty-six metres above ground. Brad McNamara, a local from Kerry who can make anything or mend anything, was part of the planning process. He took on the job of making up the steel fittings for me. When this was done they were all galvanised.

I think we were all anxious as we lugged the steel band up the tree. It was made in two sections that were bolted together and could be adjusted. I was really relieved when it fitted so well; every bolt-hole was in the right place. Brad had done a great job. We drilled holes in the tree and attached the steel band with stainless steel coach-screws. Stainless steel was used because the sap of trees generally has a corrosive effect on metal. The assembling of the deck was naturally a slow and painstaking job considering the precarious position we worked under. Supports for the deck were also attached and stays screwed to the tree as well as vertical struts that supported a chain wire fence surrounding the deck. It ended up a solid job in which we had confidence.

When that job was done we were free to concentrate on the top deck. I attached the deck to the fig tree, which was more vigorous than the mararie at this elevation. It was much smaller here too with a smooth trunk that made the top deck easier to design. Brad worked his magic with my piece of wire and some sticky tape tags to guide him. The fittings arrived and were assembled with no real problems. There was only room for one person at the top deck level so I drilled the holes and assembled the deck myself without assistance. Working on either deck was a precarious job at times but we approached the task with care and the only accident we had during the whole Tree Top Walk project was when a clamp I was using on the top deck came adrift as a strong gust of wind hit the tree and the clamp hit Rob on the lower deck. Brad made up the ladders to access the decks out of galvanised piping and we covered them with mesh and the job was done. The walkway was officially opened by the Premier of Queensland, Mike Ahern. Twenty years later the fig and the mararie are still living happily together with no ill effects from the decks.

Elevated walkways are now becoming popular, even trendy I suppose and considering the experience they offer it is not surprising. I have toured the US and looked at elevated walkways there and one magnificent example in Peru that looped from tree to tree. Some of the spans were very long but an advantage they have in the Amazon rainforests is that the trees are generally hardwoods while in Australia our rainforest trees are mostly softwoods.

I have also seen three impressive elevated walkways in Australia that were constructed of metal and I have heard of one in South East Asia as well. None of these were built before our first effort in 1986 so I believe that ours was the first in the world. Our walkway would have cost a small fraction of the other

Australian structures. The Green Mountains NHA was supported by *O'Reillys* Guest House in their endeavours and can feel justly proud of their effort. I am so appreciative of all the volunteers who contributed their time and effort to achieve something that was new to the world. It has given many people an opportunity to appreciate our rainforests from the treetops.

The Tree Top Walk has stood the test of time for twenty-one years and is still as popular as ever. The deck of the walkway has been rebuilt and is not as springy as it used to be; wires have been replaced and the structure is now subject to regular inspections by an engineer. A donation box has been installed and the contributions enabled the Green Mountains Natural Association to construct a boardwalk to access the Tree Top Walk. I have been involved in formulating interpretive signs that have been erected along the way so people can better appreciate the rainforest and wildlife.

Peter O'Reilly on the new Tree Top Walk

Remembrances and Celebrations

When I look back at the milestones that have marked our journey on the mountain I see occasions when we celebrated O'Reilly family anniversaries and other occasions when we remembered important events in the history of the National Park. We celebrated these milestones together – the Forestry Dept personnel and ourselves. It makes me realize just how closely our lives were intertwined. Protecting the National Park was a cause we had in common and I look back on those times with a feeling of nostalgia.

It was 1919 when an executive minute issued in Brisbane announced the appointment of Herb, Luke, Mick and Bernard O'Reilly as Honorary Rangers of the National Park. Later that year Mick was appointed a working overseer of Lamington National Park, and in reality he became the first Ranger of any national park in Queensland. The significance of this appointment has virtually gone unnoticed. I was appointed an Honorary Ranger by the Department of Forestry in 1975. The title was changed later by the National Parks and Wildlife Service to Honorary Protector.

The National Park was named in honour of Lord Lamington who was Governor of Queensland at the time. He visited what is now Lamington Plateau and was escorted to Point Lookout on the crest of the McPherson Range by Robert Collins in 1906 when Collins was agitating for the area to be reserved as a National Park. All the older publications refer to the reserve as the 'National Park' and I am not sure when the name 'Lamington' came into general use. As a matter of interest the National Park maps from the outset affixed the name 'Lamington Plateau' to a ridge further west that ends up in Running Creek and not the one Lord Lamington rode along. The locals and the bushwalkers know where the real one is.

The O'Reillys had already put tracks through to various lookouts and waterfalls before the National Park was proclaimed. I remember riding out to Mt Bithongabel on one of these tracks when I was still a lad and really enjoyed the experience. Everyone used these tracks before the excellent track system we see today was constructed in the 1930s. They are certainly a tribute to the men who worked on them and to Romeo Lahey who surveyed and generally indicated where the tracks should go. The accurate positioning of the tracks was left to Gus Kouskos, who was the ranger in charge of Lamington National Park.

The official opening at *O'Reillys* in 1938 of the Main Border Track that linked *Binna Burra* and *O'Reillys* would have been an important occasion for the national park movement and of course for both resorts. Representatives from the Forestry Department, as well as from *Binna Burra* and *O'Reillys*, were present in numbers to celebrate this significant occasion. The twenty-three kilometres of track follows the interstate border along the crest of the McPherson Range for much of its length.

Opening of the walking track between Binna Burra and O'Reillys, 1938

Two monuments recognising the two men who fought for the National Park ideal have been erected on the mountain. The first was a cairn of stones situated beside the main road six kilometres north of *O'Reillys*. It acknowledges Romeo Lahey's contribution to the proclamation of the National Park and the appreciation of the Forestry Department for land he'd donated that was included in the reserve. It was unveiled by the Premier, Frank Nicklin, in 1967 who also had responsibility for National Parks. He must have known the history of Lamington National Park because he asked if Robert Collins had been recognised as well.

That happened in 1972 when the relatives of Robert Collins donated a birdbath in the form of a massive concaved rock. It was erected in front of the Guest House and continues to be appreciated by the birds as well as by the O'Reilly family and their guests. When Bernard O'Reilly unveiled the birdbath he spoke warmly of Robert Collins whose foresight and positive attitude initiated the national park movement in Queensland. Unfortunately, he died in 1914 before his dream for a National Park came to fruition and Romeo Lahey successfully took up the fight.

The third ministerial conference on National Parks was held at *O'Reillys* in June 1969 and was attended by ministers responsible for national parks from the various states of Australia. The Queensland National Parks Service was well represented and I remember them proudly showing off their track system that was considered to be the best in Australia.

The third ministerial conference on national parks at O'Reillys 1969

In the 1970s the O'Reilly family celebrated two important anniversaries that took us back to the pioneering efforts of the first generation of O'Reillys on the mountain. Vince organised the first one that remembered the O'Reilly boys as they walked up the Heartbreaker seventy years earlier to claim their selections. As a reminder of earlier times a bark hut was erected on the lawn in front of the Guest House that I imagine was not up to the standard of the original built at Morans Falls. Mick, the only one left of the original five brothers, walked up to the hut with an axe on his shoulder. A group including Vince walked with Mick representing his brothers. Tom Dunne, our neighbour from the valley, always supported us on these occasions and rode up with a packhorse in tow. I also rode in on a horse that day. Items of memorabilia were placed in the hut and around it and people dressed in clothes of the era to add to the occasion.

**Keith Woolley, Mick and Vince O'Reilly -
60th anniversary of *O'Reillys* on the mountain**

Stockyard Creek Track re-enactment – 50 years of Guest House operation

The second anniversary that we celebrated was in 1976. It was the fiftieth anniversary of the time the O'Reilly family opened the doors of the Guest House and welcomed their first guests. I organised this event and we decided that the Stockyard Creek Track would be the focal point of the celebration. Weeks of work went into the upgrade of this historic old track and we concentrated on the top section around the steep side of Lukes Bluff to make it safer for a group of horses with riders of all ages. We cleared an area at the top of the cliff where an uninterrupted view could be obtained of the top section of the track.

The plan was that we would have people riding up the track to the Guest House as they did originally with packhorses trailing along behind. It would be a great sight and we were excited at the prospect. I spread the word in the valley, we needed the support of the Kerry people if our day was to be a success. I envisaged having three packhorses: one carrying cream cans representing the dairying days; one with stretcher beds that were carried up to furnish the Guest House when it opened; and one with luggage for the guests when they came.

The Kerry people responded with enthusiasm and we soon had our three packhorses and enough people to ride up the track to create a great spectacle. In fact the overall numbers increased each day when word reached other districts of our plans and I thought it wise to curb the numbers. We preferred the local people who had some idea of the conditions and what the track was like. Tom Dunne, John Markwell and Lou Stacey supplied and equipped the packhorses and Sailor, Tom's horse, was selected to carry the beds. We had a trial run down in Tom's yard at Duck Creek and loaded the beds on Sailor but he did not appreciate the beds swaying around on his back and jumped around doing his best to get rid of them. We were trying to hold him and settle him down when one of the beds came off and whacked me on the shin and boy did it hurt. With some persistence Sailor did settle down and resigned himself to carrying the beds. John's horse carried the cream cans and Lou's the luggage.

The day dawned and preparations were being made to feed the multitudes with a barbecue lunch at the top of the cliff. Among the visitors was the Minister for Tourism, John Herbert who brought a photograph of himself as a young child coming up the Stockyard Creek Track on the front of his father's horse. Professor Herbert, John's father, was a regular visitor in earlier times. The Minister for Transport, Keith Hooper, was also a visitor and had some photos of an earlier time when he worked for Luke O'Reilly and carried cans of cream down the old track. I could imagine Luke, who had a colourful turn of phrase, giving Mr Hooper some lessons on how to transport cream that may have helped him later in his transport portfolio.

We invited anyone that we could dig up, figuratively speaking, that had ridden up the Stockyard Creek Track to the Guest House from when the track was constructed in 1914 till the mid 1930s when the Canungra road was completed. Newspaper reporters were there as well as ABC television and we received some good publicity. My good friend John Persse was also there taking his excellent black and white photos that have proved to be invaluable.

I rode down to meet the riders below the cliff so we could wait for everyone to arrive and ride up together. It was a great feeling as we rode around the cliff with crowds of people watching. Sailor, loaded with the beds, was a real star and behaved himself under Tom's firm hand. I was very happy with the day. We had a great lunch with plenty of speakers who told yarns and reminisced about earlier times when the Stockyard Creek Track was the highway, the route everyone used when travelling to the Guest House. My father Mick was never one to talk much about the old days but we enjoyed listening to him tell us a few things about life as it was then.

We remembered various anniversaries of the Stinson drama and this was usually done with a visit to the site. Often, we were joined by a group that walked from Kyogle on the NSW side to meet us there. Relatives of people who died in the crash – the pilot Rex Boyden and passengers Roland Graham and James Westray – would sometimes walk with us. A younger Rex Boyden, a nephew of the pilot, commented as he looked at an unmarked hillside where a common grave contained the bodies of four men, that it would be a fitting gesture if the graves were marked in some way. I had to agree with him. I approached the Queensland National Parks and Wildlife Service and I was given permission to carry out work that would permanently mark the graves with the names of the people who had died at the site. The rocks that surrounded the grave originally had rolled down the steep side of the mountain.

I approached some Beaudesert people for assistance and the Rotary club took up the cause and was later supported by members of other service clubs. To do anything of a permanent nature we would need concrete and water and it was impossible to carry heavy material up the steep ridge above Christmas Creek. I approached the Air Force and they agreed to carry the material in for us so I assembled concrete mix in bags and a container of water at the Guest House. Keith and I left early next morning to walk to the Stinson. The gravesite was in an enclosed rainforest area that would be hard to identify from the air so we spread brightly coloured sheets of plastic on the forest floor as a beacon for the crew of the helicopter. We also lit a fire, however the smoke did not rise but drifted through the forest.

When the helicopter arrived it circled overhead and around the ridges and took ages to find us. We were getting desperate, madly waving sheets of plastic and stoking up our rather pathetic fire. Eventually, they did find us and then someone came spinning out of the helicopter on a rope down towards us. He was a young fellow of Scottish ancestry judging by his accent. When he landed on the steep side he lost his balance and went sliding down the hill on his back, head first into some prickly raspberry while still hanging onto the rope. I could not follow his accent all that well but I got the idea that he didn't like the place very much. Things were soon under control; the helicopter returned and the material was lowered down. Thanks to the Air Force the project could now go ahead.

The work was carried out by a great gang of fellows whom we would meet at 5am in a car park in Beaudesert and then head up the Christmas Creek Valley. We took on the steep climb from the valley carrying all manner of tools for the job. The evening before our last trip up it was pouring rain, which meant there could be a real fresh in the creek making it difficult or impossible to cross. A decision had to be made on whether to attempt it and Mick Moss was keen to go so we all lined up next morning and away we went.

As predicted, there was a good fresh in the creek and the last crossing proved difficult with the fast flowing stream up around my backside and flowing over slippery rocks. I took the end of a rope and waded over and tied the rope around a tree. The other end was anchored by Ian Farmers, the heaviest bloke there, and the boys waded over hanging on to the rope while carrying their gear. We were still getting some showers and it was slippery climbing up the steep side with our equipment. The gang worked in rather messy conditions and when they finished it looked good and was a credit to them all. Plaques containing the names of people buried at the site were set in place – Rex Boyden, Bev Shephard, William Fountain and Roland Graham.

We invited members of the Boyden and Graham families as well as relatives of James Westray to the dedication ceremony at the graves. Members of these families all braved the arduous twenty-five kilometres walk from the Guest House to the crash site and camped there in rather wet conditions. We passed Ricky Draper's gang of Beaudesert high school students camped on Mt Throakban with their radio equipment, on our way out. The job they volunteered to do was to relay the dedication ceremony back to the Guest House for the benefit of John Proud who survived the crash and older relatives who couldn't make the walk. There was also a lot of interest in the ceremony from the general public. The high range that runs from Mt Throakban to Mt Widgee otherwise blocked communication.

We realized it was a significant occasion and made an effort to promote the event. As a result our party included two representatives from *The Courier-Mail*, two from the *Womans Weekly* and a journalist from the *Northern Star* based in Lismore. When I look back on that trip with the generally 'out of condition' press people toiling up and down those mountains in the wet slippery conditions I am almost guilt stricken. John Pforr was another who entered the fray with his eyes closed. He was a last minute entry and came to take some movie footage of the proceedings. I did appreciate his effort and everyone else who walked out that day. A group of tired and wet people camped the night at the Stinson campsite and fortunately Jack Hurley's Kyogle mob had arrived before us and had a fire going.

When we woke next morning it was still showering but we were all in good spirits. My cousin Leo Coote, a priest, had agreed to conduct the ceremony at the gravesite.

Leo conducted a moving ceremony in the rain and involved relatives of those who lost their lives in the readings. The high school students on Mt Throakban did a good job and successfully relayed the proceedings back to the Guest House. The ceremony was witnessed by the biggest crowd that I have ever seen at the Stinson. They came from *O'Reillys* as well as the Kyogle and Beaudesert districts and further afield. Material for a documentary was also shot over the weekend that is still being shown at the Guest House.

1987 was the fiftieth anniversary of the crash and it was a significant occasion. Sir John Proud, in accepting an invitation to be present said, "I can't live forever, this will be the last one for me." We realised it would be the same for quite a number of those present.

We were pleased to welcome Sir John's wife and Sister Margaret, an Anglican nun who nursed him in Saint Martin's hospital fifty years earlier. Sir John attracted hero status and did all that was expected of him. He was interviewed when he stepped off the plane in Brisbane and during our remembrance day at Lamington on Sunday he spoke of his traumatic experience, chatted to the people and signed autographs all day.

We selected Lamington on Christmas Creek for the Sunday remembrance because that was where the survivors arrived on stretchers and were transferred into the ambulance. We had plenty of things happening that day. The army base at Canungra supplied and erected marquees with tables and chairs where people could shelter out of the sun. Rhelma, Bernard's daughter, showed slides in a marquee and related the story of the Stinson drama. Her marquee had sides to keep the light out and she must have nearly suffocated from the heat. A group of young fellows carried 'two survivors' in stretchers down from the hills to a waiting early model ambulance as we watched and were reminded of a sensational event that stunned Australia fifty years earlier.

The Python Rock Track

The year 1986 was a busy one for me and for Green Mountains Natural History Assoc. as we tackled two major projects. As well as building the first stage of the Tree Top Walk I took responsibility for the construction of a graded walking track to Python Rock lookout that would make it accessible for wheelchairs. Time to deal with these challenging projects had to be squeezed into a busy Guest House routine. Looking back now I wonder how it all happened. I am sure Vince would have had some extra duties thrust on him. The idea of doing something for disabled people came from the Catholic Parish in Beaudesert. They agreed with the idea of a track that would give people confined to wheelchairs an experience normally reserved for able-bodied hikers. The parish together with the Natural History Assoc., contributed money towards the project.

The proposal was that we would apply for a CEP grant and hire young unemployed people to do the job. The National Parks and Wildlife Service was involved in the early discussion and gave their support to the project. The Natural History Assoc. applied for a grant. *O'Reillys* Guest House, being a commercial concern, was not eligible to apply but they supported the project in many ways. Once again I had my trusty clinometer close at hand. My first job was to carry out a rough survey to find out if constructing a wheelchair friendly track to Python Rock was feasible and if so what would be the most practical route.

At that time we walked to Python Rock down an old logging track that left the road at the top of the big hill but it was too steep to be upgraded for wheelchair use. The only way we could use that route was by putting in zigzags and that is not a good way to go. Able-bodied people find it hard to resist taking shortcuts that impact on the surrounding area. Neil, the National Parks Ranger, suggested starting the track at a lower elevation near the Morans Falls turnoff, which made sense to me. It meant that the new track would not follow the alignment of the old track at all; it would be an entirely new track that would wend its way through subtropical rainforest.

I received a publication from the National Parks Service that listed the guidelines for a wheelchair track through a national park. A limit on the steepness of the grade was an obvious requirement and the addition of parking bays at regular intervals was another. The National Parks' publication was our guide when surveying and building the track and we kept within its guidelines. I had to know the length of the proposed track and get some idea of the difficulty of the country before I could attempt to estimate a costing for the project so I started surveying the track in earnest. I tried to make the proposed track as attractive as possible by passing through impressive stands of rainforest and highlighting interesting trees and vines. It took some time but the survey worked out quite well and I was pleased with the result. When it was built the track would be 1.7 kilometres in length and, except for the last small section, would pass through subtropical rainforest.

I loved surveying the track, identifying the trees and vines as I went along and evaluating one option against another when choosing the final route. When the survey was complete the route was inspected by the relevant authorities and received their approval. That was the good part, but to come up with a costing for the whole project was another matter. Constructing a track through rainforest is a difficult undertaking even for experienced workers but for a group of young people who probably were not even used to handling tools let alone building a track it could take forever. Geoff Thompson, the Beaudesert Shire engineer at the time, was experienced with CEP projects and gave me valuable assistance. I also received advice from representatives of the government department responsible for the work. It all added up to create an illusion in my mind that I really knew what I was doing and I pressed on regardless.

The size of the gang would have a major bearing on the overall cost of the project and initially I opted for a gang of five: two males, two females and someone in charge who hopefully had some experience. I was told the fifth person had to be female because I could have more females than males in the gang but not more males than females. I then opted for a gang of six and would pick a boss from that group. A costing of all the equipment needed was added to the overall figure for the completion of the project and the final figure was stacked to cover the contingencies I knew would be there. The overall cost of the project seemed alarming to me and I thought the high figure may 'knock it on the head' so to speak, but no, it was all approved, and I was given the green light to go ahead.

I interviewed potential workers in Beaudesert who came from an area that extended from the south side of Brisbane to the NSW border. For better or for worse a gang of six was selected and assembled at the Guest House ready to start work. The National Parks Service supplied two large caravans that were used as accommodation and a place for the gang to cook their meals. The caravans were parked in the vicinity of the Guest House where they could be connected to power and the workers were close to toilets and showers. They spent a couple of days adjusting the caravans to their needs while I went to Beaudesert with a shopping list. I bought axes, brush-hooks, picks, mattocks, crowbars, shovels, a chainsaw and two rider-mowers with trailers. Later, I bought a second-hand ute to carry rocks from the Guest House property 17V to reinforce the edge of the track. Although I was somewhat apprehensive about the task ahead I believed it to be a worthwhile and exciting project and was keen to get the job rolling along.

Rob, a National Parks ranger from Tamborine Mountain, came over and worked with the gang for the first two weeks. He kick-started the project by demonstrating how to go about building a track and the work ethic required to keep the project moving. The plan of action involved brushing a track close to the survey line avoiding as much as possible trees of any size. Mattocks were used to level the strip into something resembling a track. The ground was a mass of roots that had to be cut with an axe or in the case of large roots with the chainsaw. Large rocks had to be removed as well so it was a slow process. When the track was wide enough and the surface reasonably level the downhill edge of the track was secured with football-sized rocks to stop it eroding. When this groundwork was completed the track was covered progressively with good quality crushed gravel brought in trucks from near Beenleigh and dumped at the track entrance. The gravel was shovelled into the rider-mower trailers and distributed along the track.

In the early stages I traded in a few members of the gang who did not make an effort to get on with others in the group or apply themselves to the work. Fortunately, we had stable members who were generally locals from the Beaudesert district and the gang soon settled down into a compatible group that worked well together. We soon developed a daily routine that we all seemed to fit into rather comfortably. For every thing to run smoothly there was quite a bit of work needed behind the scenes. Kathy Church was the Natural History treasurer at the time. It was the busiest period in the thirty-year history of the organization. She paid the bills for materials as well as the workers' wages each week. Kathy also had expenses coming in from the Tree Top Walk construction so she was kept busy.

When the National Parks ranger, Rob left, I had more involvement with the gang and every day problems arose and solutions were found. We guided the track through the trees and it seemed to creep along like a giant python avoiding trouble spots as it went. We guided it away from gnarled mararies with their network of tough roots that would have meant hours of extra work. It brushed the impressive buttresses of booyongs and the tangled roots of strangler figs as it passed and we guided it under gardens of tree ferns and orchids. The haunting calls of the fruit pigeons from high in the fruiting trees were with us as we led that giant python out into the country that belongs to George, the famous Albert lyrebird, whose golden voice is part of the Python Rock experience. We enjoyed these highlights as we came to them and we knew the hikers and wheelies would appreciate them in the future as well.

Constructing the last one hundred metres of track around the steep rocky side of the mountain was the most difficult of the whole job and entailed moving large rocks to make a foundation for the track. The track was completed well within the time allotted so I decided to build a lookout so visitors could really relax and appreciate the view that overlooks Morans Creek Gorge to the mountains beyond. Enright's, the saw-millers of Beaudesert, generously donated timber for the structure, which was transported in to the job by the CEP workers. We decided to use concrete pylons to support the lookout that would help protect it against bush fires. Putting down holes for the pylons was a difficult job on the rocky mountainside but eventually it was all done. The gang carted in sand, gravel, water, reinforcing and cement as well as a concrete mixer and we enjoyed the view as we poured the concrete. We became carpenters then and constructed a sturdy lookout where visitors can relax and take in the wonderful scenery. I was very pleased with the finished product and it still looks good twenty years later.

Now, all that needed doing was for a layer of fine gravel to be applied to the track and then it had to be sealed. Beaudesert Shire Council supplied a machine that could be wheeled along the track. It spread two coats of bitumen to the track in a day under the guidance of two council employees and our gang of helpers. It all came together and after seven months of toil the job was completed. It was a compliment to the gang of young people who stuck to the task for seven months and could be relied on to keep the project moving.

The sentiment behind the decision to build a track to Python Rock was to make it possible for people confined to wheelchairs to enjoy an excursion through rainforest to a beautiful lookout. It was an experience that was normally reserved for able bodied hikers. Quite a number of wheelies were present when the track was officially opened and it was used extensively in its early years.

Unfortunately, the track has been allowed to deteriorate and the only thing the National Parks Service has done in recent times is put up a sign saying that the track is unsuitable for wheelchairs. On inquiring we were told that safety standards are stricter now and the track does not comply. No attempt has been made to upgrade the track to comply with these standards and the Dept. seems quite happy with the present situation. I believe the wheelchair community are being deprived of a rewarding experience and I would like to see our Green Mountains Natural History Assoc. and the National Parks Service combine their efforts to once again make the track to Python Rock accessible for wheelchairs.

The opening of the Python Rock Track for wheelchairs

Adventures and Tragedies

In the days before the SES or similar search and rescue organizations, it was our responsibility to come to the aid of people when they became lost or had accidents. The Forestry or National Parks workers were usually with us as part of the rescue team. Naturally, many of the people who needed help were our own guests but quite a number were adventurous spirits who camped at the Pine Tree.

The O'Reilly rule in earlier times was that if you were searching for a lost person you gave two cooees in quick succession. If a lost person answered they would normally give a single cooee or the cooees would be well spaced. If you receive a two-cooee response you would know that it was somebody else searching. If the lost person had been found three cooees were given in quick succession as a signal to bring the searchers home. Over the years we've been involved in literally hundreds of searches and most of these ended happily with little or no drama.

If a report came in that someone had an accident and had to be carried out there was a routine response that we followed at the Guest House and quite often the Forestry workers as well. If medical assistance was required there was often someone staying in the Guest House who was a doctor or a nurse and both my aunts, Ann and Rose, were nursing sisters. Other requirements were an axe, corn bags, twine, a blanket and warm clothes. When we arrived at the scene of the accident a stretcher was made up. This was done by cutting two thin saplings that were strong enough to take the weight of a person and threading them longways through two bags that were cut at the corners to take the poles. Two light sticks were fastened with twine at each end to both poles at right angles across the stretcher to keep them apart and the blanket thrown over it and we were ready for action. For many years they were the only stretchers that were available on the mountain. The 'home made' stretchers worked effectively and saved carrying one to the patient often over a long distance.

The Wishing Tree Track was not as well defined as it is today and people would lose their way and become disorientated at times. The crowing of the roosters at the fowl house or the throb of the engine that pumped the water or drove the lighting plant was like a beacon that guided them home.

I spoke to Jill at the Guest House recently and she reminded me of an incident involving a group of young people who walked to Blue Pool. When they were returning up the creek a heavy storm broke and it poured rain. The result was the fast flowing Canungra Creek rose and became too dangerous to cross, trapping them on the far side. A long-legged hiker called Owen managed to cross the creek and walk seven kilometres home to raise the alarm. It was getting quite late by the time we arrived at the creek and we had armed ourselves with some chocolate bars that I fired over the creek to sustain them while we erected ropes to pilot them through the torrent in safety. We all arrived home in good spirits for a late dinner and looking back I cannot help but admire the enthusiasm, the sense of fun and adventure these young people displayed. They did not have a guide with them but they acted responsibly and enjoyed the experience.

On another occasion Vince and I located a group who had gone astray and ended up at the old Forestry Camp below Stairway Falls one night. There was a fresh in the creek that made the crossings difficult especially at night so we decided to take them up on to Snake Ridge via a steep route known as Cows Skull. A cow's skull had been tied to a tree at the top to mark the route or perhaps as a warning.

There were about ten in the lost group. Piloting them up the steep mountainside with our fading torches was interesting to say the least. One of our staff, Tom, had come to lend a hand but he did not like heights so we had to guide him from one tree to another where he anchored himself. We remarked that we did not know he loved trees so much as he put his arms around them and hung on. It was daylight by the time we all arrived home. Vince and I showered and changed and hopped in the Jeep and drove to Brisbane for a wedding. I remember we regretfully declined an invitation to a party afterwards with some of our friends from out west because we were a bit tired.

A Japanese film crew had been staying with us in the Guest House for quite some time. They would often ask me where they could film certain birds or mammals so I was often giving them advice. One night while they were arriving for dinner they called me over. The boss, who had a good command of English, was not there and I was trying to decipher what this fellow was saying that sounded like 'mussing'. I was interpreting his broken English into the names of various wildlife species and the poor fellow was getting really agitated. He eventually pointed to everyone at the table and to the one empty space and then the penny dropped. I said do you mean 'missing' and that was greeted by much relieved nodding. I asked where he went and the reply was, "Look for scrub turkey mound!" which was not much help. It was summer and there was still some daylight left to guide him. Considering our rule of giving people the daylight hours to find their own way home before searchers go out we waited and just on dark he arrived in looking a bit the worse for wear to the relief of all. Some people get panicky and race off to search while it is still daylight and usually before any planning is done. It is not unusual for the 'delayed' person to arrive home while searchers are still out looking.

Vince B, who was our yardman at the time, guided a group on an overnight walk to Black Canyon. Their intention was to go to the end of the canyon and then rock-hop down the Albert River to its junction with Morans Creek and then to follow that creek back up past Morans Falls to the Guest House. It was a rather ambitious undertaking traversing rugged country with many miles of rock hopping. When they had not arrived home by lunch time the third day Vince O'Reilly and I set off down Morans Creek and when we found no sign of them we followed the Albert River up-stream. It is picturesque country with Castle Crag rising up on the eastern side and the Lost World towering over us to the west.

I was walking ahead of Vince and because there was a good flow in the Albert I waded through water and then walked over rocks along the edge of the stream. Vince called out behind me, "There's a death adder here and you've walked on him."

I was barefoot at the time and my theory was that a person walking barefoot always watches where they put their feet so I said that I would not have walked on him. I went back to have a look and sure enough my wet footprint was across the death adder's back. My excuse was that I was looking ahead to see where I was going and the death adder blended into the rocks and was difficult to see. I asked the death adder why he did not bite me and laid a stick across its back about two inches from its head where my wet footprint was to find out why. It did strike but it was a big reptile and its broad body was not supple enough to reach around and bite the stick. If my foot was an inch further back I may have been history because it was a good eight kilometres to the nearest habitation. I flicked him off with the stick into the undergrowth in case we returned this way and said, "Thanks mate!"

We found the delayed group further up stream and it was obvious that the hard going had taken its toll on the party who were tired and sore and well nigh exhausted. We decided to take them down to the Kerry Valley and go home by road. Vince piloted them out into the open country while I ran eight kilometres to John Markwell's property to ask for some assistance. John responded as he had done on other occasions and bought his cattle truck up the valley to give us all a lift out. The very tired group eventually climbed into a Guest House vehicle for the trip home.

In the days before helicopters were used, rescuing injured people from difficult terrain was often a hazardous operation. We used ropes to lift a stretcher up the steep side of Castle Crag to retrieve a lady who had fallen quite a distance. She was very lucky to have avoided more serious injuries. It was an era when you summed up a situation and acted accordingly and getting sued for doing the wrong thing never entered your head. Vince and I have been involved in retrieving five bodies of hikers generally from under cliffs. More recently we have had the help of our employee of long standing, Keith Woolley.

There was a route down off Pats Bluff that was used in earlier times that could be treacherous especially after a fire because of loose soil and crumbly rock. We received word that a young bushwalker had fallen there and as we feared the worst we waited for the police sergeant to arrive before we took action. We guided the sergeant down under the cliff and he did well because it was rough going. We found his body and it was distressing for us as the sergeant called to his two friends on the cliff top to tell them that their mate was dead. This was the second death recorded on this route that has not been used since. We lowered the body down to where it could be put on a stretcher. John Markwell piloted some army personnel from the Canungra Land Warfare Centre up the spur below Pats Bluff to retrieve the body and carry it to a waiting ambulance.

The biggest search that took place around *O'Reillys* was in the 1970s when a young man disappeared from the Guest House. He had arrived the previous day in the bus and was sitting at a table having breakfast the next morning when I bowled up in my usual fashion to tell him what walks were on and ask if he would like to join them. He said no and on further questioning added that he intended to go out by himself and did not want lunch. I spread out my map ready to offer some advice and give directions and asked him where he would like to go. He replied without looking up, "I will make up my mind when I start." That was the end of the conversation. He was sitting alone and at no time did he look at me as we spoke. He was seen walking to the Border Track entrance later and disappeared down the track and that was the last that was seen of him.

He did not return that night and we were concerned because of his attitude that morning and the fact that we did not know where he was heading and that he was alone. One of our guests returning from the Antarctic Beech Forest heard a call coming from the rainforest down towards Canungra Creek that afternoon. We concentrated our search effort that night around that area and on spots within a half-day journey of the Guest House. Next morning we notified the Canungra Police who in turn informed the Canungra Land Warfare Centre. The Federation of Bushwalkers search and rescue group were also involved. The tracks were all searched that day and it was becoming obvious that without knowledge of where he was heading it was going to be a difficult search.

Next day quite a large number of army personnel arrived from Canungra as well as a group of bushwalkers and the search of all the difficult terrain began. To make it worse the weather had deteriorated and cold rain driven by a wild southeaster made conditions difficult in the extreme. I joined a hundred or so army boys who searched the area where the original call was heard. The boys walked from the Border Track to Canungra Creek within sight of each other to make sure the area was searched thoroughly. It sounds rather easy when you say it but negotiating tangled rainforest and fallen trees down the side of the mountain while trying to maintain a reasonable distance from your colleagues on either side was not all that easy. The steep gullies seem to funnel the searchers into small groups. Nevertheless, I am sure if someone was there they would have been found.

At the end of the day we had found no clues and I can remember the dining room that night being packed with searchers as well as representatives from the major newspapers. There was a general mood of despondency at the failure of our search but we were certainly glad to be out of the rain and the cold. One of the army boys reacted to the conditions and had to be treated for exposure. It was a difficult time for us all and I know we at *O'Reillys* appreciated all the assistance we were given from the army, the bushwalking fraternity and volunteers generally.

The search continued for a week and after the more likely places had been combed on the mountain the search emphasis moved to the underside of cliffs and into the gorges. By the following weekend the search had run its course and there was still no result. You could search for years and still not cover all the rugged rainforest areas of Lamington National Park and the adjoining area in NSW but every effort was made and you could not ask for more.

The Visitors Books

If you would like to walk back in history and capture the mood of the early Guest House you have only to look through *O'Reillys'* visitors books. These books contain signatures and comments from guests that go back to 1927 and are a valuable record of our history. It is nostalgic for me to meander through the numerous visitors' books that adorn our lounge and be ushered through the years of our generation. During our time at the Guest House from the 1940s to the turn of the century many of the passing parade have enriched our lives and as I turn the pages I see a thousand stories that are worth repeating. I will choose a few that have added some colour to our lives and some good friends who blended so naturally with life on the mountain.

We can thank Ken Smith of Smith and Patterson, a publishing firm, for keeping the place supplied with visitors' books for the first fifty years. During our time there Ken often asked how the latest visitors' book was going. If it was filling up he would have another one on its way. Ken also did much of the early work organising the first track maps and folders of photographs that were sold at the Guest House as well as printing Bernard O'Reillys book *Green Mountains*. The mementos sold in the original Green Mountains Store were predominantly printed by Smith and Patterson.

A keen bird observer who visited the Guest House around the 1960s era was Sir Henry Abel-Smith, then Governor of Queensland. He would never miss an opportunity to go out to the beech forest to look for the rufous scrub-bird. He came one time just after a busy holiday period when we had a great crowd of young people in the Guest House. They were leaving on the Sunday Sir Henry was arriving and word travelled around that the Governor was coming. His room had been prepared meticulously by Pam who went back to have a last minute inspection of the room. Everything was neat but the bed was arranged in a slightly different way. On further investigation she found that the bed had been short-sheeted. There was a note in the bed that said it was hoped that Sir Henry accepted the prank in the spirit that it was given and that they've had a great time at *O'Reillys* and hoped he enjoyed his stay too.

We never found out how the Governor would have reacted because things

Peter escorting the Governor General, Sir Ninian Stephens on a tour of O'Reillys

Sir David Attenborough with regent bowerbirds

were soon put back in order. No one owned up to doing it but we had our suspicions. All sorts of harmless pranks were part of life for the groups of young people who visited the Guest House in the 1950s and 60s. There was no hard drink around in those days and people did have the capacity to enjoy life and made their own fun. I think Sir Henry would have accepted it in that spirit.

Sir Henry didn't have any bodyguards but when the Governor General Sir Ninian Stephens arrived while on an official visit to the Canungra army base he had all the trimmings including bodyguards. I was showing him around the Guest House and as he had an interest in birds I took him down the hill at the back to see a satin bowerbird's bower. We gave the bodyguards the slip and there was an enthusiastic search going on for him when we arrived back. Another time Doug Anthony was holidaying with us and Harold Holt the Prime Minister was out of the country so Doug was acting Prime Minister. He had a couple of bodyguards with him. They were fit young fellows who did exercises on the road in front of the Guest House each morning that really impressed the young female staff. The sad thing was that Harold Holt came back into the country during Doug's stay and the bodyguards went home. That's loyalty for you.

The visitors' books reflect a great era in the 1960s. The period from New Year to the January long weekend was the liveliest time of the year. At that time groups of young people visited the Guest House including some great families. The O'Gradys from Sydney with their six children would add their vitality to the place when they arrived and there would be much fun and laughter, long walks and entertainment at night. There were enough visitors from the south to have an interstate match whether it was indoor cricket with a ping-pong bat and ball or some other game. As our children grew up they became good friends with the children of families who visited us regularly. The Lane's, Casey's, Frisby's, Carmody's, O'Brien's and lots of others contributed to life at the Guest House at the time.

We seemed to have much in common with the Mitchell family from Kyogle who visited the Guest House in the 1960s and 1970s and they became good friends. Our family would enjoy a trip to Kyogle to stay with Ben and Joan Mitchell and there was something about Kyogle and the people there that really appealed to me. About that time, before the interstate visitors heard of us, not many people came to *O'Reillys* in the winter. July particularly was a very quiet month and someone had the bright idea that we should have a ball. It was to be a black tie affair and the old dining room was decorated accordingly. Ben and Joan Mitchell and their band from Kyogle supplied the music. Ben on the saxophone and Joan on the piano were both great musicians.

The first ball really stands out in my mind and we had a great mixture of ages present. My parents, Mick and Annie, as well as Bernard and Viola O'Reilly were there and the O'Gradys from Sydney also came up for the occasion. We did not have a liquor licence at the time and to have a drink on hand the price had to be included in the ticket. Serving strong drink was not our strength and Josie, who was an O'Reilly supporter from way back, was serving the drinks. She must have been making sure that the quality of the product was good enough for our guests for after a time she disappeared from view below the counter and our receptionist Esmay took over. Her experience as a barmaid was minimal and when Greg O'Grady asked for a Scotch she filled a good sized glass with Scotch and gave it to him. He said, "You had better give me a glass of ginger-ale as well Esmay." We did notice Greg was in good spirits for the rest of the evening. The night flowed along beautifully with Ben and Joan's wonderful music and Karma singing the occasional song supported by a great crowd of happy people.

I remember my cousin Luke O'Reilly in his dress suit escorting his new bride Elaine up to the dining room while dragging a beautiful specimen of a dingo he had brought up to show me. It was a young female in good condition that had been knocked by a car near the slaughterhouse on the Canungra road and had only died that night. I must have been in reasonably good form the next day because I skinned the dingo with the idea of having it mounted for a promotional display. Keith Woolley was passing on instructions from a book on preparing animals for mounting. It is rather a delicate operation and I made use of a doctor's scalpel to do the job. Obvious things like the lips, nose, ears, paws and tail all had to stay on the hide. I believe I did a good job and it was a beautiful hide.

We held a ball each year for a short time and I have great memories of them all. We really appreciated the way people supported them and they certainly added a real spark to our lives. Unfortunately, they had to come to an end.

While July at *O'Reillys* was cool by Queensland standards, Victorians enjoyed our winter climate. July was no longer a quiet month.

During 1989 we had a visit from a Chinese crew who filmed for a week around the Guest House. It was organized by Larry Zetlin, a local documentary producer from Brisbane. They also filmed at other locations around Queensland. It seems that picture theatres were big time in China and the purpose of the exercise was that this film would be presented as an example to the Chinese people of alternatives that were open to them. People from the poorer rural areas were the ones they hoped to influence. The fact that the O'Reillys went up to the mountain to dairy and switched over to tourism was of great interest to them. They filmed many aspects of Guest House life including the staff working in the kitchen and dining room as well as servicing the rooms. The entertainment was well covered too and my wife Karma organised a sing-a-long for them. They gave me three of their own documentaries that were quite good and had an educational message.

The Chinese government had become more lenient and although it was still communist in name as it is today it was embracing capitalist ideas as a way forward. Considering this it was rather a shock when the upheaval in Tiananmen Square took place while the film crew was still in Australia. Accompanying the team was a top documentary maker from China and included in the crew was an attractive lady, presented to me as Miss Woo, who would add some appeal to the documentary when shown back home in China. There was an Australian sound operator present too but generally the crew would converse with us through an interpreter so we did not get to know them all that well although we enjoyed working with them.

The story ended for me in about 1997 when a couple staying in the Guest House asked to see me. I cannot remember Miss Woo's married name but the lady was the Chinese leading-lady from the original documentary and she had married the Australian soundman who was involved in the documentary at the time. She had just heard that Karma had died and tears were streaming down her cheeks as she gave me a great hug. They were a terrific couple and are now involved in producing documentaries both in China and Australia. They stayed in the Guest House for a week and 'Miss Woo' was really an outgoing personality and at dinner she would involve the whole table in conversation.

I was of the opinion that Chinese people were reticent and reserved and possibly calculating but folk I have met from mainland China have proved me wrong. They are none of these things. It shows that the more we communicate and get to know people the less we are inclined to judge them or their race. I was in a fortunate position of being able to make friends with people from around the world and the experience certainly made me more tolerant. It has taught me to always look for the good in a person and it is usually there.

The Guest House has been a second home to many people who visited us regularly and many of these people contributed to our lives on the mountain and became close friends. There are a thousand poems like this, recorded in *O'Reillys'* visitors' books over the last eighty years but I really like Kit's very personal contribution. Kit Johnson's poem tells of her feeling for the place and how much she gained from her visit to the mountains. Kit was a loving, caring lady who would bring a different grandchild with her each year to *O'Reillys*.

I GO TO THE HILLS

"I'll have to leave here sometime, and face reality,"
Said a guest of the O'Reillys who was soon to go away,
And I couldn't help but wonder – what was real and what was sham,
But I didn't have to wonder long, for certain sure I am
That I will lift my eyes into the mountains hereabout,
When I'm far away in Sydney and my heart is full of doubt
For the future of my darlings – little Shaun who'll never see,
And Martin born a month ago, and Justin rising three,
Judy nearing teen-time, and the others growing fast.
What's ahead of all of them and will their standards last?
So I'm storing up my blessings, the scent and site and sound
Of birds and falls and forest tracks and everything around.
For when I'm sad and anxious in the unreal race back there
I'll draw upon my memory bank that I'm building here,
And its then I'll see Green Mountains,
And my heart with joy will fill,
At the thought of the O'Reillys and these everlasting hills.

by Lucy (Kit) Johnson - September, 1976.

Retirement

The year was 1993 and Vince and Lona and Karma and I were still serving on the board of *O'Reillys*. My son Shane had taken over as managing director of the company and other family members were working at the Guest House. There was less pressure on us oldies now and thoughts of retirement were with us I suppose but Karma and I had not made any decisions about it. I had already bought some land at Darlington on the Albert River from a friend and this country really appealed to me. I had a nostalgic attachment to the area for I had pleasant childhood memories of Rhelma and I camping beside the Albert River at Darlington fifty years earlier. We were part of a riding party that our Aunty Rose was taking on a three-day adventure to Westray's grave. We never made it to the grave but helped or maybe hindered the Stephens family as they dipped their magnificent fat bullocks. The grass was lush and green and there was mist on the mountains that rose up around us and I just fell in love with the place.

The more I thought about the idea of retiring at Darlington the more it appealed to me. Karma was not all that impressed at first but she enjoyed playing golf and soon realised that Darlington was only twenty-five minutes from Beaudesert Golf Course. That made a difference. Our architect, Maurice designed our house that was completed in early 1996 and we started packing ready for the move. As well as packing our own gear I had to find a home for loads of books and Guest House memorabilia that I had collected over the years. It was a difficult task for us. We had moved most of our gear to Darlington and were cleaning out Kootootonga, our home of thirty-five years, when Karma collapsed with severe back pain. She had not been really well for a while and complained of a bad back that the doctor put down to the strain of lifting Danny for all those years. Karma obtained a referral to visit a specialist and receive treatment for her back but had to wait nearly two months for an appointment. She had physiotherapy but her condition did not improve.

The specialist was pleased enough with her condition when he eventually saw her and was optimistic about her making some real improvement but the

Peter and Karma O'Reilly

Vince and Lona O'Reilly

ultrasound next day told a different story. Karma had cancer in her liver that was evident in other parts of her body and her prognosis was grim. I realize that many people have been through this experience but that does not make it any easier. The realization that we would not be together to enjoy the house that we had built and that she might not be with her family at Christmas was something both Karma and I found hard to accept.

She had many friends and the people who helped and supported us during that time are too numerous to mention. Father Bernie at Beaudesert arranged for prayers to be said in the church for Karma each week for nine weeks. Friends from Canungra and Kerry and even Brisbane travelled to Beaudesert to join the group and I found it was a moving experience to be part of it. I would have done anything to save her and stayed close to her during the months of her illness. I found it hard to watch as Karma's vibrant personality faded away before my eyes. I prayed that the Lord would cure her but the inevitability of it all was with me. The only reward for me was that by caring for her I could repay her to a small extent for all she had done for me.

When Karma accepted the fact that she was going to die she was very brave. She selected the hymns she wanted for her funeral service and gave Jean, our organist friend, advice on what should happen that day. She divided up her jewellery and personal stuff between her children and a few others and even picked out a future wife for me. My reply was that I was too bloody old for that. She was a caring person and knew that I was not an organized being and would not make much of a job of looking after myself or the new house for that matter.

In spite of all our efforts Karma died in September, four months after the fateful day we received the news that she was going to die and a month before her fifty-ninth birthday. People came from everywhere for her funeral service that was held in St Mary's Church in Beaudesert. She would have loved the day. There was lots of singing and a tribe of priests turned up as well as a Bishop who spoke glowingly of her. Police stopped the traffic as the endless funeral procession was escorted through Beaudesert on its way to the Kerry cemetery. The wake was held at our Darlington house and it gave me a lift to meet and talk to so many of our good friends. Then it was all over and there was just me and the house.

Looking after Karma during her illness, and her eventual death, strengthened me and hopefully made me a better person. Although my prayers for her recovery were not answered I was not bitter and in the long run I believe those prayers were answered in a different way. I felt the Lord was close to me during that stressful time. I was privileged to have Karma as my wife for thirty-five years but that is behind me now and life goes on.

I was not due to retire for another two years and was still involved in the Guest House. Each day I would go up the thirty-three kilometres via the Duck Creek Road. I enjoyed travelling on that rough old road and coming back at night after showing slides. It was a real thrill for me to occasionally see a lively brush-tailed phascogale, which is my favourite native mammal. They are rather aggressive carnivores and always on the move, they don't sit around like koalas. I ran a Bird Week two months after Karma died and kept running them for another six years till 2002, which was my 25th Bird Week.

I made an effort to keep the house and garden in some sort of order but I never really had my heart in it. Carmel, our good friend from down the road, would come up and knock the house into shape and me along with it I suppose. She was a good friend and support during the next couple of years when I was adapting to living alone and to life away from the Guest House. I realized I couldn't go on this way, the house needed a female to bring it back to life and I think I did too. Five months after I retired I took Karma's advice and married Annette whose husband had died four years earlier. Annette was a Bird Week regular and is a great bird spotter so we had lots in common. She is a well-organised person that I really needed and marrying her has lifted my spirits out of the shadows and I think that the house felt the same way.

The next trauma to come our way was Vince's illness. He was a redhead and subject to the sun's rays and a melanoma was found on his lungs. The doctors could not locate the primary source. He battled with it for four years but the condition eventually got the better of him. He and Lona had left the mountain and were living in Brisbane where Vince could be closer to treatment. Lona cared for him till he passed away in 1999 on the third anniversary of Karma's death to the very day.

Vince was a great strength and is sorely missed, not only by Lona and their family but by our family as well. Shane, who is in charge of the Guest House, relied on Vince's sound judgement and good business sense. The fabric of the Guest House and indeed our own personal lives seemed less substantial after he had left us. He was my only sibling; we grew up and worked together nearly all our lives. We relied on each other and had the freedom to use our different talents as we guided the Guest House on to better things. Earlier that year Vince and I travelled down to Port Pirie where our good friend Eugene Hurley was consecrated as a Bishop. He has been a great support to the O'Reilly family as I am sure he has been to many other families. The next time I saw Eugene was at Vince's funeral four months later. He is buried in the peaceful Kerry cemetery. Vince was a dominant figure in the running of the Guest House and his death seemed to me to bring down the curtain on the second generation with great finality. Both Lona and I had retired and left the mountain although we stayed on the board of *O'Reillys* for a few more years.

O'Reillys is on a solid footing with Shane and other family members adding strength to the board and being supported and guided by some excellent external board members. Certainly the Guest House had experienced great change as it moved to a third generation and that was to be expected. It is being run professionally with the accommodation and service being of a high standard. The 'hands-on' style of the first two generations that saw the birth of the Guest House and was the strength that guided it through depression and war and the difficult times that followed is not so much in evidence today. The operation continues to expand and cater for the standards of today's generation supported by a large and efficient staff. They are responding to the demands and pressures of a more complex world and the relaxed lifestyle that we enjoyed has all but gone.

As we know, family businesses are subject to the same disciplines of any business, and family members must be prepared to work hard and get on together. It is pleasing to see this happening in the third generation and the dedication they show to the Guest House is outstanding. I have every confidence in them.

And Molly was right; the world was at our feet. I believe we accepted the challenge she put before us back in the 1950s and made every effort to be part of that world. We continued the O'Reilly tradition of hospitality, of meeting and looking after our guests and we improved that old place in the hills and made many friends over the years.

Ten years have slipped by since I married Annette and they have been happy years for me. We have a stimulating interest in common and have shared some great trips to remote places in search of those elusive birds.

I am contented here at Darlington where I can now walk in the freedom of my own thoughts. As I write these memoirs I am sitting in my office tower that overlooks some waterbirds at play on a dam nearby and also affords a grand view of the country. My mind can drift off with a soaring wedge-tailed eagle taking my spirits up with it. And real joy envelopes me as I look up at the mountains that have been my life and my love for so long. These mountains have preserved precious memories that are only for me. I see the generation that went before us and I see that old Guest House standing there and the plans we had for it. I also see a magnificent rainforest that has always challenged me. And there I see Karma and Danny and Vince and our children of the mountain growing up as one family and I am with them on life's journey.

I thank you, the reader of this book for walking with me as we followed the O'Reilly story on a nostalgic journey over the years. I also thank the Lord for He has given me a good and rewarding life and may His Blessings be with you, wherever you are.

From Eagles Window looking into NSW to Mt Warning

Time Line

1911 O'Reilly boys select land on the northern slopes of the McPherson Range.

1914 Commenced construction of the Stockyard Creek Track.

1915 The National Park proclaimed and visitors stay in the O'Reilly slab huts.

1917 The rest of the O'Reilly family arrived from the Blue Mountains.

1919 Herb, Luke, Mick and Bernard were appointed honorary rangers of the National Park. Mick was appointed a working overseer of the national park later that year.

1923 Tom O'Reilly made plans for building a Guest House.

1925 A telephone line was completed to the mountain.

1926 The O'Reilly family welcomed their first guests for Easter.

1931 Family company formed to finance the expansion of the Guest House.

1931 Vince O'Reilly born in Brisbane.

1933 Peter O'Reilly born in Maleny.

1935 Laheys Ltd completed a road up the Sarabah Range. It ended at the edge of the National Park 6 kms from the Guest House.

1936 The Forestry Dept. constructs a track system through the National Park.

1937 Bernard O'Reilly found the wreck of a Stinson Airliner

1945 Mick O'Reilly returns to eventually manage the Guest House.

1947 The track to the Guest House is gravelled allowing first vehicle access.

1951 Annie converts the front of their house into the original Green Mountains Store.

1953 A slaughter house was built near Morans Creek.

1955 Vince and Peter return to eventually run the Guest House.

1967 The Guest House is connected to external power.

1968 Land Rovers are bought as people movers to start a new tradition.

1972 The first self contained units are built, the first of many.

1978 A radio telephone link established to Guest House replacing party line.

1980 Duck Creek road is constructed to the Kerry Valley.

1986 Commenced construction of the Tree Top Walk and Python Rock track.

1996 Retirement of Vince O'Reilly.

1998 Retirement of Peter O'Reilly.

2003 At 69 years and six months Peter greets the arrival of his first grandchild.